An Afterlife View of Our World

As Told By Gail Kent
After Her Passing, 1928-1996

By Gail and Marshall Kent

*Five years after she died, my wife, Gail,
began a dialogue with me integrating
our earthly and spiritual worlds.*

Published by:
ALLEUSHA PUBLISHING
1139 Third Avenue
Napa, California, 94558-3914
Orders@alleusha-publishing.com

Third Printing, February, 2016

Registered Trademark

Kent, Marshall
    An afterlife view of our world : as told by Gail Kent after her passing, 1928-1996 : An uncommon communication between a husband and his deceased wife : Marshall and Gail Kent.

ISBN 978-0-578-12596-1

Editing coordinator, Constance Wolfe
Cover by Kristin Throop, Combustion Creative
Cover Art by Marshall Kent
Printed in United States of America by Zander Press Inc., Brillion, WI,
www.zanderpressinc.com

*Dedicated to the wonder of our life
in which we all have participated
in all these years and lifetimes.*

Table of Contents

Table of Contents

PART FOUR – A View of the Beyond

PART FIVE – Our God-Given Reality

PART SIX – Let's Play God

How It All Started

Our 2 year-old son inspired us to investigate reincarnation. Here is how it happened.

Christopher was very late in talking and, that worried us, as it would any parents. Gail and I tried all sorts of stratagems to induce him to speak—with no results. Then, to our relief, when he was two years and two months old he blurted out: "It's mine, I had it first."

His next sentence was, "The fire engines are coming to our house." Gail—ever alert—asked why, and he responded, "Because the house is on fire." And indeed it was. I had purchased a used record player for the kids at the Goodwill Thrift Shop. The transformer shorted out, billowing black smoke. Although pulling the plug easily doused the fire, the house had a strong smell for quite a while.

But his third sentence is the point of this story. Walking down the hall with his mother he said, "I used to be an old man and now I'm a baby[1]." There was nothing in our house or our conversation that would stimulate such a comment. We knew the definition of reincarnation, but we hadn't talked about it nor had we believed it possible.

While his comment did not prove anything, as it was only anecdotal yet, you pay attention when you know there is nothing in your child's surroundings to explain it. I was impressed because he wasn't saying, "Reincarnation is true;" rather he was relating a personal experience: "I used to be an old man and now I'm a baby."

At that time I was an atheist, if anything. I was too busy getting on in our world to be involved in spiritual matters. I was curious, however, and this was enough to stimulate both Gail and

---

[1] Carol Bowman, *Children's past lives*, Bantam, 1998. Chronicles detailed past life memories of children.

me to read about reincarnation that in turn led us in other spiritual studies, including the mystery of the afterlife.

Since then, I have been privileged to glimpse these mysteries due to a strange and unexpected experience. Five years after Gail passed away she began writing to me discussing not only what it is like on the other side, but also providing wisdom in fulfilling one's life purpose on Earth.

I would like to share with you her insights. This wisdom stands on its own feet irrespective of whether you believe in an afterlife or not: *I ask that you judge the content of this book without feeling you have to accept its source.*

Gail's death was a terrible time for me. My precious wife of 47 years was suddenly gone. Yet as the weeks, months and years passed, I was most surprised that I was able not only to come to peace with my loss, but to transform it into a blessing. I found myself communicating with Gail: first through feelings and intuition, later through thoughts that would enter my mind to become what I call "inspired writings," a written dialogue that Gail and I carried on between us, both of us using my hands to write back and forth to each other.

It is a wonder to write a book with your wife after she has passed through death's door. At first I thought it was my imagination, as I have a good one; then, that it was just wishful thinking, but as the communications increased in volume and intensity, and as I began to review them, I recognized their enormous wisdom and organization. It took a clever stratagem by Gail to convince me that our communication was real; that it was not my imagination. Once I learned to trust the material, she became many different things to me: a teacher, confidante, traveling companion and, as always, my friend.

When I realized I was back in communication with her, I became excited. One of the loveliest things about our marriage was sharing our thoughts and feelings. Her death had yanked that away and I missed it a great deal. Here it was again, but obviously in a brand new, limited form. This limited form, however, had one huge advantage; she was on the other side with a whole new view of the cosmos which she was sharing with me. We were continuing our exploration of fundamental spiritual realities as we had for the previous forty years. To be participating in such a wondrous connection gave me an overwhelming sense of gratitude.

I would start the communication by welcoming her, comment a bit about my day and then ask her to use my fingers to write to me. She later told me that it was important to ask her to communicate because it established that she was doing so in accord with my free will.

In the early stages I both believed and disbelieved at the same time. My subconscious was convinced, as it was a primary, active participant, but my intellectual mind wasn't so sure. In fact, I doubted it and yearned for a good, hard, provable event to confirm that the thoughts were really coming from Gail. While I was determined to be open, my skepticism kept intruding.

I then had a particularly convincing experience. We are all familiar with the golden rule, "Do unto others as you would have others do unto you." It is a fine sentiment. She wrote through my hands the following: *You have heard of the golden rule, but do you know there is a higher, better expression? A weakness of the golden rule is that sometimes other people do not like to be treated as you like to be treated. For example, you might like to greet people effusively, whereas an introvert might find this disquieting.* At this point in the writing I became a bit spooked thinking she was going to try to improve upon the golden rule that has been around for centuries. She started writing, *the higher rule is: 'Be unto others'.* At this point I had already completed the statement, "as you would have others be unto you." I was surprised to find, however, my hands writing, *As you would have God be unto you.* Was I surprised! I wasn't conscious of what I had written. This thrilled me because I knew beyond a doubt it was Gail in true communication. *You want God to be kind, loving and forgiving to you with friendship and respect for the individual that you are becoming. This is how you should treat others.* I relaxed as this seemed beautiful to me and avoided the weakness she had pointed out in the golden rule.

Gail's writings make the point again and again that each of us has to find our own truth with the tools we have been given by God. Fortunately, you can read about spiritual truths in literature now available. Much of it is inspiring and beautifully written. In Gail's writings not only are the principles lovingly described, but they also state simple ways to incorporate them directly into your daily activities and difficulties.*

With this brief introduction let's move on to Gail's material. If these writings speak to you then they are for you. If they don't, just put them on the shelf and perhaps later you may find meaning in them.

---

*I remembered that during my Life Between Lives hypnotic session with Dr. Michael Newton, (Founder, Newton Institute), he stated: "Gail who seems very very advanced…" This encouraged me to think that she had wisdom to share with others. I was surprised by the amount of material that came, resulting in two books, this one and In Death We Do Not Part.

PART ONE

*A DIFFERENT VIEW
OF WHO WE ARE*

CHAPTER ONE

Questions

I invite you to join me on the journey my deceased wife and I have been taking. It is a journey of healing, full of the wonders of learning about life, the afterlife, about our place in the universe.

How would you feel to find yourself in dialogue with your beloved spouse five years after he or she passed on? My reaction at first was disbelief, which soon changed to joy and amazement. Just look at the intriguing questions she has explored with me, the answers to which I am eager to share with you:

- Why doesn't God show himself to us in some more direct way?
- Does God try to hide himself or his[2] true nature from us?
- God created a beautiful world. How can he allow such suffering?
- If there is a heaven why are we here on this difficult Earth?
- If we are made in God's image, what image is it?
- Why didn't God make us perfect to begin with?
- What does it mean when we say that God is infinite?
- What are some of God's laws?

- If we have free will, what is its purpose?
- What is my life's purpose and how do I fulfill it?
- Are we immortal?

---

[2] God is far above being male, female or both. The creative force of our universe far surpasses gender and is certainly not confined to one or the other. Due to limitation of language and ease of reading we will refer to God as masculine with no intent to limit him to only one gender.

- What is it like to die?
- What happens right after you pass over?
- What is it like later to be on the other side?
- Time: what is it? Is it always divided into three parts: past, present and future?
- It seems that prayer works sometimes but not other times. Why?

- Are we all One? If so, why don't we feel this Oneship more distinctly?
- What is the purpose of karma?
- Does astrology mean anything? If so, what?
- What is the new millennium? What is its purpose?
- Why can't we remember our past lives if reincarnation is true?

Gail provides illuminating commentary on these topics and many more. And she does this from the perspective of the other side where she can see both worlds: Earth side and spirit side.

She writes: *"Our Creator has granted us a life journey of immortal length. On this journey we encounter a huge variety of experiences: love, beauty, loss and strife. All these experiences have purpose. When we glimpse this divine plan we sense with awe our privilege in being chosen to take this journey."*

As this is a compilation of parts of hundreds of letters I have received from Gail arranged by subject, I have inserted ⬳ to separate one letter from another. *All of Gail's words will be in italics throughout the book. Words she wishes to emphasize will be in* **bold** *type.* Mine will be in ordinary type.

CHAPTER TWO

God is Revealed By His Choices

What we are and where we find ourselves are questions that have puzzled mankind throughout the millennia. Many religious texts and philosophical concepts have thrown light on these wonders, and so does one of Gail's writings.

God is the creator of this world and he placed us in it: he is the universal creator. As many religions say, God is infinite. Nothing is impossible for God. Knowing this, much can be learned if you look at the world and see what he chose to bring forth, for he creates what he likes.

It was not only the world, it was also the laws by which it dynamically functions. You can also observe, therefore, how the world is energized, how it changes. You can sense what he is from these choices too.

God communicates with you in a very revealing manner. If you want to know God, look at his choices in this world. In doing so remember that he likes what he created. If he didn't, he would have made it differently. You can look at his conception with wonder and appreciation.

The same thing is true on this side of life; we can see your world and ours with God's choices surrounding us. You live, learn and love amidst his revelations of himself, which are everywhere for you to ponder and gain enlightenment at the true magnificence of it all.

Let's view your world as God manifesting himself by his choices, both as to what is created as well as the laws by which it functions.

CHAPTER THREE

Being and Doing; The Constant Choice

Dear one, close to my heart, I am sitting here where we meditated with you beside me. The doe with her two newborn fawns was right outside while I was eating breakfast – such a symbol of the serenity of this place.

*Serenity is indeed a precious state. Notice that serenity is not a precious state of **doing**. It is a precious state of **being**. This tells you something. Your western cultural training convinces you that your response to all situations should be with an act of doing. If you perceive an injustice, if you have difficulty in a relationship, if you wish to maintain your health, you think these circumstances require that you **do** something. You think the problem is simply to decide what you should do.*

There is another choice that the above system ignores. You also have a choice to just "be." Your rational mind immediately bristles at this by logically pointing out that the injustice will not be corrected if you don't do something. You think "being" will not achieve anything.

The history of mankind is a long history of people doing versus being. The result is that you have a never-ending set of changing injustices, difficult relationships and other chronic problems. Would it not be reasonable to conclude that your "doing something" response to the world's ills is not very effective? Would it not be reasonable to try something else to see if it works better?

That something else to try is "being" instead of "doing." I agree that it is counter intuitive to think of being as an effective solution, but you will observe this pattern repeatedly: true wisdom often seems counter intuitive.

Let's look at what a state of being might bring forth. In a state of "being" you are left with your thoughts and attitudes. Your focus is away from your outside circumstances, now inward. Looking inward brings you all of the wisdom of the inner self, the subconscious. Further, you have entered a state that is most likely to broaden your perspective to view kindly both your outer and inner worlds. This will open you up and bring you understanding that will become your guide to living.

This is in contrast to doing. In the very nature of getting ready to do something you reduce your focus and narrow your perspective to what it is you're going to do. This shuts other things out. As a general rule we can say that "doing" narrows your perspective while "being" widens your perspective. Broadening your perspective is a powerful tool for problem solving.

This leads to another important generalization: narrowing one's perspective is a device of separation. Widening one's perspective is a tool to help us be closer to the We Are All One principle. The "doing" response separates, diminishing the sense of Oneness, for at the same time that you narrow your focus, you usually start separating the good guys (your side) from the bad guys (your opponents). This construct fosters confrontation. This can give us a hint of why the "doing" response does not bring peace to the world.

So you're saying that in actively "doing" it is easy to slide into dividing people into good and bad guys? You find yourself doing the opposite of being one with your world, encouraging separation and strife that simply continues our history of conflict.

Yes. This is a very difficult concept to understand. It is even more difficult to change your behavior when your entire life training has been to engage in doing. I hope you might be beginning to realize why your "doing" isn't succeeding all that well and seek an alternative.

I should add that while there is a purpose and value in doing, its value is derived from the wisdom gained by first "being." Only then can you perceive how to "do" wisely.

The above can be misconstrued to indicate you don't have to do anything, as though you should just be all the time. This is not accurate. You should act kindly. You should be helpful to your sisters and brothers. From your being you will know what to do, reflecting the primacy of who you are, a member of the Oneship. Let who you are lead you to what you will do.

You have had a thought going around in your mind these past few days. Let's discuss it.

I am thinking about the difference between "being" and "doing." We not only judge others by what they do, we judge ourselves the same way. What we are is derived from and dependent upon what we have done. It seems axiomatic that if we claim or wish to appear, for instance, as a musician, we must be able to have a resume that lists what we did as a musician. This is indeed a sensible thing. It is, however, an error to think it is the only way or even the best way to discover who we are.

What has occurred to me is that we deal in this same manner with God, believing God to be what we project he has done. In prayers we implore God to do something about this or that. "Heal John. Help his suffering." When we are at war each side wants their God to join them in smiting the enemy or protect them from the bullets coming their way. We do this even when both sides believe in the same God.

We are greatly puzzled by God and what we regard as his actions. Some of us believe we could greatly improve on what God does. I, for one, would eliminate all childhood diseases and starvation. Wouldn't this improve the world? My point is that even though we believe in God and worship him, his acts of doing leave us mystified. Perhaps we should stop trying to measure God by what we think he does and try to know him by what he is.

Put another way, by looking at what you think God does, you look at disconnected events and thus adopt a narrow view. The narrow view restricts the level of understanding you achieve. Broadening the view is what is needed. And how do you do that? You do it by attuning to what God is. The moment you do this you broaden your vision and increase your understanding.

It is not easy to attune to what God is and give up thinking in terms of what you perceive God did or didn't do. It is a matter of looking in the right direction. Stand right where you are but turn away from perceiving God as a doer and look at what he is. With this you will see the path before you and know what your first step should be.

In my own experience this opens the mind to much more.

If you perceive the cosmos as a huge environment with incumbent laws all created by God in which you are placed, his scheme of things begins to reveal itself. The material world does require that you do. So you do. But that is not the end. In life what you do is the result of who you are. But in living, your deeds modify who you are and this in its turn determines what you become. This circular back and forth duality is your tool to evolve and grow spiritually.

*But what are you growing toward? Each of you would find it fascinating to read in the Akashic Record,[3] the very long resume of your past lives, which gives great details of your actions. I have seen this vast record of how you have evolved, which is a distillation of who you have become. Right now you are the distillation of those myriad separate events and circumstances of your past lives. This demonstrates the importance of what you **are** over what you **did**. Do you see this?*

I do. All my efforts, all my energies and all my striving should be directed on becoming the person I wish to be. Actions

---

[3] The mystical literature contains many references to the Akashic Record. It is a spiritual library of each soul's total lifetime experiences in both detail and essence.

and doings are only subordinate tools to my becoming. This clears away a lot of the underbrush that often gets in my way.

Let's carry this one more step. To attune to God is to return to him. His primacy is simply stated as: "God is." When you return and attune to him, you too must become: "Marshall is." If you would become as God, then you must share his attributes. God is love. You must be love. God is creative. You must be creative. God is. You must become. To understand this becoming you must know the role of memory.

CHAPTER FOUR

Essence Memory, Who We Are

It is all very good to have these potential attributes of what we can become, but looking at how people behave in this world I can see that one lifetime doesn't give us enough learning time. We need to learn and sustain the wisdom we have so painfully accumulated in this life (to say nothing of previous lives). From your vantage point, how is this done?

Memory is the means to preserve wisdom and creates the individual you are becoming. Memory is also fundamental to reincarnation. These points will become obvious as we go on.

Memory consists of two aspects, both of which go beyond what you can recall with your conscious mind. The first aspect is detailed memory, which is easy to define. Detailed memory contains the specific details of a situation, people and events. You are right now sitting on the couch with your Dell computer on your lap while listening to Saint-Saens Piano Concerto, Number 5. I could recite many more details, but this gives a sampling of what your detailed memory consists of at this moment.

The second, essence memory, is more difficult to define. If you take a life experience, which will have a myriad of details associated with it, there is the essence of the experience as well. The essence is derived by abstracting the essential meaning with lessons learned from those detailed circumstances. From our writing this letter there will be a document that a year from now will primarily contain the essence of the experience you are now involved in. The details in the above paragraph such as the make of your computer will seem unimportant compared to the essence of the understanding you are trying to record.

This is true of every thing and every circumstance. There is both detailed memory and essence memory in each experience.

We need to flesh this out further. In a past life you could have been a violinist and your favorite composer may have been Schubert. In your next life you would have no memory of being a violinist or liking Schubert, yet you might find that you take easily to music and learn quickly to play the piano, for example. The violin and Schubert are details held in the detailed memory and are set aside in each incarnation. An affinity with music, however, is in the essence memory and is brought forward to your new lifetime.

It is interesting to note that this discerning of the essence is one of the major activities that each of us is engaged in on my current side of death. We review our previous life experiences to distill the wisdom they contain to add to our essence memory, setting aside our detailed memory.

Now why do you suppose God made memory with these two facets? I will use an analogy to understand this learning system.

When you were learning to read you had to sound out each letter to pronounce the words you were reading. Confronted with the simple sentence, "Jane is running" required recalling the "j" sound and joining it with the "a" sound, followed by the "n" sound. Then it got tricky and you had to remember that the "e" was silent. And so it went tediously. When you finished the sentence with the "ing," only then could you reflect back on what the sentence actually meant. You gave attention to the detail of each sound in order to start learning to read, but this lessened the ability to understand the meaning of the sentence.

With a lot of practice you were able to develop the skill of reading without stopping to sound out each letter. It was only then that you could grasp the meaning of what was written, which after all is the purpose of reading. By doing so you left behind the detailed memory and used your essence memory of the letters and their character. In other words your goal is an amalgam of all the reading you had previously done. You could not have become a good reader if you had not made the transition from detail and specificity to essence[4]. This same pattern

---

[4] The finding of an analogy in this world that echoes a spiritual truth is a tool of great value and is stated in the Hermetic statement, "As above so below and as below so above."

occurs with the various lives in which you have reincarnated.

Stripping away the detailed memory of your past life while leaving the essence memory is the best mode for enlightenment. Any specific detail would get in your way, just as sounding out each letter while reading gets in the way. **This is why you do not generally remember your past lives.** *In this way you are able to bring into each life the essential meaning and understanding of what you have learned during previous incarnations. You can therefore build upon the wisdom you have already accumulated over many lifetimes. If you accurately observe your world you will see that God wastes nothing. Do you think he would allow the wisdom you gained in any single lifetime to be wasted?*

Observe how some in life seem to be able to ride over difficulties with ease while others have to labor mightily and progress slowly. Others observe difficulties as a matter of luck. Actually, it is the result of the different levels of wisdom in the essence memory each person brings into this life.

Now I hope you can see how memory is essential to your individual being. Further, it is a fundamental part of the reincarnation process. Who you are at any given moment in the long series of incarnations is, in effect, your individual essence memory at that time. Sounding out the letters in reading is not the purpose of reading. Similarly the details of any life experience are not the purpose of living; rather the goal of living is the accumulated essence of the lessons learned in your journeys.

One of the joys of teaching is hearing the experiences of my students. One student from Alberta, Canada told me this story. He was four years old when, as World War II refugees, his family emigrated from Holland to Alberta. As they were farmers they were given some farmland. There were a number of Dutch who came to the same rural community and the locals resented their intrusion. He was sent off to kindergarten speaking very little English. During the class he needed to urinate, but didn't know how to ask. Being embarrassed by the whole thing, he held it as best he could hoping for some kind of a break. But it never came and he wet his pants. The teacher scolded him soundly and all the other kids laughed in derision.

At this point a psychologist could tell you he was in the midst of a trauma that could have profound negative effects.

But it didn't affect him negatively. Although he did feel devastated in a strange and hostile world, he told himself: "If I can stand this, I can withstand anything." Later he said this was the making of him. For the rest of his life he felt capable of enduring anything that came his way.

I would suggest that this reaction was the result of his essence memory. During his past lives he had experienced many difficulties and resolved them to such a degree that he felt great confidence. This essence of confidence he brought with him into this life was an already established reaction.

You generally do not remember your past lives, but there are exceptions. In these cases there is a compelling sense of unfinished business with a past life that tugs these memories into the conscious mind. In our middle son Christopher's case it was a sense of the wonder of it all that allowed him to recall being an old man.

Although there is considerable variation, the availability of these past life memories comes in spurts and generally diminishes as the child grows older. The reason for this is that too much past life memory interferes with functioning and learning in our current situation. Children in their innocence are wonderful teachers.

Other exceptions to remembering the details of a past life include déjà vu, spontaneous recall, dreams, regression hypnosis and reading the Akashic record. Generally these occurrences are brief flashes. When one does remember details of a past life it is almost always a past life that has relevance to the current life and may help in problem resolution.

One is also able to remember past lives when one has mastered the ability to grow in his current life. In other words, the recalled detailed memory will not encumber progress in this life; rather it will aid it.

The subconscious is a repository of both detailed and essence memory. Your conscious awareness aided by your sensory systems observes and digests new, specific experiences that are passed to the subconscious. The subconscious stores the specificity of the experience in its memory banks. The subconscious then beautifully abstracts the essence of the experience and makes it available to the consciousness, which will use it to react to subsequent situations.

Because essence memory is such an important concept we should describe an example. Let's take a person now living, a woman in her fifties. Who she is, is her essence memory. All the lessons she has learned in her past lives have been digested and provide the basis upon which she acts and reacts to the relationships and events in her current life. This includes what she likes, what she dislikes, what she fears and all sorts of things that make up her personality and character.

In this life she abhors violence and is very uncomfortable in any kind of a confrontation. She doesn't know why, she has always been this way. Her past life experiences as retained in her essence memory give the answer.

Her past lives contained a great deal of violence that resulted in losing loved ones, homes and the things in life she valued. She had many confrontations, some of which she lost and some she won. Even for those she won the victories came at the expense of a relationship she valued. Her essence memory warns her that violence and confrontation will bring misery into her life. This is why she has a gut reaction to avoid them.

In past lives she may have drowned a number of times but seldom with any real trauma. It passed quickly and she was soon over here being greeted with love. In several other past lives, however, she burned to death in gruesome ways. Accordingly, in this life she doesn't fear the water, but gets panicky if she thinks about being caught in a house on fire.

While she has no conscious memory of the details of any of these past life experiences, the abstracted lessons are very much a part of her present character. She doesn't need the detailed memory of them in order to put into practice the wisdom of those experiences. If she were consciously aware of the vivid detailed memory of being burned alive it could be so devastating to her present situation that she couldn't properly function, much less learn anything new.

In this description I have taken just two themes that contributed to her essence memory and thus, to the person she is in this life. All one's attitudes, character and personality are fashioned in a similar way; you are your essence memory. This essence memory is constantly being built upon as you journey through life.

You particularly become aware of this continuity when you pass over and go through the life review process, which utilizes the Akashic Record. It can be described as a huge bank of detail and essence memory, a most impressive memory system. Spiritual time which unifies past, present and future provides the medium in which the Akashic Record can function. It is much easier to read the Akashic Record on this side than it is on Earth, although you know of people like Edgar Cayce[5] who read it often while on Earth.

When you go through the life review process, you review your Akashic Record. This is generally confined to the immediate past life. You also read the Akashic Record of those with whom you had relationships. Thus you are able to know what your loved ones were feeling as you related with them. This is a tremendous learning process with many surprising revelations.

Essence memory describes how you become who you are and why you behave as you do. It does not, however, describe the teaching tools that God has created for you to learn to be wise.

---

[5] Edgar Cayce (1877-1945) was an American prophet and seer whose more than fourteen thousand documented readings were ostensibly received from the highest source. They are studied in depth and over three hundred books have been written based on his readings. The Association for Research and Enlightenment Inc., the organization devoted to his work, is headquartered in Virginia Beach. Internet address: www.edgarcayce.org.

CHAPTER FIVE

Looking at Karma as a Friend

Very closely allied with essence memory is the law of karma. Some people, when they first become acquainted with karma, view it as an inescapable taskmaster. Fortunately, when you get into it you realize it is much more a friend than a taskmaster.

Tell about how you and I first viewed karma.

We realized there was no scientific proof of karma because much of it operates invisibly. Although the word karma sounds foreign and mysterious, it means the same as the Old Testament law: "As ye sow so shall ye reap." I remember well the first time we considered karma. We had no idea if it was true, but it was a fascinating theory with many possibilities. It intrigued us that there might be justice in the world after all. It made us feel good that perhaps the bad guys were not getting away free and clear, and also that the good guys were being rewarded.

But as we pondered further and observed life we learned two things: karma does exist, and it is not a system of justice. It has nothing to do with punishment. Yet much has been written about how you cannot escape your bad karma and inevitably you are going to have to pay for your transgressions. Although it seems to work that way, that is not its purpose.

I wondered about murder. If I murder you and my karma repays me with my own murder, now we have a new murderer who also in turn will ostensibly have his karma bring about his murder. And so it continues. How does it stop? Somehow a person's bad karma is erased.

Further reading introduced us to the law of grace, which

allows bad karma to dissolve; but for what purpose?

It then became clear that the law of karma is neither a justice system nor an accounting system. It is a teaching system! In each experience we have is an opportunity to learn something that we did not fully know before. If we don't learn our lesson and thus act inappropriately, we experience "bad" karma.

When we haven't learned our lesson, our "bad" karma confronts us again with the same sort of difficult circumstance giving us another opportunity to learn to behave better. In this way our "bad" karma returns to us. Maybe the next time we will learn our lesson. If so, the law of grace erases our bad karma and no longer do we have the same negative results. We do not attract to ourselves this same level of difficulties. If they occur, we now know how to handle things suitably.

There is no account with your name on it that shows all your bad karma, which in time you are going to have to expiate by having done to you the same deeds you did to someone else.

My dear beloved Buck (my nickname), you are right. None- theless, God's inspired laws result in the same consequences as if you did have personal karma. The mystical literature is full of descriptions of karma that attribute this personal account to each of us. This personal account, however, is not needed to bring about your growth.

Let's illustrate this with an analogy. If you run and jump into a patch of cactus you will get many painful spines in your body. Until you learn not to jump into the cactus patch you will have many hurtful experiences. One such experience would be enough for most people to realize cactus is not for jumping into. This would be karma acting instantly.

Now say you scramble through some poison oak. It will not be until the next day that your itching and discomfort begins in earnest. In the previous 24 hours you may have done many things so it would be easy to miss the connection between the poison oak exposure and the delayed itching. This is how it is with your behavior. You have difficulty in connecting what you do with the consequences that follow.

Through karma you would continue to go through poison oak until you learned your lesson that poison oak is not for touching.

Was the cactus or the poison oak deliberately trying to bring pain into your life? Were they out to get you to pay up for your bad karma? No, they responded quite impersonally. In truth, they didn't know whether it was you, your neighbor or a wild pig. Not having learned the lesson, however, you continuously stumble into the same bad behavior with its unhappy consequences. In this same way you do not have a personal account of bad karma. You escape the consequences only when you learn the lesson: to avoid the poison oak.

I see that, Gail, but would you care to explain why it is that God constructs it this way? It seems as though he is deliberately making it hard for us. It is much easier to learn not to jump into cactus as it only takes once to absorb the lesson. Why do we have to have a time lag between our action and the consequences that makes it difficult for us to connect the two?

If all your lessons could be learned with instant karma you would all be behaving in a most correct but hollow way. You would be robots, very well functioning robots, but robots still. This is the automaton solution that God did not choose.

The law of karma works on the principle that there will be a delay between the cause and the effect, often a considerable one. To further compound the problem the connection between cause and effect is invisible. If I murder you and am immediately murdered myself by someone else in fulfillment of instant karma, there would be no more murders on Earth. If I mug you and am immediately mugged myself, I wouldn't be very eager to ever mug again. Everyone would be going around being very good to each other, not out of brotherly love, but self-preservation. The understanding that We Are All One would not then permeate your souls. Although you would have free choice it would quickly be reduced to one mode of behavior.

If God wished to create perfect automatons I'm sure he could have. You are the evidence that he preferred something else. That something else is your individuality and your free will, which allow you to learn through teaching systems like karma.

In his wisdom God created a time delay between an act and its karmic resolution that gives us time to ponder our situation to make better choices. Free choice then has a very wide menu. Thus, you see a great diversity in people's choices. Through the course of many lifetimes greater wisdom develops on Earth. Mankind comes gradually to the knowledge that you are indeed all One. This feeling of being One grows from the inside reaching outward; it comes not from the outside corralling you into restricted behavior. Can you see how this timing delay is essential to the fulfillment of God's plan? Do you see that this is the means by which you can become an enlightened companion to God? God created you with the potential to become god-like in a way no automaton could.

*What matters in your spiritual growth is the quality of your being and who you are rather than what you do. Instant karma would have you doing all the "right" things. He, however, gave you free will so you can develop and grow into your individuality. For example, God gave you his attribute of being loving, but as yet to be developed by you. He wants you to choose to love not because you are hardwired to be so, but because your heart wants to love. You are loving because of your individual desire and free choice from which will flow the **doing** of loving things.*

I think the above paragraph is beautiful.

Here is an example of bad karma caused by my own ineptitude. When I was young I expected everyone to do things correctly. If they didn't I felt justified in being angry with them. I had a tendency to view people critically. I needed to learn to be patient and accepting of others and their mistakes. After all, I made plenty of mistakes.

I made a four-day reservation at Curry Village in Yosemite National Park for Gail, our four little kids and my father who was visiting. When we arrived at the registration desk they could find no record of our reservation or any evidence of my paying a deposit. They also informed me that they were booked full and had no space for us. I got quite put out and did not speak courteously. We got into a confrontation.

We finally left the office with no campsite. I fumed with the thought of having to drive five hours back to Napa with no vacation at Yosemite. I was the recipient of my own bad karma or ineptitude. I felt like a failure to my own dear family. You could say I was right, as I had made a reservation and paid a deposit, thus they were wrong. I felt I had the right to be angry with them and felt self-righteous about it, but that obviously turned out to be ineffective behavior.

My father had witnessed all of this and said quietly, "You stay out here and let me go in and see what I can do." About ten minutes later he came out with the reservation completed and tents assigned. He explained patiently to me, probably for the hundredth time, that the way I behaved had been unsuccessful in solving a problem. An irate confrontation does not solve problems; it can create them.

Underneath my embarrassment I was very impressed. I thought long and hard and realized that when I knew I was right (in my view), I could be confrontational to the person I viewed as wrong. The lesson I needed to learn was to be considerate of other's mistakes, as I make mistakes myself. By learning this I could avoid getting into similar difficulties engendering more bad karma.

This next letter discusses why with karma our difficulties appear as they do. Why do good and compassionate people often suffer greatly? Further, the letter reminds us that the Oneship is by its very nature all-inclusive even though we may wish it weren't.

When I was on Earth we puzzled about that, Buck. You and I observed that there were some really cruel and difficult people in the world, some as bad as Hitler and Stalin. We also knew there were peo-

ple of outstanding spirituality. Remember how impressed we were with the Dali Lama simply for his genuine compassion? The vast breadth of difference between the unspiritual and the spiritual of this world seemed inconsistent with the comparatively small difference in their lives played out. It seemed as though the truly cruel did not get struck by God's lightning and, in fact, some of them led relatively charmed lives. We saw others who were really trying to live in a spiritual and compassionate way, but were buffeted by occurrences in their lives that they didn't deserve. Think of the persecution of the Dali Lama and his Tibetan people by the Chinese government. That is not easy to reconcile.

Thus it seemed karma was out of joint or so long delayed in its action that it wasn't meaningful. How can this be explained? You need to return to the understanding that karma is not a justice system based on an eye for an eye, nor is it an accounting system to enforce behavior. It is a teaching system and a marvelous one at that.

When you are teaching kindergarten through twelfth grade do you give the same homework to all the students? More accurately do you use the same tests and grade the results in the same way for every student no matter the grade level? No you don't. If you did, the less developed students would fail. They would not advance, as they would be so overwhelmed with what they were supposed to know, but didn't.

It is the same with karma. You would not give low marks to a first grader who could not spell the word spiritual, but you would give low marks to a twelfth grader. In any given time you need to learn what is appropriate for that stage. If you fail to learn the lesson, you receive it again, usually in a different format. You are not given lessons way above your head. If this were done you would be overwhelmed with these difficult concurrent lessons and could not function.

God is merciful. He will relentlessly give you lessons, but only those that are appropriate for you. Further he will see that you have the tools needed to learn these lessons. You may not recognize these tools. In fact, you probably won't, as they are part of the lesson.

You are all God's children no matter how poorly some of you recognize that. Thus the stumbling, inept soul who is judged on Earth as being evil does not generate in his life all the retribution that you feel he deserves. He is not escaping karma; he is simply being given that which he has the capacity to digest. From your narrow perspective he seems to get off easy. There is no bad and good karma, only appropriate karma.

The more advanced soul has lessons to learn as well. And basically they are more difficult lessons. It is acknowledged that he is performing at a higher level and yet must undergo struggles. These challenges will manifest in his life as difficulties that you, in your narrow view, may feel are undeserved.

Karma is more than a teacher; it is God's means of balancing cause and effect. It is not a balance between good and evil or reward and punishment. It is a balance between two relating parts, which are neither good nor bad. It is a tool whereby things remain connected to one another because we are, after all, One.

Buck, you always liked the duality evidenced by centrifugal and centripetal forces that keep the Earth orbiting around the sun. They are, of course, the effects of momentum and gravity. Neither is good or bad, nor are they opposites. Rather, they are two principles that operate together to produce a singular effect. Stripped to their basic properties, this brings two things together in a harmonious unity. Karma too brings two or more things together within the pattern of the One.

This amalgamation is a most important aspect of God's natural laws. Think of all the spiritual concepts that share this function, each in its own unique way. Love brings unity. Forgiveness brings peaceful harmony. Meditation unifies; it brings you to your higher self and your higher self brings you to other entities' higher selves and ultimately to God.

Karma also unifies. It allows different parts to relate to each other in a vast variety of ways. When the parts conflict with each other it allows them to work it out and eventually reach resolution. Karma is therefore closely related to patience. Patience and karma succeed in the long run as God intended. Notice that all during the fractious period no matter how acrimonious or prolonged, the two parts are always relating to each other.

We are all relating to each other. This is because we are all One. Your first introduction to karma is not unlike being introduced to the boogieman. If you don't do right he's going to get you. Then you discover good karma and open up your bank account and launch a savings program. This helps because now you are trying to do good, albeit in self-interest. This should introduce you to the joys of doing good for itself alone. Then you love and forgive without thought to your karma, but simply because it feels right. To love is salutatory to your awakening being. In forgiveness you experience giving up burdens you don't want. As you do this you become conscious of the Oneship with God.

Have you ever thought about karma and your higher self? You think in terms of karma being what you have done in relationship to someone else, someone outside yourself. In contrast your higher self is something that is within you.

Karma is largely what is going on inside of you. The center point for karmic action is within. It goes well beyond simple accumulation of credits or debts that one must resolve. To expiate karma does not require that someone outside you do to you what you did to someone else. For example, you were cruel to a friend. The simple view of karma is that you now need to experience cruelty from a friend. In this view your friend is obviously an outside agent fulfilling karma. This incorrect thinking makes you view karma as outside yourself, as something that impinges upon you.

Karma is within you, not only because we are all One, but also because the self is the place where karma occurs. Karma is a teacher attempting to bring about greater understanding within you.

When you are cruel to a friend the stimulus for this poor behavior was inside of you, and came from your attitudes and ineptitude. You can regard karma as the teacher that is trying to convert this inept-

itude into enlightenment. Again this is addressing what is within you.

This brings us to the higher self, also a teacher, which is within you at a higher spiritual level. What is it trying to teach? Your higher self is trying to bring about greater understanding in you. It strives to transform your ineptitude to enlightenment, similar to how karma works.

Karma and your higher self work together to promote growth. How is it that you expiate karma or escape its debts? As answered above, you do so by learning the lesson contained in the circumstances. By learning the lesson and becoming less inept you rise above the karmic debt and, by God's law of grace, become free of it. Ideally all this is accomplished within you without any outside agent.

If you are deaf to the teachings of your higher self and persist in remaining inept, then you will experience something negative like a friend being cruel to you. You will continue to receive and attract similar situations, which, incidentally, will get progressively more difficult, until you do pay attention, listen and learn. So would it not be sensible to try to communicate with your higher self to begin with and listen to its urgings? Make friends with your higher self.

Earlier I gave you a life example of my bad karma in getting reservations at Yosemite. I would like to give you an example of good karma that illustrates how the conversion of ineptitude to wisdom helps you.

I was a low bidder on constructing the jockey quarters for the local fairgrounds. I was awarded the contract and as I was laying out the foundation I realized the architect had made a mistake in the plans. His outside dimensions were about twenty feet shorter than the actual dimensions for each room. I was entitled to extra compensation for the additional footings I needed to build.

I submitted the bill and was paid for it. In this process, however, I found out that the contractor who came in second had discovered this mistake while calculating his bid. He had called up the architect to inform him of this error. The architect should have issued an addendum to all the bidders correcting the error.

Instead he told only that one contractor to include the cost of the additional foundation in his bid.

Here I was a young whippersnapper in his twenties starting out, while the second bidder was an established and respected local contractor. It also was true that one of the members of the Fairground Board, Dick Pagliuso, was in the ready-mix concrete business. The second bidder, who was a good customer of Pagliuso, told him of his talk with the architect. Dick immediately jumped to the conclusion that I knew perfectly well the architect made a mistake and kept quiet about it so that I could come in with a lower bid and also get an extra payment. I thus gained an enemy in the wrong place.

It is customary for the owner to withhold final payment amounting to 10% of the contract price from the general contractor until the 30-day lien period expires; this allows the contractor time to pay all his bills. When this occurred I invoiced for my final payment, which was then due and payable.

As punishment to me Dick Pagliuso told the Fairgrounds Board to withhold that payment for six months. I did a lot of pleading to no avail. As I was just starting my business this delay in payment really hurt.

I knew that I could resent this action and continue the bad feelings. I also knew that was not the right thing to do. I had seen the importance of bringing healing into relationships that had gone sour. I also learned that it was up to me to make the first move. As you will see, this new wisdom benefitted me.

The next time I needed a quote for ready-mix concrete I went into Dick Pagliuso's office to talk to him. When I walked in he said, "I never thought I would see you in here again."

I told him, "Dick, you did what you thought was right and I have no quarrel with that. In truth, however, I did not see the architect's error until I was on the ground laying it out. I am a little chagrinned that I didn't spot it." From that point on I had a good and friendly relationship with Dick.

Being new in town I didn't realize Martinez had a substantial Italian community. Whenever an Italian wanted to know about contractors they would call up Dick and ask about them. Four or five years later I had a new, major client named Anthony Seguso. Later on Tony told me he had called Dick Pagliuso and asked him about me and received a glowing report. I ended up building two restaurants, an office building, a mobile home park and best of all entered into several business partnerships with Tony that were mutually beneficial.

The above example includes ordinary, real-life occurrences. Events such as these could be explained easily without any reference to the law of karma. Yet karma is made up of ordinary experiences as well as extraordinary ones that are not so easy to explain.

CHAPTER SIX

Your Mind and Your Constructs

Gail, sweet one, in driving up to the ranch your dialogue came through, but I noticed you stopped without finishing. Am I right that you were trying to avoid giving me more than I could remember and hopefully as I now begin you will pick up where you left off? I will, of course, accept anything that comes or doesn't for that matter.

So here I am in our elegant cabin at the ranch looking out these four windows into the redwood grove that you and I loved. The sun is shining through the branches with its godlike illumination. I'm sitting comfortably on the couch with a fire going. I've got a CD in this computer playing dream melodies, all the lovely old chestnuts. In short all is right in my world. It is an ideal time and place to invite your mind to join mine in holy dialogue. Thank you God for letting this be. You are so kind.

Buck dear one, we have made much progress in our ability to communicate. We are now ready for longer communications covering wider areas. First I want to speak directly to our readers, as it will help make clear what you are trying to say. Then I will launch you on one of your favorite subjects.

Dear reader, Buck is my husband of many lifetimes. He has always been fascinated with how things work. He has been much involved in design and construction. For his job, he needed to know how one thing affected another as well as a view of the overall device or building to be constructed. In addition he has shown an insatiable drive to integrate all things, material and conceptual, within his purview. The fact that they appeared to have nothing to do with each other just added to the challenge of integrating them. You may already have noticed he is quick to see how a function exists because it is fulfilling the We Are All One principle.

His next fascination was to see what common dynamics, tools, vectors and energies make up the integrated whole. He loves abstract thinking as long as it illuminates the practical. To me this is his uniqueness. He perceives the whole by knowing the practical shown by the detail.

Buck, I want you to start writing about what you call "constructs." I will insert from time to time my comments and clarifications and generally steer the discussion.

In learning how to more fully utilize our minds we need to know more about how they tend to work and what tools we have to help us on our journey.

Our creator gave us minds with free choice. We accomplish two things with this gift: We "are" and we "do" however, we tend to focus in one mode or the other. When we are busy doing we are not so aware of being. If we wish to perceive our "being" we need to slow down our "doing." This is only a general truth. There are important exceptions.

We will deal first with doing, as it is much easier to comprehend. When we do, we do so by making constructs. What are constructs? Constructs are thoughts or attitudes as well as physical objects.

If I design and build a house, that is an obvious construct. The house is there to see, but constructs are not limited to physical things. In fact, the material construct was really started by a mental construct as I was designing the building in my mind. If I harbor resentment and fume about it in my mind I am also making a construct of anger and bitterness that will affect my life and others. This bitterness construct has an effect upon the world just as surely as a highway (also a construct) does. If you doubt this, look at your world and see what bitterness has wrought.

In effect we have taken the idea of physical construction and applied it to all things, which our minds build. Please bear with us and you will see why calling them constructs is illuminating. For one thing the word construct informs you that someone, sometime or other, built it, and can also modify, remodel or even demolish it.

This use of the word "construct" shows that each of us is a builder. We are constantly building our relationships, and ourselves which includes our relationship with God, whether we believe in him or not. We are also continually remodeling our environment. With our constructs, we build and rebuild our own reality.

Whether you want to or not, you build with every thought and every action. This realization may make you more cautious of your acts and thoughts, but it can also bring you the power to command who and what you are. It is like giving you a new set of tools.

Mankind has created a huge footprint on this Earth. Every single manifestation of this footprint began with a thought in someone's mind. Only after the mind initiated an idea did it become a physical manifestation. The mind is also the initiator of ideas and perceptions that don't become physical, for instance, resentment, which can in time become physical.

The next big thing to know is this: We create our constructs with our free will and in that sense we are their masters. Once a construct is created, however, it in turn affects us. In this sense the construct can, if we are not careful, become our master and alter our reality.

What Buck is saying is that we do not simply make constructs at random. We make them for a purpose such as building roads so that we can get from here to there more easily. They become our servants and we can indeed get from here to there more easily.

Sometimes, however, constructs become our master. A prime example of how a construct becomes our master and our whole society loses is illustrated by Buck's grandmother. She was a physician way back in the 1890s. Buck, tell about your Grandmother.

In 1889 my grandmother married a young holistic minister who was also very idealistic. He believed he should help his flock in every way he could. For instance, he imported a breed of cows from Ireland that was very small so that an elderly couple could keep a cow for milk and butter. A regular sized cow produced too much milk and was harder to handle, to say nothing of the amount of feed it consumed.

My grandfather could see that the health of his flock was also of prime importance. So he sent his bride off to the Chicago School of Medicine to become a doctor. She did so well that she graduated at the head of her class. This presented a huge problem to the cultural construct of male superiority. Who would be valedictorian? Certainly not a woman! But since her grades were the highest they couldn't very well substitute the second highest student as the valedictorian. Their solution was simply not to have any valedictorian at the graduation ceremonies that year, thus preserving the faulty construct that men were smarter than women.

She returned to rural central Illinois with her husband and set up practice. At this time alfalfa was being introduced as a crop and was a real moneymaker. The farmers' wives had an immediate use for this new wealth; they threw out the black strap molasses and bought that lovely refined white sugar. They also stopped using home-ground whole-wheat flour and bought wonderful white pastry flour, which they now used daily, not just for special occasions.

Goiter, a disfiguring disease, was prevalent at that time in Illinois. Women were particularly prone to it. It consisted of a swelling, often of considerable size, on the front of the throat, which could often be larger than the woman's breast. Can you imagine how ugly this made a woman feel? Not to mention its impact on the women's health.

My grandmother noticed that the goiter either began or worsened when families switched to refined foodstuffs. She recommended that a family return to the molasses and whole wheat flour. When they followed her advice, this therapy reduced the goiter problems. My grandmother had no idea that the cause was an iodine deficiency. This was not discovered until about forty years later.

She had, however, stumbled upon something that could alleviate the condition and might hasten the understanding that an important mineral was missing.

She wrote to the Chicago School of Medicine reporting what she had observed and wondered if some follow up studies might be useful in developing a cure for goiter. The School's answer was that they were scientists, not cooks, and that diet had nothing to do with curing diseases. And that was the end of that.

Because of the cultural construct that women and women's work were trivial, our society for forty years was deprived of medical relief to a physical condition that caused great personal grief. The grief was restricted not only to the disfigured women who had goiter but also their husbands who were upset to see their wives suffer.

This shows how society as a whole loses when it has an attitude or construct, which restricts what any member can contribute to the society. This applies with equal validity in matters of race, sex, age, etc.

We have described basic examples of constructs and how they should be our servants, not our masters. Most of what we do in this world is a construct with the same potential to be our tool or our master. This world of constructs is all around you. It is in your government, your job, your family life, your recreation and your dreams.

I would like to give another example of a cultural construct, which was a big part of my life experience. When I was growing up it was generally understood that women were not equal to men in their abilities to drive or fix a car, handle money matters and a whole host of things. My twin brother, who also worked his way through university, as I did, could get a much higher paying job as an electrician's helper than I could. After high school I worked for a year as a waitress, which, even with tips, was not high paying. Our culture and the people in it had made a construct that women should be in the home, not out earning wages. And if they had to earn wages it should be only in selected areas deemed to be fitting for women's abilities. It was no accident that there were far more female nurses than male nurses and more male doctors than female doctors.

In my last lifetime with you I watched this particular construct change and be remodeled. Typically the new construct recreated some of the same difficulties, but in different places. I wanted above all else to have children and to be their mother. I did not want a career. Fortunately for me this coincided with the cultural construct of what society felt I should be doing. It made it much nicer for me because I had a husband who told me when all those babies (four in six years) were coming, that the purpose of his career was to buy the time and wherewithal to allow me to mother our family. And he really believed this. He gave up his career at 44 without regret partly because he had completed that task. It also enabled the two of us to fulfill other dreams, once the children were off to college.

When the women's movement began to gather momentum, I was made to feel that I was betraying the sisterhood because I was not out in the workforce. So again the culture tried to make the choice for me. There was now a new construct that said I should have my own career. I didn't agree with that new construct and spent time with my retired Buck rather than working.

There is no holier role to play on this Earth than being a mother and no role where you have greater opportunity to practice love. You are constantly reminded again and again that over-permissiveness, over-discipline, over-protection, etc. lead to imbalance and problems. This is a world of dualities that operate together. To go to one extreme or the other is to ignore one of the dualities which will soon arise as a problem. In such ways motherhood gives you the opportunity to bring love to a love-starved world. It also presents you with high-caliber learning possibilities. How could our culture be so silly as to make a construct that somehow motherhood is inferior to a career?

Please note the temporal nature of your mind-made constructs. You build these constructs, tear them down and rebuild again. Nonetheless, this activity serves a useful, even holy purpose; it gives you an arena in which to exercise you free will. In exercising you free will you see the results of your actions and are given the opportunity to improve by trying again.

What we construct with our minds has a vast influence in how we enjoy our lives, how fulfilled we become. Our lives are full of these examples.

Here is another illustrative story:

I had a good friend who helped me record traditional jazz. He was a fifth generation Chinese American named Charles Han who was raised and lived in the Chinese section of Oakland. His ancestors panned gold during the California gold rush. As happened more than once when a Chinese camp began to yield gold, the American miners would gang up and run them out. His great grandmother remembers rushing off in her nightclothes with her family and looking back to see the American miners burning down the Chinese camp.

Charles was the oldest of four boys. When he graduated from high school in 1929 at the beginning of the depression, he had to go to work, joining his mother and father in supporting the family. Although he was bright he never had the opportunity to go to college. As things improved his three younger brothers attended university with two becoming doctors.

He spent his working life in the supply depot of the Alameda Air Station while his brothers had very successful and financially rewarding careers. Here is where the construct comes in. The Chinese culture was such that Charles was as proud as his parents were in making it possible for his three younger brothers to get their university degrees. He never felt resentment that he had been unable to go to university because he had to work. This Chinese cultural construct that Charles adopted served him well in being pleased with his life and his brothers' success.

Someone from the more individualistic American culture given the exact same circumstances would probably have a different construct. It would be easy for one to feel that they had received a raw deal, leading to resentment, not pride.

We think our life fulfillment is derived from outside circumstances. The above true story shows that it is not the external circumstances, but the internal constructs that determine our fulfillment. It is well to recognize the results of our mind-creating constructs. No place is this better applied than in the bitter resentments that you so diligently construct and harbor.

Dear one, it is a good to write to you. Do you know that we are both being of service when we communicate like this? We do it because we love to learn with each other and like touching each other if only with words, but we are also serving a spiritual purpose. At this time there are many who are serving a spiritual purpose. We are all doing so as part of a new millennium, which is a huge symphony with many skilled players each on his own instrument attuned to the same cosmic pitch. Each instrument contributes a special timbre to the overall sound.

*The whole orchestra is playing the **We Are All One** symphony. Listening to it brings you to the emotional understanding that there is no separation. When your senses experience separation your intellect constructs separation in your thoughts, but the music allows you to feel the oneness.*

As I said there are many working on their own chosen areas of enlightenment. You and I have a special niche to fulfill. We have a special separation to address. If you look at our lives you can see that our experiences have prepared us for this. We have been given the tools and the circumstances to do our job.

The senses and the intellect of the peoples of Earth have constructed a separation about death. Your senses note that one who has died physically goes away. Your intellect observing this constructs the thought that the deceased are now separated from you in all ways. Your intellect then paints all aspects of death with separation. It assumes without any proof that you can no longer communicate with the deceased, that any thorny issues cannot be resolved but remain frozen by the death separation. Many assume also that the deceased entity in the afterlife cannot grow and develop but remains at whatever stage he was at death. These stagnant or frozen concepts around death are another manifestation of separation just like ice separates itself from the remaining water.

One of my and Buck's roles is to be an instrument in the orchestra to convey the truth that there is no separation. Our particular instrumental part is to allow people to see that even though there is physical separation there need be no separation in mind and heart. You can communicate with someone who has gone on before you. You can learn, interrelate, resolve and grow with your departed one. The essence of your relationship was never in your physical selves even if you thought so. It was always in your heart and mind.

Your relationship with God has never been with a physical God. Your relationship with him has been with your heart and mind. As above, so below. Your relationships with your brothers and sisters reside primarily in your heart and mind. Buck and I are to use our experiences both past and present to open the door for others to allow themselves to understand this non-separation, to show them how one can actively, joyously continue their relationship. There is physical separation at death. There will also be separation of mind and heart if you so construct it but that does not make it real.

These writings between Gail and me demonstrate that communication is possible between the living and the dead. There are many who have created a construct in their minds that death is a complete separation. There are also many through the ages who have made the opposite construct.

We limit ourselves when we construct beliefs based on what we believe God is incapable of creating. Wisdom grows by being open to new possibilities and examining them.

CHAPTER SEVEN

Astrology, A Teaching System

Astrology is an influence, not a determinant. No matter what your astrological chart shows, free will predominates as each individual's gift from God. Further, the birth chart is a set of tools. Astrology does not predetermine which tools will be selected or how they will be used; the free will chooses.

You are on this Earth to learn lessons as you go along your spiritual path. How are those lessons presented to you? How are you guided to the classroom that is appropriate to your individual growth needs at a particular time? Astrology plays a vital role in presenting the aspects needed to bring this about. Astrology gives you a matrix, a set of personality traits denoted by the sun signs that best suit you to address the lessons your incarnation has set for its goals. With your new astrological personality traits you can approach a lesson you failed to learn before in a past life from a new point of view. This dissimilar point of view will let you respond in a new and probably more appropriate manner, allowing you to learn new knowledge.

Gail is making clear that you are not your personality traits even though they very much feel like you. They are tools given to you to experience in different ways the events in your life in order to evolve toward wisdom. A concert pianist can with consistent practice and his inner artistic sense incorporate great skill in the use of his tool, the piano. Yet he is not the piano even though he would be hard pressed to display his talent without it. It is the same with your astrological personality traits.

Buck is an Aries with the common Aries traits of having a temper and being impatient. These were two areas that in previous lives he had not fully worked out. There was more for him to learn in regard to each of them. Thus Buck and his guides chose for him to be born within Aries in order to provide him with the classroom that would allow him to learn further about these two issues. He couldn't escape observing the negative consequences of having a temper and being impatient. As a consequence he has made great strides with these in this lifetime. There are many on Earth who are struggling with these same traits. Each of us at various points in our series of lives, have or will have to come to terms with traits like these.

Each baby born comes with a set of astrological parameters that are chosen to help that baby progress on the spiritual path. This individual with its free will can choose how and to what degree it will utilize those traits to learn his lessons. Thus you will find in each of the astrological signs individuals who live and practice the sign's traits at a highly evolved level or at a lower level. Since there are only twelve signs and each soul has many lives, it is implied that you are born in a given sign quite a number of times. It can be said that you need to learn each lesson in each sign before you are capable of comprehending it completely. Think about that. What a comprehensive way to go about it.

No single astrological sign is evolved above another sign. In each sign the individual can live a very advanced life or unenlightened life and still have a personality consistent with that sign.

Just to provide balance to this there are other influences such as genetics and the environment. But like all things we attempt to separate they are, in fact, not truly separate. As you are now discovering, the environment affects genetics. There is also your individuality that is the sum of all your past experiences and learning. This latter, your essence memory is many lifetimes wide and is the most profound influence of all.

I will conclude with the obvious statement that the invisible connection between each baby and the planets is the result of the We Are All One principle. The baby is one with the planets so, of course, there is an influence. Is that more difficult to credit than the butterfly flapping its wings in New Guinea affecting the climate in Ohio? Science accepts the latter in chaos theory and in this new millennium will begin to accept the connection between the baby and the planets. The reason astrology has persisted even in this so-called rational age is that it is a cultural construct supported by many people. Buck has the traits of an Aries and I had the traits of a Gemini this last life. I was even born a twin.

<hr/>

Oh, dear Gail, it is delightful to be with you again talking about planets being one with us, while here I am on the couch where you so often meditated. I am inhaling the scent of jasmine tea I just made and listening to sweet music.

The planets are physically predictable in location; however, they have their invisible modes. It is these mode that manifests the various characteristics and personalities of each planet as described by the astrologists.

The visible and the invisible are constantly interrelating. To understand the immense variability that is possible, let us think in terms of numbers. We have nine single digits in our numbering system, ten including zero. From these ten you can create an infinite set of numbers. By man's definition you have either 8 or 9 planets, which is almost equal to the ten digits in your numbering system. So why is it so surprising that you can have almost infinite personality possibilities in astrology?

There are an infinite number of factors that comprise the individual. This should not be surprising because God created you in the image of himself. If God is infinite, which he is, you must be infinite too. Many religions state that there is a spark of the divine in each of us. The word spark is used to symbolize the initiating energy that starts an expanding process that becomes much greater than the spark alone. This in a generalized way is saying that God gave all of us his attributes, but in nascent form. Thus we have all these potentials awaiting fulfillment in our God-given environment of many learning systems. Our basic nature is infinite and therefore the factors that comprise us are infinite too. We don't sense this infinitude because so much of it is only in potential form, but we are in the process of expanding this understanding.

Going back to the beginning we have a universe created by an infinite God who manifests as ever-changing harmonies. You are an integral and congruent part. You, along with the planets and everything else, vibrate in an ever-changing attunement to universal harmonies. As babies you are open to these harmonies in a way that diminishes as you grow to adulthood and learn from your culture to close your minds, particularly to the invisible.

Astrology is a teaching system that allows you the freedom to see your world and yourselves through lenses of differing personality traits. If in one lifetime you get stuck in the mud, say with addiction, you can be reborn in the next life with a different set of personality characteristics with which to address this muddy morass and come up with new, more appropriate responses to promote your wisdom.

CHAPTER EIGHT

It All Fits Together

Let's recapitulate. We are beings created by the creative force, God, to seek our own individual ever-evolving truth. We have been granted Godly attributes in nascent form. Our purpose in life is to develop these attributes in order to fulfill our potential. God has placed us in an environment with various teaching systems to aid us in our learning, such as karma, reincarnation, essence memory and astrology. Additional learning systems will be discussed as we proceed.

It bears repeating that God gave you free will so you can develop and grow into your individuality. He gave you his attribute of creative potentiality. He wants you to choose to be creative not because you are hardwired to be so but because your hearts yearn to be creative. You are creative because of your individual desire and free choice to be so, often against considerable odds. You are a creative energy from which creative, innovative things and actions spring.

Our gift to God is our individuality, which in time, will bring to fruition all of the attributes God has given us. All of us are on this path and all of us in time will fulfill our purpose.

Important aspects of this learning environment include a loving God who has given us many blessings to savor with pleasure. He does not judge us by the inauspicious things we do in our ineptitude; rather he sees our true intentions and provides us with the tools for these intentions to grow toward the joyous fulfillment of our nature given to us by him.

We also are an integral part of an all-inclusive Oneship. You will already have noticed that I have difficulty in separating the various subjects without bringing in others. This is because the subjects all interrelate. Free will activates karma, which stimulates us to learn our own truth, which evolves with the development of our essence memory. None of these things stands in isolation. In understanding how they work together, you will realize they powerfully enhance each other and can help you find joy and serenity in your life.

It is time now to move from the generalized topics of who we are and what we have been given to the more personal view where our individual choices manifest in our individuality.

PART TWO

A PERSONAL VIEW

CHAPTER NINE

Communications Are Core

When Gail and I first met at Antioch College in Yellow Springs, Ohio, the very easy way we could talk to each other made us think that maybe the other was "the one." We each wanted to reveal to the other our emotional, mental and physical selves without cover-up or pretense.

I remember our first date when she kept me waiting for almost an hour. I still dislike waiting but in my youth I abhorred it. Her delay ordinarily would have made me not want a second date. For reasons I didn't understand at the time, however, when she finally came down the stairs to the common room where I was waiting, the thought appeared clearly in my mind that this was the woman I would marry in spite of the fact I hardly knew her. I had never had such a notion before.

The reason she was late I soon found out was that her boss at the drug store asked her to stay longer. As she was working her way through college and needed the job, she didn't feel she could refuse.

We loved talking and finding out about each other. It felt like we had known each other for years and were just catching up. We accepted that feeling with no realization that it could actually have been true.

Gail and I had each grown up knowing that we sought a life-long, loving relationship. Gail particularly knew that this meant we needed to be able to communicate openly, often and with a passion for sharing. Fortunately, we were able to let that grow between us over the years. Looking back we both could see that the difficulties we had with each other were often due to kinks in our communication, so I think it is appropriate to share with you some of her writings about communication.

After she died I had felt Gail's presence and received short messages that seemed to occur spontaneously. I longed, however, for deeper communication. This began to occur with writings about five years after she passed on and has continued for ten years.

I realize that mind-to-mind communications without some known means of contact are something many of you may be skeptical about. When it occurs, it is not something we are used to. We don't recognize it as something we resonate with or can identify. It is something we can ignore altogether more easily than we can a ringing telephone. Maybe we ignore it because we can't be sure of it. In the following Gail talks about opening up to this mind-to-mind communication.

❧

My dear Gail, I love your name. You would think in time I would get used to this writing and feel confident that I will be able to communicate with you easily but I don't. I still am apprehensive that I won't be able to do this. I wonder sometimes if not taking our ability to communicate for granted actually aids in continuing. Please use my fingers to write what you wish.

My Buck, who always tries so hard, in spite of your trepidation you must admit that it works. Yes, it is good not to take this or anything else for granted. You show respect for what you have been given. Our communications will never be like a production line that can crank out writing after writing. Each is to be hand crafted.

Mind-to-mind communications have never been like the telephone. Mental communications are fuzzier with less clear definition. That does not make them less real. It is a different mode altogether and takes getting used to.

When I was with you we would have spontaneous mental communications at times. They were usually short in duration. Now we have learned to call them forth and share considerable information.

What is wonderful about this is that a huge new channel of information gathering and exchange becomes available. If people would open their minds to the possibility of mental communication they would begin to have access to much, much more. It is a use of the invisible laws. For example, the law of love is felt by all of us and the results of this law are seen by all of us, yet the law of love is invisible. We will devote a whole section to the invisible laws later.

Human consciousness's current state of evolution is finally recognizing what a large role information plays in life. You are experiencing a vast increase in information exchange. You are, in fact, only entering into the beginning stages of this expansion.

The supreme pattern of God includes a vast network of the channels of interrelated cross communication. This is all very basic. You can say that gravity communicates in the form of the gravitational force. Scientists speculate that gravity transmits its force via a particle called a graviton even though with much searching they have yet to find it. In time they will. Other forces also communicate with particles that are well known like the photon. When you love someone you are communicating. All that goes on has a commonality of connections in the Oneship.

If you think in these terms you will sense more fully all the abilities that are available to you. There are possibilities out there of which you have no idea; yet with openness you can learn how to partake in them. Communication channels for all kinds of information are unlimited as they are God-given. These channels are accessed regularly often without your being aware of it happening. Your subconscious often gives you information whose source is beyond you, such as thought duality discussed later in this chapter.

The widow of a business partner of mine told me one amusing example of unexpected communication between heaven and Earth. As far as I know, Dewey and her husband Bill never believed in psychic happenings or any other such "nonsense." When her husband died I took her to lunch to commiserate over what it's like to lose your spouse.

Bill could fix anything, she told me, having that natural gift. In rearranging things after his death she was in the midst of shredding a lot of papers when the shredder suddenly shuddered and stopped working. For three days she tried various ways to fix it including kicking it, to no avail.

One day in frustration she said out loud, "Bill, fix the god damned thing." A moment later from across the room it made a funny noise and then a whirr, and started up. It has worked ever since.

❧

For me one of the supreme moments of communication with Gail was as she lay dying. In the emergency room when I gently shook her awake, she looked at me with her half paralyzed smiling face that seemed to be saying: "Thank you, I appreciate you, and the love we share will be ever ours." The look in her eyes was one of encouragement. She communicated confidence that I would have the strength to carry on in her absence. And it seemed that she wanted to share this experience of dying with me. All this came to me clearly, but without words.

Previously Gail and I had had some discussions about what we would do in the event either of us would be dying, but were unable to communicate verbally with the other. We had agreed that the survivor should pose questions *and* answers so that a squeeze of the hand could communicate yes or no. It puzzles me how we knew to agree to this before the problem arose.

So when I sat down next to her in the emergency room, I began to ask her questions.

"Can you hear me? Squeeze my hand for yes if you can."

She responded – her hand tightened around mine.

"You look like you are at peace. Are you?"

Again she squeezed my hand and gave me that lovely half smile.

I had heard about "near death" experiences and I knew Gail

was going through the tunnel to the light to be greeted by a spiritual being. Unfortunately, this time, I feared that death was just hours away.

I asked, "Do you feel surrounded by the light of love?" Gail squeezed my hand once more.

Then I found myself asking, "Is Jesus holding you by the hand?" A very hard squeeze. Although I was beside myself with worry, this exchange was beautiful and it felt holy. Gail (and I, to a lesser extent) had always felt a strong connection with Jesus.

I still wonder how I had the presence of mind to ask her the questions that I did in the emergency room. I am impressed that I had somehow sensed what was going on so that each answer could be a positive one. While part of me was rattled, another part of me was taking charge, almost without my will.

The whole thing amazed me. Gail was dying and she knew she was, so what did she do? She communicated her passing with me so that I shared it. It was the most momentous day in my life. Writing about Gail's dying brings tears to my eyes but also awe that I could share such an experience. I wish I could adequately convey the immense beauty of watching my beloved friend and companion of 47 years, with whom I experienced so many adventures, joys and difficulties, finding and feeling the true peace of God. It was the most tender experience of my life.

Here is what Gail wrote about it six years later:

I wanted to convey to you a lifetime of thanks for your companionship. When I saw that you sensed this, I smiled. I so wanted you to know how I felt. I didn't know my face was half paralyzed. I felt like I was smiling at you as I always had. It was such a good feeling to smile at you. Do you ever sense that I am smiling at you now that I am out of my body? It still feels good to me.

Yes, it feels like invisible sunshine.

You were wonderful the way you asked those questions so I

could squeeze your hand.

You did have help in asking those questions—from your higher self—but I know it would not have happened if you had not been listening, truly open to the spiritual wonders that we were both experiencing.

Now it takes great courage to be open. And, it is particularly hard to be courageous when you are losing your loved one. As you experienced, Buck, when you were losing me you felt as if all your courage was used up, and you needed a good deal more to get through, but you did it—you kept yourself open.

Many of us, one time or another, have felt we understood or received thoughts from another person. This is particularly true with loved ones. You know what they are thinking even before they utter a word. The means by which you receive these thoughts is scientifically unknown.

When Gail was with me on Earth we occasionally communicated mind to mind, but it was usually spontaneous. When we intentionally tried to communicate this way most often we failed; now that she is on the other side, we have been much more successful.

Gail tells us that this occurs much more often than we realize. In fact, she describes it as a regular tool whereby we can be stimulated to gain wisdom.

*Your very thoughts can be dual as to their source. You think your thoughts are solely yours, generated only by you. Only on special occasions such as my communicating with you now, do you feel that someone else is entering your thoughts. Right now you know that my thoughts **and** your thoughts are going through your mind, so here you have thoughts that have two sources, yours and mine. This does not occur only on special occasions.*

Let's put it in a general statement. Thoughts may have dual sources: the first source is the thinker who generates an idea, or a thought. This thought by its very nature attracts to it like thoughts that have been generated by others. These can be higher thoughts if the thinker's original thoughts were highly attuned, or unfortunately, lower thoughts, again if the original thought was so attuned. The second source we will call the contributor.

When she first presented this, I had never felt that someone else was contributing to my thoughts. The contributor apparently does not come with a caller ID or announce himself. This may seem underhanded, but there is a real purpose for it. Using myself as an example, if I knew the identity of the contributor I might very well react negatively to the idea because of its source. This would not be in my best interest. I should be looking at the content of the idea and not its source. It is best for us to concentrate and evaluate the content and not be distracted or prejudiced by the source.

This is equally true for a source you greatly respect. If I knew the contributor to my thought was Buddha I would accept it unreservedly. This is not how I develop my own truth. To be overwhelmed by the source bypasses a very important step in making this wisdom my own. I need to ignore the source to discern the truth in the content and decide with my own capacity to absorb this wisdom.

This is why thought contributors come to us unannounced. Additionally, if a contributor gives us an idea and we think it is our own, we will entertain that idea in a more open way. If we like the idea it is much easier to incorporate into our own truth when we feel it was our idea in the first place.

In our inspired writing I am contributing over 80 percent of the thought. This is because you are starting the writing with a blank agenda so that I can take over the subject and direct where I'm going with it. Your thought portion is quite small because you make no attempt to direct my overall message. You only try to set down the words and the phrases as they come to you in small segments. As we practice this inspired writing, we get better at it.

There are times when my contribution hits a resonance in your thoughts. Then your thoughts and my thoughts are one and the same. Being so, you cannot say that it is your thought or my thought. This occurred when I told you, "Be unto others as you would have God be unto you." That is why I didn't give you that earlier. I knew you would love it but I wanted to wait until it would resonate as our thought. Remember how good that felt? It is an example of an "Ah ha" moment.

People who are psychic are those who are able to diminish what their mind is thinking and allow other entities to enter their thought process. Psychics and channellers cannot receive 100% of their thoughts from another entity. The ratio may be 95% to 5% or 80% to 20% or even much lower like 60% to 40%. When it gets down to 30% to 70% the message is pretty contaminated with the thinker's own viewpoint and wishes. This latter explains why there is much psychic material that is not very high-grade. Do not judge this harshly. They are all trying. They need practice and show courage in trying to develop themselves. It does point out the wisdom that you never should just accept someone else's truth including what is in this book. You should evaluate the content and create your truth.

We on this side use this thought duality to help you. We do not tell you what to do; we contribute to your thoughts and give you new alternatives to consider, which is exactly what you do in your thought process.

*Think of it this way—thoughts can come from the thinker **and** the contributor. This is the duality. If the contributor's portion of your thoughts were limited to only that which is exactly the same as the thinker's portion, nothing new would result.*

Since it is God's plan that there be growth, there has to be some means to let growth happen. So he allows the attunement between the thinker and the contributor to do more than simply echo the thinker's original thought. This added idea or increment of thought goes from the contributor to the thinker even though there is nothing in the thinker's mind that exactly corresponds to it. As a general rule the contributor's new increment is closely related to the thinker's thought. Thus we are allowed to have the holy wisdom seep into us at a rate that we can absorb and make our own. This is how we gather our own truth within us.

There are exceptions to this general rule. A genius is one whose ability to absorb is significantly greater. He or she receives a contributor's thought with comparatively huge increments of new ideas. This same thing occurs with the true saints. They get advanced inspiration because they have a demonstrated ability to absorb it.

Now here is where God does a clever thing. He makes it easier to receive a more holy thought of greater dimension than to receive a lower one. In other words, when the thinker generates a thought, the default is to have his thoughts elevated by good thoughts rather than lowered by bad thoughts. This provides a gentle trend upward for the soul's evolvement. And this is precisely what you are doing on Earth. We are becoming more spiritual all the time. It may not feel this way, but it is nonetheless true.

These ideas are not easy to grasp. It is such an important concept that I want you to write about it from your different approach. To do so will make clearer what is happening.

When you attract only thoughts that are equal to your own, no growth is stimulated. What happens is a simple reinforcement of where you already are. Because we don't advance if we attract just what we already are thinking, God incrementally allowed new thoughts to the contributor's communication. These new thoughts can be either higher or lower than the thinker's original thoughts.

Numbers can illuminate how things relate so let's assign numbers and designate the lowly thoughts with lower numbers and advanced thoughts with higher. Let's assume a scale of 0 to 30. If we are thinking at the level 15 and attract thoughts of level 15, we have not been given something to help us learn. So God worked it out that we not only would attract a 15 but also a 16. The 16 would be new to us, but still relevant and thus a stimulus to advancement.

In addition God has given us free will. Therefore he gives us the choice not only to attract and consider higher thoughts, but lower thoughts as well. Using the numbers again we could attract a contributing thought not only at 16, but also a 14 as well. Thus, any individual can exercise his free will to choose higher or lower thoughts as revealed to him by the contributor. If this were all there is to it, we humans would likely not advance much, as we would have an equal probability of choosing the higher or the lower.

God in his wisdom did a brilliant thing. He increased the scope of the increment of higher thinking we are exposed to, to be larger than the scope of the lower thinking. Using numbers, your thought is at the 15th level. You attract contributors at the 15th level plus increments of 16th **and** 17th on the higher side. On the lower side you attract only down to 14th. Thus, God makes it easier and more likely that you evolve upward on your journey even though you have the free will to persist downward as well. You have the stimulus from contributors ranging from 14th through 17th, and your free will is not violated.

Gail, is this what you wanted me to write?

Yes it is. Now let's go on to other aspects of thought duality.

So far we have talked as though there is one thinker and one contributor. We do this to convey the basic concept. The contributor, however, is often plural. In other words a number of entities contribute concurrently to the thinker's thoughts. To some extent it is inaccurate to say our thoughts are dual in nature because they are in fact multiple. Even now, I am not alone in communicating with you. It is sort of like I reach out and touch others' thoughts and bring them back with me to touch your thoughts. Your higher self is one such entity that I reach out to.

This multiplicity operates on the lower side as well. When you lose your temper more than one angry entity joins you; in fact, many do. That is one reason anger can be powerful and difficult to control. I hope this also makes it clear that the contributor does not have to be some higher being. The contributor(s) can be in the same morass as the thinker. The result is a mutual reinforcement of this morass. You can see how a movement like Nazism could take hold. Ordinary people end up doing terrible things and we all are puzzled as to how this could come about. It is because of the reinforcing nature of a contributors' lowly thoughts to the thinker.

Let me move along to brighter thoughts. In meditation you could describe what is happening as you, the thinker, deliberately trying to open your mind to allow the contributor to enter your thoughts. You also deliberately set your mind to its highest level in order to attract a corresponding high level of attunement. So you see from practical experience you have learned to use this duality of thought source even if you did not quite understand what it was.

I told you about duality thinking in which the thinker and the contributor participate in the thoughts. The thinker is you and easy to understand; however, the contributor is more mysterious and has a different role. You should write about this, as you have delineated it in a helpful way.

I will try but I am puzzled as to why you want me to write this.

The contributor can be any thinking mind in the universe. That includes all our brothers and sisters living now on Earth. It includes all those souls, who like you, Gail, are on the other side. It includes entities and spiritual beings that have never incarnated on Earth. I presume it also includes thinking beings from other civilizations in this universe and other universes. It includes God. With such a broad bank of thinking minds, it is well to remember that you attract that which is in close harmony with your thoughts. This means that many of the possible contributors almost never contribute to your thinking. I presume this actually helps us, as some of the advanced spiritual thinking might well be too powerful for us to handle, to say nothing of the very low thinkers that we would like to stay away from.

God has given us free will. This prompts the question of whether the contributor can control your free will, as he is involved with your thought process. Fortunately, and wisely, no, the contributor cannot exercise your free will for you. That is reserved for you, the thinker. This means that even though your thoughts consist of those from both thinker and contributor, only you, the thinker, control your life. The role of the contributor is to provide you with new ideas to consider in pursuing your truth. It is like going into a restaurant and being presented with a menu. It is the contributor's role to provide the menu items, and your role is to make the choice. As I understand it this does not mean that you cannot come up with new ideas or new menu items yourself. The contributor just provides additional items, particularly those that would not normally occur to you.

The above will help people see that having a contributor to one's thoughts is not in any way a threat, but an enabler that allows you to process and benefit from new ideas, all of which are in your total control. You can perhaps see how beneficent God is in providing you learning tools such as this to explore your world and discover its magnificence.

I would like you to write again. Please go into how the thinker/contributor dynamic is a teaching system to help us grow spiritually.

The thinker attracts the contributor's thoughts because they are similar, in this case like attracts like. It should be understood that the contributor is not necessarily aware when someone else is receiving his or her thoughts. It is like the radio broadcaster sending out a message with no idea who might be listening. My guess is that the more highly evolved one is, the more conscious one may be of actually contributing in this manner. Gail can you tell me if this is true?

Yes, the awareness of being a contributor starts out as a very vague feeling. An advanced spiritual being, however, knows full well what he is doing and to whom and why, while those who are angry don't know they are contributors. When you can perceive how kindly and cleverly God made this world you can live more easily in gratitude and serenity. God Bless.

There are further aspects of thought duality to explore but the above describes the fundamentals. When this duality is joined with Gail's essence memory you can see how God has created a vast learning environment where we can grow in wisdom and understanding. Reincarnation gives us many lifetimes to advance at our own individual pace. Essence memory allows us to accumulate our insights gradually but allows us to become our most integrated self.

CHAPTER TEN

Difficulties in Your Lives

If our purpose in life is to learn, then we must expect to be given new lessons with more homework.

Gail, do you remember when you told our first born, Gordon, that next Monday he would be starting school? When Monday came he dutifully went, came home and began playing. Tuesday morning he was very surprised when you woke him up to go to school. "You told me I was going to school Monday and I did. Why do I have to go again?"

"Gordon, you go to school on Monday, Tuesday, Wednesday, Thursday and Friday, but stay home on Saturday and Sunday." Off he went, a bit unhappily. He really was unhappy on Sunday when he found out he had to go to school every Monday through Friday of the school year. We humans are like children in our understanding; we believe the construct that we have but one life to live and orient ourselves to that, believing we will leave all those problems behind when we pass over. But, if our lifetimes are destined to be filled with a never-ending list of difficulties what's the point in trying?

God is merciful. As you advance on your spiritual path you will find you become more skilled in using the tools he gave you to solve your difficulties. You will become an adept learner. Believe it or not you may actually begin to enjoy your competency in being a problem solver. You quickly solve the old problems that used to bug you and move on. In fact, some of these old problems are actually fun, like the steep ski slopes after I learned to ski.

We shall talk about reversals or more accurately what you perceive as reversals and problems. Life on Earth does not seem to run smoothly. It seems that life always includes problems. You solve one difficulty and another takes its place. This happens so consistently that you can't decide whether the world is getting better or worse.

You need to take a broader view. God has designed the world so that each of you has to constantly recreate yourselves. This gives you the opportunity to create yourselves into something better. Facing reversals keeps you from settling down into complacency. It requires you to keep applying yourselves to finding and revising your truth. Thus you learn and advance.

If you recognize that this is what is occurring you can see the constant flow of problems as a positive element in your lives. If you address yourselves by learning to recreate yourselves, you will be more in harmony. What you do instead of solving the problems, is to take the easier road by sweeping the problems under the rug, sugarcoating the reversals into victories and searching for someone else to blame for your problems. This misdirected energy simply compounds our difficulties.

As Winston Churchill put it, "I'm always ready to learn although I do not always like being taught."

With life's constant flow of problems, it seems like no serenity is possible in your world. Realizing that the problems aren't holding you back, but rather remaking you into something better, you will find your problems diminish into something lighter and easier to handle. Further, the solutions to the problems will come more easily to you and will be simpler to apply. Although it may seem counter intuitive, you will find serenity in acknowledging that each problem is an experience for the purpose of redefining yourself.

After you have had constructive experiences with problems, you will find that new problems and reversals are not so overwhelming. This again amplifies your ability to rise above the problems and feel peace in this world. Buck, write about your skiing metaphor that illustrates this.

Gail and I learned to ski in our forties. I remember the first time I went down a steep slope. It was really scary. I skied down very cautiously, slowly and it wasn't a bit fun. After I got the hang of it, the very same slope was exciting; I looked forward to racing down. It is the same with life's reversals and problems. As you learn how to handle a given problem, meaning you learn how to recreate yourself and not focus on the problems themselves, you will remodel fear into joy.

The first time down the slope it was the steepness that was the problem. The steep slope represented a threat. If I had addressed myself to changing the slope by getting bulldozers out to make it less steep, I would have missed the fundamental idea that the very steepness of the slope can bring joy. If I had become mired down in getting and paying for bulldozers I would have found myself with a huge, difficult-to-manage problem.

The problem is not the steepness, which is outside me but rather my skill in skiing, which is inside me. By converting what is within me rather than bulldozing that which is outside of me I magically changed an outside fear into an outside/inside joy. And this is done without changing anything outside me.

This is precisely what we do with our problems; we miss the point and come up with solutions that become in themselves bigger problems.

The attitudes of many on Earth are counter-productive because people do not understand what is going on. This is because people tend to see the world as only a material existence. Opening your mind and heart to the invisible allows you to find joy where before you found strife.

You would think that people would jump at the chance to have joy instead of strife. Instead they find the idea fearful and refuse to be open to it.

If you perceive that God has placed you in an effective, educational environment, then if you bring yourself into congruence with that environment you will learn and advance rapidly. You cannot bypass experiences and lessons or skip grades. In that sense there is no short cut even though there are many books that purport to tell you how to do just that. You can learn your lessons much more quickly when you realize the Earth is but a means for your return to God. To use Buck's analogy: stop trying to bulldoze the ski slope; instead learn how to ski.

Buck, write about the practical steps to do this.

The very first thing to understand is that fixing the world's problems is not where you need to focus your energy. Your work is to learn the lessons the world's problems present to you. This may sound like double talk so let me reexamine the skiing metaphor, which I think makes it clear.

Focusing on correcting the steepness of the ski slope is a big and discouraging task. It requires the input of much money, energy and time. It also requires the agreement of a lot of different people, which is not likely to occur. In being unwilling to accept any solution except our own "right" solution to make the slope less steep, we bog ourselves down with terrible problems, none of which will easily be solved. Unintentionally we blind ourselves to the real solution which lies within ourselves and not outside in the steepness of the slope.

In gaining understanding of what Gail has said about the primacy and efficacy of the learning environment, we can change our focus if we learn to ski. As a solution this is almost magical. First, it requires no changing of the slope whatsoever. Secondly, it does not require that you recruit legions of others to help you reduce the steepness of the slope. Learning to ski is totally up to you. It is within your power. Thirdly, it magically transforms a fear/threat situation into one of joy that you happily volunteer to enter. Can you see what immense burdens are released when you change your focus? You can do it.

I would simply add that this change of focus is difficult, but that does not make it less vital. The amelioration of the material ills of this world is not confined only to material intervention. In truth the greater aid to the material ills comes from the invisible raising of the consciousness of man. One can partake in this by changing one's own focus.

Observe that the injustices and inhumanities in the world have been going on throughout history and have been combated all through history as well; nonetheless, they persist. Something different needs to be tried and needs to be tried by you within your jurisdiction.

First, you need to realize that you cannot be the instrument to solve everyone's difficulties or needs. Instead, you can be compassionate as you become aware of injustices and needs, but without attempting to solve them. There are several reasons for this. You may not be the appropriate instrument for this particular difficulty. Also the person or people you are trying to help have their own free will. They may simply choose not to accept your help, advice or aid, no matter how appropriate you feel it is.

Once on a tour bus in New Zealand we got a flat tire, which stopped us beside an empty playground. A number of us got out to stretch. Gail, you and I ran over and started playing on the equipment. Gail was going down the slide and I was trying tricks on the rings. Then we both went ape style hand-over-hand on one of those elevated horizontal ladders. Here were two gray-headed people cavorting on children's playground equipment. With the tire fixed we got on the bus and went our way without another thought.

On the bus was a younger lady, who unbeknown to us marveled at the child-like joy we unselfconsciously displayed. She was recently divorced leaving her with a dour outlook on life. She watched us incredulously at first, but then realized we were happy and full of life. This inspired her to put aside resentment of her ex-husband and seek enjoyment in her life without trying to please others or worry about what people thought of her. I'm sure we looked silly doing what we did, but the minor stimulus she received from us cascaded ultimately to change her whole life. She decided right then that she was going to taste those same joys. Within a year she had met and married a fine man who appreciated this quality of hers. She knew this would not have happened with her previous resentful personality.

Gail told me this from the other side to illustrate how we can give aid without knowing it. When you know you are helping someone else, it can frequently place a burden on them because you expect them to respond. Sometimes your unconscious example can be more effective than offering direct aid.

While there is wisdom in what Gail has said, there are many paths to God. It is also true that you need to find and follow your truth.

❧

Another foggy morning. Here I am enjoying fresh plums from our fruit trees.

Do you remember when you heard yourself at a board meeting spontaneously saying, "The fruit trees don't like to be pruned, but nonetheless they produce more fruit?" The other board members would have been astonished if you had told them that you had just received that statement from your higher or inner self. You had not previously thought about it, or composed it; it just came out whole all by itself. I wish to write about its more universal application.

*As souls go through many lives there are quite a few things that happen to you that you may not like, particularly **as** they are happening to you. You feel unlucky, unfortunate, undeserving and sorry for yourselves. You think you would be better off if you were spared these difficulties. In fact, you go to great effort to try to make sure that such things do not happen to you in the future. You even mistakenly think that your goal in life is to achieve happiness by eliminating "bad" occurrences. Yet bad things continue to occur in your lives. Problems may change but they never go away; new ones crop up to take the place* *of the old.*

What you don't see in all of this is that you, like the fruit trees, protest the pruning with no realization that it is being done for your benefit so you can produce more fruit. And what is the fruit that you should be producing? You are to develop your truth to fulfill your nature as given to you by God. More specifically, you are to develop the wisdom within yourselves to understand that you are perfect creations of an all-loving God. Your fruit is that wisdom.

Seen in this manner the pruning you experience makes a good deal more sense. If these "bad" experiences in your lives bring wisdom then you can see the "good" in them. This understanding will also bring about a change in your goals. To achieve happiness by eliminating "bad" things in your lives is neither achievable nor desirable. To achieve wisdom, however, is possible and desirable.

If you realize this, what effect will it have on the fear in your lives? The future is where your fear lies. You are fearful of what the future will hold for you. Behind all your fears is a huge, dark unknown: the inevitability of your death or the death of your loved ones. This background casts a pall on all your other fears. If all things that happen to you are for your benefit, what is it you have to fear? Fear promotes separation in all its forms, particularly separation from God. The We Are All One principle and fear cannot co-exist together. All this shows that wisdom could be described as the realization that you need have no fear. If your goal is to gain wisdom, the corollary is to shed fear.

If you, the fruit tree, recognize that the pruning you experience (i.e. pain, difficulty) is actually promoting your wisdom, then what do you have to fear? Previously you were fearful of the pruning and had the goal of trying to prevent any cutting from taking place. With this new understanding that pruning is beneficial, the fear in your lives is greatly reduced. In this cultural counter intuitive way you achieve serenity. Serenity is to live without fear. Now you see this can be achieved by accepting the pruning and thereby diminishing the fears. Your world has so many things backwards.

There is a greater state than happiness, and that is joy. Joy comes from within and is not dependent upon outer circumstances, as is happiness. Joy is the clothing you wear when you are near God. Wisdom is what brings you close to God. Learning is the means to wisdom. Everything that happens to you is for your benefit. A narrow view of your experiences will blind you to the benefit the experience contains. Broadening your perspective will allow you to see the benefit in every moment of your lives.

Now Buck, the above is insightful but quite abstract. Your readers need your practicality to bring it down to Earth. Please write about how you experienced this.

I do believe that whatever happens to me will be for my own good.

Let's talk about a horrendous experience. My biggest fear was the possibility of losing Gail. She was my center of gravity. Having her die before I did seemed the ultimate abyss. My biggest fear came to pass: she died. How could this possibly be for my benefit? How could I possibly look upon it as being good for me? How could I even contemplate that I may have chosen to have this happen to me?

My perspective is now broadened by almost twenty years of living without her. I have gained much in wisdom, a great deal with her help as this book will attest. I do now see that her death was indeed, in part for my benefit,

I have discovered as my own truth that there is a direct correlation between joy and the wisdom I possess. The wiser I am the more joy I feel no matter what is happening outside of me. I repeat that wisdom is the realization of who you are, who God is and how to live in his universe. If I am wise, I am joyful, at peace and I feel serene. The masters all know this. When Gail died, my own level of wisdom did not vanish or take a step backward; it now jumped into action. I had a certain degree of wisdom I could use to help me in this trauma. It was difficult, but then I had much practice with difficulties so I just got on with it. The thing I wish to state is that outer circumstances, including the death of my beloved, were not the keys to my serenity and well being; wisdom was. This means that as I gained wisdom so did I gain in serenity. The pruning of my tree, difficult as it was, produced more fruit of wisdom. It did for me and it can for you.

Sometimes it is not only one tree that gets pruned but a whole orchard as Gail illustrates next.

The World Trade Center disaster can be described as inhuman behavior on the part of the terrorists. It is hard not to think they should be punished. Yet God does not punish them. What happens is that God uses this occurrence as a teaching device to all his children, victim and victimizer alike in accord with his We Are All One principle. Such a disaster changes your perspective.

The World Trade Center disaster took many of you out of automatic pilot, which you slip into without meaning to. It placed you in an environment where you consciously let the petty go and grasped what had true meaning in your life. You had a new awareness of what is truly important. You treasured things you used to take for granted. With every change of perspective there is a loosening of your old stuck-in-the-mud view of things and an opportunity to acquire a higher, broader level of understanding. All this comes with acceptance of the difficulties in your life if viewed from a new perspective.

Each of you learns from every experience you have. Your choice lies in what and how much we learn. It is with this constant stimulation to change and to broaden that your growth occurs. God has so created the world that this growth, however slow, does not go backwards. There is a gentle flow to things that moves us ever upward toward God. This is true for everyone, including even terrorists.

The entire history of mankind has always shown humankind to be rebuilders of great energy. You also have had much practice in recovering from all kinds of losses. In fact, in looking at history, the World Trade Center is a small and comparatively minor area to rebuild.

Turn your focus on what is happening within you and others because of events like the World Trade Center. This is where the advancement will occur.

My sweet Gail. How is it with you? I was telling someone about our communications. They immediately thought that I would be asking you all kinds of advice about how to live my life. They thought it would be wonderful to have some entity on the other side with all that prescience telling me what stocks to buy or sell. They couldn't understand that this is not what we do. I know I have to live my life, do my own homework and learn my own lessons. None of this can you do for me. What you can do and are doing is to teach me fundamental wisdom about how God and life function.

To me it is far more valuable to learn that our thoughts are dual, that gratitude is necessary before we perceive perfection and that we should be unto others as we would have God be unto us. That wisdom is vastly more important than having your advice on how I should handle a problem I have with one of our children. The latter seems such a fleeting situation, whereas wisdom is eternal. We always loved to learn, particularly spiritually. Here we are doing just that and it is wonderful. Thank you.

Several years ago I had a scare with prostate cancer, which is quite common in men my age. My PSA tests started jumping; a good indication cancer was a real possibility. For various reasons I didn't get the biopsy test results for several months, giving me plenty of time to worry.

I knew that Gail would know if I had cancer and hoped she would tell me. She didn't, but she did give me some wisdom that was instructive. She reminded me that all our experiences contain learning opportunities. Often we don't recognize these opportunities because we are so concerned with the future that has yet to happen. Our lessons are usually right in front of our faces in our now.

With these thoughts I began to think of my current status

and when I would get my test results. I thought that perhaps I should be learning what it feels like to be really threatened with cancer. Perhaps this would make me more sympathetic to others in poor health. I realized that when I went to a medical appointment I could be more compassionate to the other patients around me. So as I waited I sent healing thoughts to the various people there with love in my heart.

Later Gail told me she did indeed know I was cancer free, but had she told me I would not have learned to be more empathetic. Now I enjoy giving out healing when I go into the hospital or clinic.

Here is one of Gail's letters that touched on this.

My dearest friend, our mutual love of spiritual wisdom is one reason we can be doing this inspired writing. As to day-to-day problem solving, you have that well in hand. It would be a waste to involve me with your life circumstances. There is one exception to this that occurred. (Don't you love the lack of rigidity?) When you feared you might have prostate cancer I did give you advice as to what you were to learn from that experience. (I did not tell you, however, what you wanted to find out.) I did this because I knew you were not seeing it properly. With my help you did understand more clearly the lesson and benefited thereby.

For each soul on Earth there is help available for every problem. I'm speaking primarily but not exclusively of the invisible side of life. Each soul has a connection with its inner self. Each soul has a connection with God. Each soul has a connection with other souls including a guide who wants and can help him or her. These souls have individually faced the same difficulty and surmounted it. They now are in a position to help others work out a solution. Because each soul is part of the all that is One, this gives each soul access to the all that is One and the vast wisdom contained therein.

Most people do not feel this access to wisdom or know of the channels to which they are connected. Let's review a few of them. You can, through meditation, access your inner selves and God. Because your thoughts are dual, consisting of a thinker and a contributor, you can ask for help that will attract a contributor with the wisdom you need.

Your conscious awareness is the first tool given to you to solve problems. You can use your conscious awareness to analyze the problem and clear your thinking. In this way you can think anew outside the boundaries you have created. It is a worthy tool to broaden perception; you should not hesitate to use it. With it you can determine the needs of others, the needs of yourself and whether your chosen response harms anyone. You can also discern what lesson is contained in the circumstance. This is difficult but well worth it.

If you find your conscious awareness going around in circles or more simply just overwhelmed by a problem, all the other sources mentioned are available to help you. And don't forget that the solutions to most problems are helped by widening your perspective. It is very important to keep these other sources consciously in mind. One very common aspect of a difficult problem is that you feel alone in having to cope with it. Just knowing you are not alone and have these places to go for help will create a better environment for solutions to appear.

If you only realized the vast network of aid contained in the Oneship that is for your individual counsel, your fears in life would atrophy. You really have been made invulnerable, but you just don't realize it. To become aware the first prerequisite is to believe that such a network is possible. As long as you think such a network is ridiculous, impossible, or too fantastic, you cannot become aware of it. You must keep coming back to the necessity of being open.

Your individual conscious awareness is such a limited tool, how can you expect it to know what is possible in God's universe and what is not? Start by imagining that you don't know what is possible or impossible. Then open your mind to the idea that some very strange things could be possible. This is different from jumping to the immediate belief that strange phenomena are true. To open one's mind is not *the same as committing to a given belief. With an open mind you will, by observation, discover new wonders in this already wondrous world.*

You should be patient with yourselves as you try to become aware that your difficulties are but opportunities for enlightenment given to you by God.

CHAPTER ELEVEN

Fear in Your Hearts

Fear is an integral part of the difficulties we encounter in life. We all have fears, which can easily get out of control. Sometimes fear acts as a good motivator, as it keeps us from doing foolish, dangerous things. Then there are those who enjoy the adrenalin rush which fear can bring. But mostly fear is a debilitating and unhappy state that we wish we could control better. Gail has some interesting things to say about fear, its role in our lives and how it can be a more positive force.

Dear Gail, yesterday was the anniversary of the day you passed on and I didn't even realize it. I don't know whether to be ashamed or pleased. Ashamed because I forgot the day that was so important to us or pleased because I am letting it fall behind me. Please write to me.

*My Buck, be pleased. You never showed much talent for remembering anniversaries and the like. I always felt that this was because you were so engaged in your **now**. And the now is what you should be engaged in.*

Neither you nor I will forget the day I came over here. It was a most powerful experience. That experience is part of our being. There is no need for an anniversary remembrance to bring forth its value; it is already part of us.

That day was important to me for many reasons. It was a lesson in fear. The fear of an anticipated event or condition is often worse than the event itself. Often the fear of a future event is in error, as that specific worry never will happen or the actual event is positive.

My mother dying of TB when I was twelve made me fear death. All those health nurses warning me about getting TB made me afraid of death. Then as you know when we were raising our kids I worried that one or the other of us would die. Also I loved you so much I feared losing you. All this made death frightening.

Then when our kids left for university we started traveling. We managed to get into several life-threatening situations, like Tiananmen Square during the demonstrations. We became quite fearless at looking death in the face. Remember walking across those wet slippery logs on our trek into Machu Picchu with a three thousand-foot drop one step away?

The result of all this was that I had mixed feelings about death. You do too right now, I know. I had no idea how I would feel when death actually came.

When it did come I knew it was death. There was no fear there as I realized this. In the beginning I was concerned about the effect of my death on my family, particularly on you. Somehow later I was not fearful for you or my family. That was strange. All my life I had been concerned with the care of my family. I had been willing to devote much energy to promoting their well being. Yet here I was feeling calm when I knew my passing would be a trauma to you all. The reason was that my perspective had widened greatly. I could see clearly that my death was my choice and contained lessons that each of you in my family had entered into. Further, I knew each of you would grow beneficially from the experience. I also felt each of you would gain in wisdom. This made me feel pleased in a way I had not experienced before as a wife and mother. The word Godspeed had a whole new meaning for me. It meant I could lay down my concern and active participation in your lives and give you over to God. He and I would speed you on your path.

My passing was also a lesson for me in being instead of doing. In the death experience you are much more a passenger than a driver. In this it is similar to the birth experience.

I understand that those of you who are constant doers often have difficulty with the death experience because you feel frightened by the loss of control. In this sense the understanding and practice in being is good preparation for getting the most out of your dying experience.

After completing the dying experience you do return to a mode in which you can elect to be a doer. It is a different kind of doing than what you do on Earth. Nonetheless, the doers of Earth will like this new type of doing and adapt to it quickly. I tell the doers this so they need not be frightened.

❧

How are you sweetie? I love you. I feel the love flowing between us. It is good. So much of me is you.

It does feel good. It is inexpressible isn't it? And feeling it is better than knowing it anyway.

We didn't finish yesterday. Fear on Earth has an all-pervading power. God gave us choice and so many Earth decisions are made with fear being the dominant factor. Fear is a confession of vulnerability. Yet God made you invulnerable. When I died at the hospital, the staff saw me as vulnerable to the stroke I had. That is the narrow perspective. In the wider perspective I was not vulnerable. After all I am still here enjoying my life.

When you come here you feel much less vulnerable so the influence of fear disappears. Some whose earthly life was dominated by fear find it hard to give up this fear attitude. Therefore, if you can reduce the role of fear in your life, it is very helpful when you pass on.

❧

Think of that huge body of interplay that we have partaken in over so many lifetimes. Our love of wilderness in this last life brought us back to those cave dwelling days. Remember when you spoke at Kiwanis and showed slides of one of our African trips? They wouldn't believe that you and I had rented a four-wheel drive vehicle and traveled around on our own with no guide, camping on the ground in our tiny tent. We watched a hippo feed three feet in front of us while lying in our sleeping bags looking up at his huge mouth and belly. We loved that there was nothing between them and us. We were excited to be back among them after so long a time[6].

Not being afraid is the key to life. The good things in life and fear do not go together. You cannot love and be fearful. You cannot have joy and be fearful. You cannot truly be grateful and fearful at the same time. You cannot fulfill your spiritual self if you are fearful. You cannot communicate with your higher self if you are fearful either of meditation or being creative.

Fear separates you from God. There is no "evil" in the world, but fear is the closest thing to it. The more advanced you are spiritually the less fear you have.

Your reasons for fear are all self-made constructs, but you can remodel these constructs to remove fear from your life by understanding God's gifts to you. There are three great gifts, each of which removes fear from your mind. The first gift is that we are all One. If this is true then it is impossible for you to be separated in any way. Nothing important can happen to you that would not happen to the All. All the strife is but a temporary illusion that cannot affect you, unless you choose to let it.

The second great gift is that you are immortal. You are forever. So what do you need to fear? You need not fear for your loved ones either as they too live forever.

The third gift is free choice. You therefore do not need to fear having to do something you do not wish to, for you can choose not to. There are many who think of karma as being something you cannot escape. You can escape your bad karma in an instant if you choose to learn the lessons contained in that bad karma. If you do this you will feel so much better allowing yourself to understand that the bad karma

---

[6] In regression hypnosis we discovered that we had had previous lives together in our caveman days with wild animals around us and felt at home with it. In this last life together we made several trips to Africa on our own with no guides and slept in our little backpack tents out among the big animals and surprised ourselves by not being afraid. We later concluded this was because we sensed these past lives in just such an environment and we enjoyed being there.

was actually a gift awaiting your acceptance.

You can choose to give up fear. If this seems too daunting then give up your fears little by little, but move in the direction of removing all fears. As you abandon fears you will increase your fulfillment.

Many wonder what is the purpose of old age? The apparent downward spiral of energy, health, ability and mental acuity seems an unfair burden. This can result in a great fear of being older. There are many purposes to being older, but one is to give you an opportunity to gain a greater understanding of fear. Old age gives you a choice of embracing fear or embracing joy. As you look at older people you can see those who have let fear control them and those for whom fear has little place in their lives although they are much closer to their day of death. The latter understand the opportunity given those who reach the older years. Again, it is a gift if we can just see it.

We also talk much of being open. You cannot be open and fearful at the same time. Fear closes you down. Fear requires that you separate yourself from that which you fear. Separation is never the path to God. Openness, on the other hand, allows new things to enter your life without fearing them.

When I was first dying, I was somewhat fearful. I feared the consequences to my family and to you, Buck. But that quickly went away as I progressed into death. I gave up my fears. In their place I had the great joy of coming home. I want you to observe that the consequences of my death for you were the same whether I was being fearful or whether I was not. So what purpose is there in fear? Put another way, fear acts principally to close off the fearful.

*At my death you too had a tussle with fear. Your perseverance and choice and perseverance to be open was a tremendous antidote to fear. You felt the effects of this choice almost immediately. You never sank into depression. You never went into denial. You never felt it was all so unfair. You embraced your **now** life without my physical presence. Do you see what magic there is when you refuse to let fear control of your life?*

Once you recognize that fear is unnecessary, you walk into the sunshine.

Today let us talk about how you grow spiritually. You grow by changing. It seems self-evident because if you grow from one stage to another you have obviously changed. This is not how many people view it. Some go to great efforts to preserve the status quo and prevent change in themselves and where they are. This is like fighting the tide.

The entire universe is governed by change. The universe is energy and energy is the engine of change. So in your microcosm you should shift your energies from trying to avoid change to seeing how change can help you find fulfillment. Many of you love the changing circumstances in the movies or on the TV so why not love the changing circumstances of your life?

How do you do this? The main reason you try to avoid change is fear. You feel threatened by what may come about by change and so resist it. From your narrow perspective this is not unreasonable. After all you don't control what happens outside of you. What is outside can have a tremendous effect upon you. The World Trade Center is just one such example. From your logical viewpoint, however, would it not be true that if change did not threaten you, you could welcome it and use it to move in the direction you wished to go? Understand this and act upon it and you will find that change can be your friend.

You also avoid change within you. Here too you are afraid of what you might become. The underlying problem here is that inwardly you are afraid of who you really are deep down. This leads you to fear what you might reveal or become. When you strip everything away you are not sure you will like what is your core.

This belief or fear is based on an assumption that you are indeed separate from everything else. This separate thing could be pretty ugly. To overcome this you need to realize that you are not separate, but are an integral part of the whole. That whole is God. God is good, therefore you are good. The ugliness that you may sense and fear is not in your core, but on your surface. It is the result of your separatist thoughts and actions. This surface can be recreated into something better.

As you make this change from constant separating actions and thoughts to those of joining and sharing, a wonderful truth will become evident. How you think inwardly will attract to your outward environment commensurate experiences. There is often a time delay in this coupling that may puzzle you. Nonetheless, what you give out is what you will receive, as many religions have told you.

Accept change as your friend. Do not seek ways to resist it. Instead seek ways to make it your helper. You can do this by elevating your thoughts. Realize that fear of what might happen to you is chaining you to stagnation. All this will help you grow spiritually.

It is good to join with you this moment. Let us talk about fearlessness.

Fearlessness is a quality of God. In fact, it seems strange to think of God being fearful. Why would he be? You're right; God has no cause to be fearful. He is forever; he is the Oneship and he obviously has free choice. But as we have said many times, so have you; yet you are fearful.

Fear, which you choose to build in your mind, prevents you from the realization of yourself. It is a powerful stimulant to your wish to separate things in your life. You work very hard at separating yourself from that which you fear. To accomplish this you build boundary after boundary. You also fear for those whom you love because you see them as vulnerable to fearful threats. You try to include your loved ones within your boundaries so they will be separated from threats. By choosing separation instead of unity you establish an incubating environment for difficulties. Thus you spawn a whole series of problems that take many lifetimes to unlearn or undo.

Your ultimate goal can be said to be that you are to become like God. God is love, so you should be love. God is a creator, so you should be a creator. God gives blessings, so you should give blessings. It is also true that God is fearless so you should be fearless. By becoming these attributes you draw yourself consciously into the Oneship and make your holy contribution to it.

Do you see how this works? You feared losing me. Remember going down into Royal Gorge? I didn't fear that nearly as much as you did for me. Even at the time you knew your fear was ineffective and useless, but it was still difficult to set it aside. You did have the courage to let me do the trip, which I very much wanted to do. And it turned out as I had hoped. It was a lovely family adventure, one of our last. The trip would have been even better if you had not been fearful for me.

When you can cast aside your fears, life comes out into the sunshine and joy is natural. Whenever you bring yourself closer to God, closer to the Oneship, you feel joy. The same is true when you embrace love, creativity, and fearlessness and also give blessings. It all makes sense and can be said to be quite simple in concept although difficult in execution.

You went through an interesting evolution with my passing. Before, your biggest fear was that I would die and leave you. When your biggest fear materialized, all you had left was fear for yourself and what my death would mean to you and your life. About yourself you had always been fearlessly courageous. This characteristic of yours came to your rescue and you faced your future without me with strength. I think you were more surprised by your strength than anyone. With my help, which I was able to lovingly give you, you started on the healing path. I could not have helped you if you had not been open to it.

There are many on this side who would love to do the same thing, but are thwarted by the ones they left behind not being open. Understanding fear and having a goal of fearlessness will help a great deal in being open. Notice I said having a goal of fearlessness. I did not say being fearless, which is very difficult. Having a goal of fearlessness is much easier. Fear closes you down. Fearlessness opens you up to life and joy.

In Royal Gorge in the Sierra Nevada Mountains you hike down over a thousand feet to a small river rushing with great energy through a granite gorge. There is no road, so it is true wilderness. The whole family was going, kids, wives and grandkids. It was just the thing we loved doing. Gail had already shown signs that she didn't have the vigor or stamina she once enjoyed.

Several nights before we were to go I hardly slept; I worried about what we would do if she had some kind of heart problem at the bottom. Daylight came. I didn't want to worry Gail with my fears so I simply asked her if she really felt up to it. Her answer was so quick and positive that I made no attempt to talk her out of it.

We had already decided long ago that we were not going to allow fear to curtail the adventures in life that we cherished. If we died in the process, so be it, as we were living life as we wanted to. Practically, we had observed that adventuresome people seemed to live as long or longer than those who fearfully stayed at home. We were not going to avoid living by being afraid of possible death.

With this history I then tried to set aside my fears about Gail at the bottom of Royal Gorge. We had a wonderful time. After she died I was so glad we had had that full experience and I knew we had done the right thing.

Everyone knows what it is like to be afraid. Most people assume they would be very happy never to be afraid again. And yet there is much evidence that this is not the case. Many people like horror films. Then there are those who are attracted by all kinds of dangerous activities from jumping out of airplanes to climbing mountains. The fact that others have died doing these things is not a deterrent, but an attraction.

After one has experienced and survived a fearful thing, one feels a pride of self, a joy and a strong feeling of being alive. This sense of being alive is so attractive that people will go to great lengths to achieve it. Fear is often the door to this feeling. Mountain climbers and others will tell you that living on the edge gives a clarity and exhilaration to being.

The same thing applies to the feelings of the heart. Teenage girls sometimes like to be "drama queens." It excites them to be involved in grownup-like relationships before they are really ready to handle them. Teenage boys do the same thing with dangerous actions. Some don't outgrow this even as they get older.

What is going on here? First we start with the duality of your world. Fear is one polarity and then there is the opposite polarity of fearlessness. If done properly the partaking in this duality will result in a third state of heightened awareness of life. You can't exactly describe what this heightened awareness is, but you have no trouble recognizing it when you feel it.

The other element that is functioning here is the process tool. Some things only manifest themselves as a process. For example, music can only be heard as a process. Dancing, unlike a finished painting, is a process that ceases to be once the process is stopped. The process of fear followed by the overcoming of fear is a tool to achieve this exhilaration of life.

Fear is similar to the function of discord in music. In your musical demonstration you showed that straight harmony can be boring, almost to the point of ceasing to be music. Yet discord, which sounds grating when played alone, can, when played in sequence, add color and meaning to the harmony to create tantalizing music. Often, the discord in a piece of music doesn't even sound like discord. It can be the loveliest part. In your piece, "La Vie Perdu," you play an undiminished seventh chord that creates a ravishing focal point for the entire piece.

So what is the role of fear? **A Course in Miracle**[7] *clearly says that fear leads you away from love. This is correct and yet in the process of our evolvement, fear can be used to elevate us closer to God. If you remain in a state of fear, that is, if you halt the process without resolution, it is debilitating. If you continue the process of fear and the overcoming of it, then you experience your invulnerability. Invulnerability is part of the reason you feel this exhilaration.*

There are other ways to achieve this same exhilaration, the

[7] *A Course in Miracles* by the Foundation For Inner Peace, 1975.

feeling of being truly alive without fear. Holy men are well aware of this. They could describe it this way: you experience the sense of the exhilaration of life's invulnerability because you have become attuned to the Oneship.

≈

There are terrible things happening on Earth, but that is all against a background full of wonders and things to be treasured.

One of the very best ways to become more aware of the good things in your life is to understand the role fear plays in your perception. When you are fearful you see many dangers. The fears in your mind crowd out the myriad small things that are so meaningful partly because they are not attention getting like fear.

Fear is demanding. It requires you to stay alert to fend off the threat, making your mind unavailable to see the good things in your present. Fear will not allow you to look forward to your future with joyful anticipation. By choosing fear you let it contaminate your future.

It is very difficult to let go of fear even if you understand the heavy price it is asking of you. Buck, do you remember when we entered our sixties and we received all those insurance company letters urging us to buy supplemental insurance? They depicted the unhappy diseases and conditions that could happen to us that Medicare wouldn't cover. Of course, they were all real possibilities that could indeed happen. We decided we were not going to worry about them. We let our very good days continue as they were unfettered by these fearful possibilities. We realized we could die in an accident, which would make all that worry and fear of diseases irrelevant. As it turned out we thought about a number of different difficult medical conditions we could get but never considered a stroke. So we didn't think about what actually became my transition. Again, our worrying didn't apply to what was in our future. To a large degree we did enjoy our final years together, treasuring them for as long as they lasted. We were not robbed of the sweetness of those days by volunteering to cloud them over with fear.

Even my last day, traumatic as it was for each of us, was a day you have described as the most tender and awesome day of your life. As we both loved learning, it was a successful day, rocky indeed, but successful.

I still feel inspired by that day. I think it wonderful that as you were leaving this world, you were thinking of sharing that with me. I also realized that within me (and I'm sure in each of us) there were other modes that could come forward to handle the situation. Whatever part of me asked and answered those questions so you could respond by squeezing my hand took over for my quivering, rattled, devastated self. Seeing that beatific half-smile of peace and love on your face still brings tears to my eyes so I can't see what I am typing.

That fateful day began normally with my dear wife waking up beside me. We looked out of our floor-to-ceiling windows at the lily pond and saw three deer drinking. It seemed like the peaceable kingdom. We talked about a ski trip we were planning to Lake Tahoe the next week. We loved the winter mountains, skiing down the easier slopes followed by a warm and cuddly evening together. It always felt good in bed to wrap my arms around Gail.

She got out of bed first and started filling the tub with hot water for her morning bath. Since teenage days she had suffered from scoliosis with its attendant sore back, which was helped by hot water. I went into the living room to do my daily stretching exercises. A bank of low clouds had moved in from the west, causing a light fog to hang over the redwood trees as the deer wandered off down our hill.

When I finished my short routine, I came back into the bedroom and on to the steamed-filled bathroom to shave and take my shower. I found Gail in the tub gripping the safety bar with one hand and the other arm flailing about, and worst of all with her eyes unseeingly looking to the left. Instantly I knew something terrible had happened. I shook her by the shoulders and pleaded, "Gail, talk to me." It was awful. There was no answer or recognition, just a bewildered and fearful confusion, as if she had suddenly found herself plunged into a shadowy other world. I knew it was a stroke, heaven forbid. It took strength to pry her hand loose from the safety bar. I took her into my arms and carried her to the bedroom, where I laid her on the bed and dialed 911. I couldn't think of what to do except to dress her, hold her hand and remind her, over and over again, that I loved her, would not let her go and that everything would be okay, but I was so scared that this wasn't to be.

The paramedics were quick, efficient and kind. They put her into the ambulance and took off at high speed for the hospital, siren wailing. I raced behind them in our pick-up truck, praying that this would not be the last time Gail would see our beloved hill and home that we had built with our own hands.

In the hospital emergency room, after they had her hooked up to various monitors, I was again by Gail's side, holding her hand. The bewilderment and confusion had left her face and even though her eyes were closed she suddenly had a look of peace and contentment. Though I thought she needed rest, something prompted me to gently shake her awake. When Gail opened her eyes, a streak of hope shot through me. Still holding her hand, I moved my face into her line of vision. Her blue eyes softened beautifully in recognition. The right side of Gail's face was paralyzed, but she nonetheless gave me a lovely half smile that I shall never forget.

It seemed to me that her beautiful blue eyes projected a love such as I had never seen. I realized at that moment that Gail knew she was dying. I never experienced such love and tragedy at the same time and yet somehow it was very beautiful as if God touched us. Here in this storm of fear that was in my heart was a lovely jewel of transcendent love.

It seemed so appropriate for the two of us to be communicating mind to mind as she was leaving. Communication was always central to our companionship.

What we were doing was attuning ourselves to the godlike at-

tributes within us in harmony with the We Are All One principle.
Such attunements do stay with us and become part of our individual
selves at the very same time they exist in the Oneship. In this manner
we step forward on our path.

One of our first communications two weeks after Gail died
caught me by surprise.

Neither Gail nor I wanted a public memorial service, a
grave or the like. We both wanted to be returned to the soil where
our ashes might contribute to something living, without a plaque
or such, just a simple recycling. So for our family memorial gathering, on Easter Sunday as it turned out, I had decided to plant a
tree and mix Gail's ashes in the soil under the tree.

Forty years ago, when we first bought our 13-acre knoll,
we planted a black oak tree right by our house and it is now a big
lovely tree. We had always talked about planting another one but
had never gotten around to it. Now another black oak seemed to
be the most appropriate. I telephoned our local nursery; they had
no black oaks. They couldn't even order me one because it was the
wrong time of year. I called other nurseries in adjacent towns and,
sadly, no black oaks. I went to the library and looked in the yellow
pages for all the nurseries within 100 miles and I called each one. I
had luck with only one. They said they had a shipment of 10 black
oaks coming in on Good Friday and to call back.

When I called on Friday, they told me they had rejected
the shipment of oaks, as they were not of good enough quality. I
was terribly disappointed and reluctantly concluded that we would
have to plant my second choice, a redwood tree. But we already
have quite a number of redwoods on our hill and one more didn't
seem unique or special enough to honor Gail. I had tried my best,
however. Saturday I went down to the local nursery that I had first
called to buy the redwood.

I confess that shopping and I do not mix well. If I must
shop, I walk straight to what I want to buy, and then I pay for
it and leave. Many men are like this. I think most wives shake

their heads in despair over their husband's peculiar ways. Gail, of course, liked to browse around.

There I was walking into the nursery toward the redwoods when into my mind came this thought, "Don't be so silly. What makes you think they know what they have in their own inventory? Walk around." I immediately knew that this was Gail's thinking. After living with her for 47 years I knew how Gail's mind worked and this was her style, not mine. Being committed to staying open, I immediately changed course and headed up an aisle of plants not knowing where I was going. There, at the very end of that aisle, up against the fence—lo and behold—were three black oaks! One of them had an outstanding shape and I would have picked it out of 100 trees as Gail's tree. It had the most wonderful character. I found myself laughing and, in my mind, giving thanks to Gail.

Of course I bought that tree. It seems as if Gail arranged the whole thing including the frustration of finding the tree in the first place. She would know that would get my attention. What a lovely, humorous and gentle way for her to let me know of her presence and how she could help me. I felt so amazed and over-joyed to hear Gail's wonderful voice again. Much to the peculiar glances of the customers around me, I laughed out loud. I feel certain now that Gail's presence was not a figment of my imagination. Although I couldn't see her, I was absolutely positive that Gail was standing there beside me. My fears dissolved.

Later I had a number of feelings that Gail was close, often with a simple message of love and sympathy. They were short and came spontaneously. They seemed like real contacts with her but in a fuzzy and unique way. Still it took five years until these inspired letters first came through.

Gail and I studied various schools of mysticism for 40 years. Every time we reached a new understanding of the questions that puzzled us, we would find that this insight stimulated a whole new series of questions. We read many instructive books, but wished somehow we could have a direct dialogue with someone on the other side who would comment on the very subject that was then puzzling us.

Now that is actually happening with Gail's passing. As I tap into her spiritual view of life after death I want to share what we have been discussing these past years.

❧

Life is endless and endlessly fascinating. If you could see the panorama of it all, many of your fears would evaporate.

Of all the difficulties you face in life, the worst is fear; fear of sickness, fear of starvation and fear of death contribute to not seeing things as they really are. But even these have a vital function to play on your journey to fulfill your nature.

Fear motivates you to do many things, some of which you can call good and many others you can call negative. No matter which it is, fear will keep you searching. It is by seeking that you grow. If life is too easy you may settle back with little progress on your path.

It may seem that I am saying that it is best for you to be in constant agitation. It would seem to indicate that the serenity you seek is impossible in this world, as it would inhibit growth. Fortunately this is not true. Our God is merciful. We need quiet along with our agitation, just as after eating we need a period to digest what we have eaten.

You will find that serenity is a reward you attain by your growth. As your understanding expands, your fears diminish and your periods of serenity deepen. Another way of saying this is that if you develop the attributes given to you by God, such as love and patience, you will find peace.

What you all wish is to speed up the process and in this way take much of the sting out of our difficulties. There are many, many ways to learn and one of the most helpful is to think of God's attribute of inclusion that is within you. Fear and separation are twins. Fear promotes to the urge to separate yourself from that which you fear, but a goal of inclusion will bring you into greater understanding.

Inclusion doesn't necessarily mean you have to immediately embrace what you fear; rather it means you should stay alert to its presence. Fear tends to perpetuate itself even after the reasons for it have disappeared.

≋

I walk down my hill via the long driveway to get my mail. It is dark as the mail delivery comes late. I carry a flashlight but seldom use it. When it is on I can see where my feet are going within the small circle of light but little else. I turn it off and I see so much more: the dark trees pushed against the night sky, the planet Venus and Jupiter too, the stars of such wonder revealing themselves. All these are invisible when I choose to guide my feet by the flashlight's beam. I'm glad I've always wanted to see beyond the limited pedestrian view at my feet to include instead the vastness that is. I walk in the dark so that I may see. I walk in the dark that I may know the magnificence of God. I love all his creations including myself.

Why do I use my flashlight? So that I can see where my feet are going. Why do I need to see where my feet are going? So that I don't stumble or fall. In other words I use my flashlight to avoid fearful consequences. I use my flashlight out of fear.

Whenever you are fearful you narrow your vision to that which you fear. This obscures the vastness of the One from your view. You become limited. Your awareness is actually confined within the boundaries of the light cast by your flashlight. This results in separation from true reality.

The next chapter tells of a tool you may use to lessen your fears and reveal the path to take.

CHAPTER TWELVE

Patternmatics, a Useful Guide

Does your life work for you?

Or does a significant part of your life seem undeservedly difficult, a series of circumstances that occur without apparent reason, or worst of all, totally beyond your control? Do you struggle to get some semblance of satisfaction with life only to have an interruption come out of nowhere, to upset you and disturb your being? If so you are not alone. A huge number of people know exactly what this feels like.

Why is this so? There are patterns to life—some you see, some which are hidden. The fact that you do not see hidden ones does not diminish their effect on your life. The law of gravity behaves the same whether mankind believes in it or not. Life patterns also operate with or without your consent. **You can be sure those areas of your life that give you trouble are those where patterns you don't see are operating in your life.**

You can vastly improve your life by becoming aware of these **hidden** patterns. Doing so will increase your ability to foresee the result of your actions and the actions of others. With this expanded predictability you can attract what you want in life and reduce the negative effects of difficulties.

To make it clear let's use an analogy. Two people mount surfboards out in the breakers off Waialua Beach. One is an experienced surfer who recognizes the pattern of the breakers; the other hasn't a clue and sees no wave pattern at all. (It is difficult to believe anyone could be so naive, but pretend this is true). This clueless surfer is out there hanging precariously onto his surfboard. He no more gets on top of the board to catch a much-needed breather when along comes a wave that throws him off his board.

Desperately he grabs the board again trying to climb back on before it zooms out of reach. After a struggle he succeeds only to be thrown again by the next wave. These seemingly random waves are giving him fits.

The experienced surfer is in exactly the same situation; he, however, recognizes the patterns of the waves, anticipates them properly and delights in a great run. Instead of a disastrous environment he enjoys the situation so much he paddles right out again to catch another wave, voluntarily putting himself in the predicament the other person can't tolerate.

We have two people placed in identical external circumstances yet each responding in opposite ways. For one, life (i.e. the wave) is catastrophically unpredictable and he can prove it by what is happening to him; he is a victim and, of course, an innocent one. He feels his only recourse is to get the hell out of there or more accurately get out of that hell. For the other, life is sweet and exciting and his only regret is that he will have to quit and go back to work.

The key to the difference between these two outlooks on life lies first in the perception of the wave patterns and then in their utilization. Of course, a good deal of practice is involved, but observe that the practice would have been fruitless if the surfer did not first understand the wave patterns involved.

In this same way if we fail to see our life patterns, we encounter difficulties. If we recognize them and practice understanding them, we live with joy. The first step is to be alert to these patterns and see how they affect us and others. We can use the patterns as our tools to accomplish our goals, such as a thrilling ride on a wave. Our problems, however, come from those patterns that remain hidden from us.

In actuality, we are already making use of the patterns we perceive. We all recognize that to get a good job we need an education. Further, to get an effective education we need to study. Here is a pattern many of us have used and have put a great deal of effort into because the predictability of the pattern is reliable. Hard work and study equal a good education that in turn equals a better, higher paying job. This pattern and predictable result warrant our efforts. If the pattern did not exist few of us would bother with the task.

It is also a common observation that we can recognize other people's bad behavioral patterns more clearly than we see our own. An obvious example is the alcoholic who is the last one among his friends and family to recognize his destructive drinking patterns. His agility in denying the obvious is remarkable. To overcome his problem he needs first to see that his drinking patterns do spell "alcoholic" and then, and only then, can he begin recovery and straighten out his life.

Patterns go well beyond this. There are many important life patterns that we only see in bits and pieces or fail to see altogether. In general, realize that if there is a hidden pattern in our lives causing us difficulties, we can, by recognizing it, put our energies in a direction that will bring us satisfaction not pain.

The same thing happens when you bake a cake. You have a recipe, a pattern, which you follow and if you are a good cook (accurately following the pattern) you reap the predictable result of a delicious cake. The key is to recognize the pattern, follow it and get the intended results. This way you can choose what comes to you in life, a piece of cake or an inedible mess.

Going back to the two surfers most of us would agree that our lives contain experiences of both the skilled person who enjoyably rides the waves and the battered one wishing all this were happening to someone else. What gives us difficulty we usually describe as bad luck. We believe this bad thing descended on us without warning, which we don't deserve. It seems so unfair because it came to us at random. It is as if we were a non-participant and suddenly were grabbed by the neck and thrown about. This is the precise area of our lives that we should like to understand but we don't know how. How can you improve on random bad luck? If it's truly random, you can't improve it and that is why you feel helpless; but was it just bad luck?

When we cannot see patterns in the difficulties we are experiencing, would it not seem reasonable to try to identify them? I realize you may be thinking there are no patterns but please do not persist in believing so, or you will remain stuck and dissatisfied. If you are not looking for a pattern you will surely not recognize it, even if it is there. With each discovery of an unseen pattern you will improve your life.

All human knowledge is derived from the recognition of patterns. This is a very broad statement but nonetheless true. Without discerning the pattern of the seasons, all agriculture would be impossible. And that is just one example. Patterns manifest as distinctly in the spiritual realm as they do in the material world. Astrology is but a compendium of patterns long recognized. As we perceive and understand our spiritual patterns, we take a step forward in our evolvement.

This is achieved by broadening our understanding of patterns both in material and spiritual realms. Einstein's $e = mc^2$ is a pattern whose identification has had a great effect on this world. All nuclear power, whether good or bad, is based on this formula of converting mass to energy. Before Einstein everyone was oblivious to the pattern even though it operated faultlessly. With this pattern recognition we have solved many problems.

Try to think of anything we know or do that doesn't derive from a pattern. You will find it difficult. As patterns are central to all human knowledge *they also are central to your life.*

Look at the following apparently random set of letters.

A llhu ma nkn owle
dg eisd eri vedf
romt hedi sce rnm
ent ofp at ter ns.

To some the above is meaningless. Others have already discovered the pattern, that the four lines have meaning. What appeared as *without* order turns out to be *with* pattern. It is a statement in English in which the spaces between words have been shifted to spaces within words: "All human knowledge is derived from the discernment of patterns." Just as simply and easily the patterns ruling your life can be converted from random meaningless "bad luck" to instructive guidance.

Science is not exempt from this same problem of hidden patterns. In fact, science could be described as the art of revealing hitherto unseen patterns. In the last several decades' science has had to do just what I'm asking you to do: Assume there are patterns where you think there are none.

Science defined chaos as a condition without patterns. It has now found patterns in chaos and very beautiful ones at that. In a 1960's era Webster's dictionary chaos, is defined as any condition or place of total disorder and confusion, in short a patternless condition. Now with Benoit Mandelbrot (a stellar mathematician) we discover that chaos has beautiful patterns, which we call fractals, and even more remarkably; fractals are everywhere. All this beauty and understanding lay hidden from us because we thought chaos was without pattern, for we defined it that way. In getting at this knowledge we had to change the very definition of chaos.

We, too, can discover that the chaos in our lives has patterns that we may utilize in spite of our current view that bad luck is without pattern. Finding these patterns is the key to new understandings of what makes the world tick and how we can ride the waves to our joy and satisfaction. So, too, you can see beauty where there was none.

To become more familiar with patterns we need to discuss them from an even wider point of view.

Almost all human knowledge has been derived from someone's discernment of a pattern. Michael Faraday experimented for years before discovering how to generate an electric current. Unwittingly he and other scientists were limiting themselves to a pattern by assuming it would be done with a static apparatus. Then he discovered this significant expanded pattern: If you *move* a wire within a magnetic field, electricity is generated. Simple, but it took one of our greatest minds nine years to discover this.

We are immersed in a world of many patterns, some of which we have discovered and many others of which we have no inkling. The uncovering of many more patterns has brought about the current explosion in human knowledge. For example, Watson and Crick discovered the double helix pattern of the chromosome and ushered in a burst of biological knowledge.

I chose the word patternmatics to describe this because, like mathematics, patterns have application in all fields of study. In fact, mathematics is itself an intricate, fascinating series of patterns and as such is a subsidiary of patternmatics.

Since almost all human knowledge comes from pattern perception, we can reasonably conclude that it is possible to discover new knowledge about ourselves by seeking the hidden patterns in our lives.

CHAPTER THIRTEEN

Gratitude: We've Got it Backwards

God loves us and has given us the tools we need in order to advance toward joy and enlightenment. One such tool, gratitude, is an effective means to bring about much satisfaction in our lives. Although gratitude is easy to understand, it is not always easy to use. We feel justified in perceiving our lives as full of disagreeable, unjust things. How can we rationally feel gratitude?

Dear Gail, here I am at the small rock pile in the sagebrush desert we discovered years ago. I am totally by myself. God seems very near and the world so perfect. I hear God's voice in the wind through the piñon pines.

Sweet Buck, what could be more perfect than the butterfly that just jiggled by. Perfection is everywhere when you give gratitude. It is by feeling gratitude that perfection reaches through to your perception.

Again the world has it backwards. Most withhold gratitude until they experience something to be grateful for. You feel it would be a grave error to express gratitude for something that didn't deserve it. It is as though gratitude were something scarce that should not be spent carelessly. In actuality gratitude is a precious commodity, not because it is scarce, but because it is so powerful.

You think something good comes first and then gratitude follows. Yet the reverse is actually true; **gratitude comes first and then good things happen.** *Something good does not bring forth gratitude; rather gratitude brings forth that which is good. I know you realize this and reap the rewards. Others would receive a great gift if they would try it. Gratitude is not something you need to conserve. In truth, the more you use the more you have. It is not a crime to give gratitude for something that on the surface appears undeserving. Grat-*

itude will lead you deeper into feeling perfection. This is particularly true with respect to life's adversities.

Buck, your ability to feel gratitude was key to your response to my death. You kept returning to the gratitude you felt for sharing my life, my love and our learning. This gratitude made it possible for you to perceive the perfection of my passing. Having experienced it, the word perfection is not too strong a word for me to use with you. To some it will seem an ugly, gross exaggeration.

When I died there was an ambiance of great sorrow. You, Buck, in your gratitude to me for spending my life with you brought forth a positive, loving presence in that soup of sorrow. This in turn brought healing to you and through you to our family. Although this might be hard to understand, that was perfection in action.

In experimenting with gratitude I have discovered two benefits. First, I realize and feel gratitude for things I used to just take for granted, such as my Napa hilltop. Secondly, in ways I do not understand, feeling gratitude seems to attract into my life people, things and experiences that I enjoy.

Dear Buck, you are an enchanted oasis, as is every soul. The meaning of this oasis is not that you are all alone in the middle of the desert, but rather that you have within all that you need (metaphorically): water, sun, greenery, sustenance and a cohesiveness of being.

When you realize God has made you self-sustaining, many good things come to you. You have less to fear. You feel good about yourself. You feel capable of pursuing fulfillment. Perhaps most important you feel gratitude for what you have been given. Gratitude opens the door to so many other wonderful things.

If you can begin to feel gratitude for things that at first appear to be unwelcome, the outer covering will strip away and you will see the perfection within.

All is within the mind. As Edgar Cayce said so simply, "The mind is the builder." With it you can construct a world much more to your liking than what you have so far perceived. God has given you the key, yet you leave it unused by limiting your perception. As you begin to truly see who you are, you will realize how glorious it all is: All life on Earth is singing but you have turned the volume so low you can't hear it. Turn it up and listen. There is so much more for you to see and listen to. There is so much more for you to feel. Welcome these into your life.

❦

Dear Buck always the puzzler. Write down your thought.

If God's spiritual laws assure that you receive your due without his intervention it seems that gratitude might be somewhat redundant. What are you thanking God for if he has not intervened on your behalf?

*You are right that your gratitude should not be based on thanking him for intervening on your behalf even though many do just that and it causes no harm. Your gratitude should be in recognition of the beneficence of his spiritual laws and the totally beautiful creation in which he has placed you. You should thank him as he has given you everything you need to have an abundant life filled with love, communion and joy. You should thank him for his three great gifts (**you live forever, you are given free choice, and you are part of the Oneship**) as well as his many other gifts, along with his creation of you in the first place.*

You should also thank him for the generosity in providing his law of gratitude. Under this law if you give gratitude you will attract to yourself the good things in life. By giving gratitude for what you have, you show the capacity to appreciate what you receive. Thus more will be given to you.

Live in gratitude that God has given you your own soul. You can say, "Thank you God for the blessing that is me." That, of course, is just the beginning. Be thankful for colors, plants, the sky and so many other things that fill your life. Be thankful for the good people who are in your life. Be grateful for your relationships with them, which we will take up next. Your gratitude should not be based on a particular nicety that has come into your life, but on the wonderful panoply in which you are immersed.

Living in gratitude heals.

Perfection as used throughout this book refers to the process by which we find ourselves; the process of developing our God-given attributes to their fullest potential. As we all observe, the world at any given time is imperfect. This imperfection is the result of the pace of our learning. As we learn our world improves because of **the perfection of the learning process**. The value of the teaching systems that God has created for us becomes apparent when this is realized.

CHAPTER FOURTEEN

Relationships: The Learning Arena

You spend much of your lives in relationships, which offer you so many learning opportunities. Relationships always offer the opportunity to grow whether they are loving or rocky; that they present difficulties along with fulfillment simply underlines their importance. How you grow is up to you. You can make things worse or make them better depending on your understanding and intentions.

You try to develop the relationships you want, particularly close ones. If difficulties arise in these, you are prone to think of how you would like the other to behave, how you would like the other to think and how you would like the other to feel about you. You fall into the habit of thinking that the other person needs to change in these various ways while you continue more or less as you are. You don't think as much about how you could change your behavior, thinking or feeling.

There is a secret here. You could assume the best way to change another is, either overtly or covertly, to direct or manipulate them toward your point of view. That is typical of the earthly approach: work directly for what you want. This approach doesn't work very well, especially in the long run. You may gain temporary success only to find that the other is building up resentment.

The secret is that by being willing to change yourself, you are more likely to be successful in creating a relationship to your liking. Now it may not be the relationship you originally thought you wanted, but it will be one that is both good for your partner and good for you.

Since your description of the relationship you wanted was all about how the other should change and little about how you could change, what is there for you to alter in yourself? You feel you already bring what is needed for the relationship to prosper. To seek the overall view let's talk as well about what helpful adjustments you could make in yourself.

You could try to have within you an attitude of respect for others seeking their truth. You may feel your partner has taken a wrong turn, and he may have, but you must respect his seeking. A productive talk is more likely to occur if you have an attitude of respect.

In truth you only have jurisdiction over changing yourself; you do not have jurisdiction to change someone else. If you invade your partner's jurisdiction and take it over as if it were yours, things will worsen.

Further, you need to understand that it is not up to you to make a unilateral decision of what your relationship should be. Your partner needs to be involved in making this determination as well. In some ways it is best for neither of you to make this determination, but simply to let it grow as it chooses, an organic relationship, if you will, without the use of pesticides and chemical fertilizers.

In essence, by giving up control you create a garden much more likely to be bountiful. You do not need to control what the relationship is to become. You do not need to direct the other person's behavior and growth. Discussion with respect is helpful in keeping communication flowing, but trying to control the outcome shuts your partner down. Positive behavior by both of you is more likely to occur if communications are open and done in mutual respect. Giving up control need not be frightening. In fact, giving it up leads to the delights of watching a new flower bloom.

This reminds me of the art of picking wild blackberries; you don't pick the berries you want, you pick the berries the bush wants to give you. This is also the art of close personal relationships. Failure to realize this leaves you scratched and scarred.

There are other changes you can make within yourself that will do wonders in improving your relationships, but this is enough for now. I need to add that the above applies particularly to adult relationships. It also applies to parent/child and child/ parent relationships, but other responsibilities each way complicate that issue.

Hello Buck, it is not only your fingers I use directly, but also your mind. I communicate through your inner self to your conscious mind through your fingers.

You and I thought that God had deliberately made the romantic relationship between a man and a woman paramount in the scheme of things. The highest potential for learning, the highest potential for realizing that we are all One could be realized in a long-term male/female relationship. This is the prime arena. God gave it the function of reproduction to enhance both joys and challenges in a learning environment. He made women appear to men as beautiful and men appear to women as desirable. And as you say the rest is our history.

The spousal relationship is both the playground and the classroom. You should delight in both. You should also be willing to labor in the process, as the rewards in advancement are great.

What are you seeking in this relationship? It can be described in a number of ways, but I will describe it as congruency, an unromantic word. You are to experience and learn the techniques in becoming congruent. Male and female are both equal, being so created by God. We are not the same, not even close. It needs to be understood that spiritual congruency does not mean the fitting together of equal, identical things. In fact, the fitting together into congruency may require that one be the opposite of the other such as pushing the plug into the electrical socket in which neither is superior.

The sex organs so central to the male/female relationship fit together with joy. I assume this is congruency even though they are in effect the opposite of each other. Is this right?

Yes, but do you need to be so openly graphic about it? Some of our readers will find such descriptions uncomfortable.

Your goal is to bring the mind, body and heart into congru-

ency. All three are different aspects with different sexual approaches. They can be joined as three manifestations that fit together consistently with a singularity of purpose.

In the male/female relationship you develop your skills to bring two equal but different entities and energies into congruency. In this way the power that God invested in each can then work together to achieve the common goal. In romantic relationships this goal changes constantly, but in time will focus on the development of your truth in fulfilling your nature.

I need to add that there are many on Earth who are not involved in a male/female relationship nor do they need to be. Their purpose in this particular lifetime has a different direction. In previous lives they may have had such relationships, but in this current life they are learning other lessons. Again the key is to seek your truth, which does not have to include a male/female relationship. In fact, there is no external thing, relationship or experience that you need to have in any given lifetime. That is one of the accommodating beauties of God's world and is one of the results of having free choice.

～

Dear One, here I am at the ranch after a busy weekend. I had a glass of wine and dinner on the new deck, which we have partly finished. The sun hasn't yet burned off the fog.

Dear Buck, those redwoods make such lovely groves. We should talk about blessings since you are in a blessed place. What is a blessing? It is something that you can both give and receive. And herein is the key to both giving and receiving. They are acts of joining, sharing and an expression of the Oneship.

When God gives you a blessing and you receive it with gratitude, it is a way of acknowledging the We Are All One Principle. On the other hand when God gives you a blessing and you are not aware of it nor do you feel gratitude for it, you are responding with separation. This has been your problem all along. You choose separation, not join-

ing. As long as you choose separation you will continue to have strife and difficulties, and won't achieve the peace and serenity you seek.

You choose separation when you assume that death is the inevitable and complete separation from your loved ones. This is an incorrect assumption. People have plenty of experiences demonstrating that death is not the ultimate separation. You and I are having such an experience.

There are many who feel that if something is not "proven," it is false. This is close-mindedness. This "separates" you from many truths including this one. There is no need to believe that the deceased can communicate with you. You need only be willing to acknowledge that it is possible. This will open the mind to recognizing such experiences when they occur. If you are close-minded you could have such experiences and never know it. It is your choice. Which do you prefer: shutting yourself off or becoming aware?

There are also the blessings you give each other. Now these may seem very paltry compared to those of God's. You now have gratitude for God's blessing of your being in the redwoods on a soft lovely day. How can you give a blessing to someone else to compare with this? In one way you cannot and yet in another way you can give an even greater blessing to someone else.

You have been created by God to be a wondrous being. When you open yourself to someone else, you are indeed giving a blessing of great magnitude. Others may not accept your blessing; they may not even be aware of the great gift that it is, but that is not as important as your giving it. This someone else may also ignore the blessings of God. There is no need to be hurt by this; being hurt is giving in to separation again.

There is risk in opening and giving yourself to others. There is also joy to be had in sharing. It helps here if you see that this opening and giving of yourself is more of an attitude than an act. It is more a state of being than a state of doing. With this understanding you can be open to someone you simply walk by on the street as easily as to members of your family.

When you "do" something for someone else it is so easy to build up an expectation of how they will respond, which tends to lead to disappointment. When you are simply "being" open to another, expectations don't arise as quickly and you are saved from disappointment.

Expectations are really a manner of closing down options. You expect one thing and so you are disappointed when another thing happens. You therefore increase the possibility of your being disappointed because you have now defined fewer possibilities for your happiness to occur. Rather than limiting your opportunities, you should include more possibilities to please you. You can accomplish this by your attitude of "being" without expectations.

The above is particularly true in relationships.

Good morning my beloved. I feel you wanting to write to me now. That is such a nice feeling; I bask in it.

My dear husband, today let's talk about fights and failures, but we need to start at the beginning.

Your purpose on Earth is to learn. By definition learning means that you are attempting to understand something new. If it isn't new, then you already know it and you are not learning something new. Thus true learning means you are thinking or doing something new.

How skillful are you at doing what you have never done before? Not very. This means that those who are truly learning the most will appear as quite unskillful. A very good example of this is teenagers. They take great risks as they learn to be adults, independent and self reliant, and because they have not done it before, they are not very good at it. Not being very proficient means they will do foolish things, appear irrational and engage in all sorts of teenage behavior. If you thought of them as stumbling apprentices you would be more understanding.

Now let's apply this same pattern to a long-term female/male relationship. You all dream of this being a cozy, frictionless joining, and it can be, but this comes as the reward for creating a learning environment in your relationship. In a learning environment you run into this same lack of skill in learning new ways and often find your significant other being foolish, irrational and stumbling. You, too, will be foolish, irrational and stumbling, but this won't be so obvious to you. You can isolate or separate the episode into a fight with its causes and effects and define it as a failure if you take the narrow view.

As I have emphasized, however, solutions are found in widening one's perspective. Let's take the narrow view of the fight and expand it. Imagine it no longer as a fight but as two brave people trying to learn something new and realizing they will stumble as they progress. Of course, they will make mistakes. Of course, these mistake will upset the other person, but this is all to the good if you view it properly. So instead of being discouraged by a fight, be encouraged and learn as the circumstances beckon you. If you regard these failures as simply ineptitude you will find yourself being more tolerant.

I would like to go one step further. When a loved one dies it is only logical to assume that they pass over with a number of these failures or learning opportunities still unresolved. With a narrow perspective this can seem tragic to the survivor. Again, however, by widening the perspective, you see that it is just a stage in an ongoing process taking lifetimes to complete. You can continue to learn and grow with your departed one and resolve the unresolved. Godspeed.

Dear sweet friend, no fog this morning so it will get hot. I'm getting ready for another trip to the Sierras. The aspen leaves should be turning.

Buck, how lucky we were to always be each other's best friend. Husbands and wives have responsibilities and expectations of each other, which can be either a joy or a burden.

Friends are different even if only by degree. A friend allows you to be who you seek to be. A friend does not have fixed expectations *as to what you should do. Oh I know that there are friends who make heavy demands on each other. In these cases I would ask you, are they friends or codependents? No, true friends help you find your truth. This truth may be very different than their truth, but they accept your seeking your path. In fact, some friendships are based on the fascination one has for someone who approaches life differently. This open tolerance and even admiration for differences is a quality to be sought.*

Do not misunderstand. This is not an argument to downgrade the married state or the closeness of a family. Each has its virtues. It is an argument to bring this quality of open, tolerant friendship into intimate relationships. This will only improve and deepen them.

Your friendship attitude can and should be extended to the weather, trees, flowers, animals and in truth your entire world. Why did you and I love the wilderness so? It was because all life forms in the wilderness are following their own truth, their own nature, and by so doing creating a vast balanced ambiance that we loved. Why did we so love wild animals? Why were we going to Africa on our own with those big animals right outside our tent? Do you remember the two enormous rocks twenty feet from where we slept that turned out in the morning to be two sleeping rhinos?

We have always been drawn to those creatures and people who follow their own path, fulfilling themselves as they celebrate life. This includes what the Earth calls the non-living as well. Why did we delight in those magnificent thunderstorms in the Southwest? They too are living things that seek their own natures. All things are living or they wouldn't be. How can you look at the Iguazu Falls and not see that it is living? Vitality, energy and fluidity just ooze out endlessly. Waterfalls are fulfilling their inner purpose as given to them by God.

God's entire universe in which you find yourself immersed is worthy of your complete acceptance, respect and love. You can be friends, best friends, with all of it. Walk in friendship with all that you see, hear, feel, smell and touch. If you do, you will know joy.

Can you not see the wisdom in this? Wisdom can be defined as finding God's intent. It is God's intent that you are friends with his entire creation. There is nothing that he created which you cannot embrace.

CHAPTER FIFTEEN

Love: Romantic and Otherwise

How beloved you are. Our last lifetime together was a wonder. I remember very well hugging you after you died. Your body was still warm but I could feel it begin to cool. That may sound creepy to anyone else, but I never found anything about you creepy. It helped me say goodbye. All of those people were wonderful at the hospital.

Do you remember when we were first married how good it felt to lie in bed hugging and cuddling? Any way we lay down with each other we seemed to fit so very well, as though we were designed to hug that way. I remember telling you that if I had to choose between making love to you or being able to hug you, I would choose the latter. That's just how good it felt. Luckily we had both. It was not an either-or choice.

Yes, I remember. That was characteristic of our lives together. It was not either this or that. We had both. In Cincinnati where I grew up this last life, the German men, like my father, were very attracted to the Irish women because they were full of life and exciting to be with. And the Irish women found the dependable, hard working German men attractive. So a Feinauer married a Flannagan and became my parents.

When I was young my Prince Charming was going to be both at once. He would be dependable, hard working and at the same time be exciting and full of life. He would not be either-or. If I had looked around me I would have realized how unusual that was. I also wanted us to be in love and romantic all our married life not just in the beginning. When I found that man I would be a perfect wife for him as he would be the perfect husband for me. Youth is full of ideals.

But that is what you were for me. You were ever dependable and wanted to be the breadwinner. Also you always surprised me with what you could and would do. I can't imagine many men doing as you: buying a panel truck, building a bed and small kitchen in the back and with our 8-month-old first born, driving around the country to decide where we would live [this was before RVs]. *And you wanted it to be our decision not just yours. Our life seldom was either/or. It was both. We were so fortunate. No wonder Betty Bethards* [a Bay Area psychic] *said we had a marriage that was one in ten thousand.*

Do you know Gail that the single thing I am most proud of in my life is that I fulfilled your adolescent dreams for a husband? You told me that a number of times; it made me feel so good. As we matured as adults we came to appreciate that part of the satisfaction in marriage comes from resolving the frictions that any male and female find in joining. You and I had our share, but these never dented our commitment to each other. I also knew I wanted to have a life companion and best friend in my wife. And you, my beloved, were that and more.

Yes, Buck, we have appreciated each other. We have also appreciated our learning opportunities. Did you ever think when we got married that here we would be, more than 60 years later, with you alive and me dead and yet still learning, still communicating, and yes, still loving with all our hearts?

I feel it necessary to state here that the love I share with Buck, now that I am on this side, is not exclusive. It is a joint love of life. That sounds strange with me so-called dead. Perhaps better would be to say, "Joint love of being."

I want you, Buck, to have a female friend. The inclusiveness of all life is the basis of our love. Others enhance this love. You have sought, as you should, a special female friend. You and I are both incurable romantics. To live without this aspect would not be a full life for you. I know how loving you can be. I would feel it a waste for you not to find someone to give that to.

And yes, there is room for you to learn and grow to be even more loving than you were with me. Here again a misunderstanding can occur. It does me no honor for you to place limits on yourself in how you relate to another woman. Particularly, you should not think that your relationship with her must somehow be less than your relationship with me. Limiting yourself is not what you are about, nor is it the wish of God.

In truth your relationship with her will be different than your relationship with me. This is as it should be. In your relationship with her you will be encountering new experiences, new personality traits. This in turn will stimulate a response in you that is also new and different. This is how you both will grow. Celebrate romance. So my dear, cherish every moment.

There is much love in the world. Anyone anytime can join in this love. In so doing love is both received and given. This is especially important to anyone feeling lonely.

Dear sweet one, I rededicate myself to you and the work we are doing. I love you. I want to be of service to the Oneship. I ask you to help me to be a communicator with you and with all the spiritual beings that are helping this world remember God.

My most precious Buck, take heart. Our communications will all come because that is what the spiritual presences want to happen. I love you too. I also love the Oneship and I love God. From this comes JOY, which you feel too. It is in the love that flows out of you that causes the joy to flow into you. **When love flows out something else must flow in.** *What flows in? The law of congruency governs. What flows in is congruent with what flows out. Therefore if you truly feel love and you let it flow out unrestricted, you will have joy flow in unrestricted. It is simply elegant.*

The reverse is also true in that if you let bitterness flow out of you then you will attract bitterness or perceive reasons to be bitter.

Outside events will then seem to justify within you a bitter response.

This is why Jesus taught that your thoughts are so important and that love is the answer.

You on Earth are so absorbed in dealing only with the material, you don't see how powerfully influential your mental perceptions are. You believe the material is the only way to promote relief. If no material benefit occurs you assume no benefit has been achieved. That is untrue. The mind has tremendous power and effect that often does not manifest a material change. All of the many steps you individually take to return to God seldom involve a material event. They are mostly internal events. It is true they may subsequently cause a change in your behavior that will show up externally, but that is an after effect.

The other thing you greatly underestimate is the ability of one mind to reach another mind. (You and I, of course, are doing this now.) When you see a drunk lying on the sidewalk and you send love out to him as inclusion in the Oneship, it seems to have no effect. The drunk is still passed out. But what you don't realize is that his inner self, his subconscious, does indeed register your joining. This is of great benefit. If you pay attention you will feel the response of the drunk's inner self. It is a form of greeting that acknowledges the Oneship. Every time two or more minds join in the Oneship, the Oneship strengthens. There is no greater labor or spiritual honor than in strengthening the Oneship. Do so consciously, deliberately, and feel the results in your heart.

Thank you, Gail. This throws new light on what we can do in this world. It so often seems our own individual efforts are totally smothered by the enormity of world problems that we feel hopeless and powerless. What you have said allows us to participate positively in bringing peace and serenity ourselves and others.

I particularly like your explanation that when something flows out of you, something else will flow in to take its place. This explains how we attract to ourselves all those events that we consider external and beyond our control. The mystical schools have always said we create our realty but it can be difficult to see how this is so. I now understand one mechanism to accomplish this, which allows karma to work; we are at all times sending out and receiving. It shouldn't surprise us that what we send out and what we receive are not two separate, unrelated things. They, like everything else, are one; therefore what you send out determines what you receive.

~~~~~

Dear Gail, it is a lovely rainy day, good to be inside dry and warm. Share this good feeling with me.

Dear Buck, I do share your feelings, and can almost sense the wind blowing through the pines, and see the dark sky. There you are sheltered in the house that you and I built. In front of you is the window you made in the same proportions as a Chinese wall hanging. I always loved that window and how it shows sky, roof and bamboo, which are now swaying in the wind. God does make all things beautiful. He gave each of his children the power to make things beautiful as well. You don't take full advantage of that power.

Love is at the core of all things. If God withdrew his love from you, you would cease to be. Although your very life depends upon it, you often do not recognize it. Love comes to you from God pure and constant, but it can come out of you distorted. Ironically, it takes work to change the love energy into the distorted form that you give out, while it takes no work or energy to let it pass through you as unadulterated love.

Why do you do things the hard way? Why do you allow yourself to be your own worst enemy? And why do you take such delight in blaming things and people outside yourself for your errors? No wonder you find the world so puzzling. You are looking for solutions where they are not. Love is your solution.

Even love you do not understand. Love is your respect, your acceptance, your appreciation of everything that is seeking the fulfillment of its nature. And you ask, what is its nature given to it by God?

With that very question you lead yourself astray. You start right off judging and separating, which is the opposite of love. Simply observe what its nature is. Don't meddle with it. This is another amplification of the mystical phrase: "You need do nothing."

Divine love does not come in pieces. You cannot give a piece of divine love to this person and withhold a piece of that love from another person because in your judgment they are not entitled to it. God has entitled all. Don't argue with God. Don't argue with love; just give it.

Do you really believe that this world would stumble if you were to make a practice of love? Would criminals go unpunished? Would chaos reign? Again you have it backwards. As so often is the case, it is the culturally counter intuitive that works, and since it is counter intuitive, you hesitate to try it. In actuality your intuition is the most reliable part of your thinking.

Illogical as it may seem, if you loved as I have defined it, the world would be greatly improved. And don't be misled in thinking this could only occur if suddenly everybody decided to do this. The world would change with just your love. Oh I know you find this very difficult to do, and from your perspective it is. And that is precisely the key; it is your perspective that is hindering you. Broaden your perspective and it all becomes much, much easier.

Beloved Buck, It is a fine morning. Love is my favorite topic. It is both much more and much less than what you on Earth think it is.

It is less than you think in this sense. Love on Earth is given many meanings, some of which seem very beautiful. Take for example the love given to a child by its parents. They do genuinely love that child. But then in school, the parents are so very pleased when their child is the best in the class. This love can become a put down for all the others and a means of separating their child from other children.

So much of earthly love is conditional. If you fulfill these conditions (your part of the bargain) then I will love you (my part of the bargain). And then there is the corollary, which says I withhold my love because of what you did. Further I will continue to withhold my love until you straighten out and comply with my vision of what you ought to be. Many a husband and wife have at times withheld their love until such time as the offending spouse has come "back in line."

So much of earthly love is doing. We don't feel we are loving unless we do something to back up our love. We also don't feel loved unless some action is taken that proves it. Love is a state of being from which actions, if any, flow out automatically.

There is nothing inherently wrong with your manifestations of earthly love. It is just unfortunate that you use the same word "love" to describe both earthly love and the way God loves. Language is full of words that have two or more meanings. But it does seem as though there is confusion over the distinction between divine universal love and earthly love.

~

Beloved Buck, you are feeling very good and that is fine.

Today I would like to talk about how one practices with love. The most important thing you have to do today is love. Every action, every thought should come from love. You have no idea how much this would change your life.

*Do you remember when we studied **A Course in Miracles** that it seemed so very difficult, even impossible, to be as he said we should? Just the one example that we should love all people equally from Hitler to our own children seemed altogether beyond any mortal's capabilities. Then he goes on to say that until you can do that you cannot be with God.*

To give love in every action and thought is difficult. Love should place no demands nor should it expect returns. If you do even one loving thing or think one thought, however, it is quite effective in transforming how you feel about your world.

So try to do things with love this day. Have that in the forefront of your mind. You will notice an immediate change. Then think the next thought with love. It will become easier and easier. You will inevitably run into a hard place where you will not respond with love. That's okay. Accept it and go on. Get back in the mode of love. This will do much for your life. Your joy will come more easily

❧

Today we shall talk about being beloved. Each of you is beloved by God. How you individually learn to see your fellow brothers and sisters as beloved is a process, as is how they see you as beloved. Your path to enlightenment follows a gradual awakening that you are worthy of being loved and know the joy of finding others beloved.

With your earthly experience it is difficult to know, feel and transmit pure love. An analogy that will be helpful is to think of how you feel about children. You watch with wonder as they respond energetically to their inner being with such zest, absorption and freshness. When you don't judge their behavior, but watch their spontaneity, they are beloved by you. They don't even have to be your children. You accept and feel pleased with whatever it is that they do. (As an adult you wish you could yourself return to that same natural spontaneity.) Even when a child is behaving badly he has a charm and appeal that makes him beloved. This is what it is like to find others beloved.

To feel that you are beloved is similar but different in that it reverses the flow but not the content. Buck, do you feel beloved?

Yes I do. I feel beloved by you, Gail, as I did when you were on Earth. Sometimes it is palpable and that is wonderful, like now, for love, though intangible, is very powerful. I also feel beloved by God because I feel his blessings. Here it is a lovely day with the spring leaves pushing out and there is beauty everywhere I look.

*It is good that you do. Do you notice that you feel beloved not by your wish to receive it, but rather in your appreciation and gratitude? Your state of being is what brings this pure love into your life. It is not the result of **doing**. Do you notice the difference between the* word loved and beloved? It has a prefix, "be," telling you again that "being" is the key. This is a pattern we have talked about before. Your spiritual awareness comes through who you are rather than what you do.

It is also who you are that enables you to find God and your brothers and sisters beloved. You become a dynamic part of the Oneship. This immerses you in being beloved where joy awaits you. Because of the prevalence of either-or thinking on Earth I must make clear that I am not saying you should either "be" or "do." (Either-or thinking frequently leads to confusion.) What I am saying is that what you **are** comes first or is primary. What you **do** comes second. But you should certainly both "be" and "do." I am trying to convey the idea that what you are determines what you will do, not the other way around.

When you meditate, being beloved is one of the states that you may experience. Meditation is the practice of being with the absence of doing. This condition ushers in connection and understanding that feeds the soul.

Ideal meditation wherein the mind is completely quieted is elusive for many people. The inner monologue is hard to shut off. Fortunately, this failure does not mean your meditation is useless. Anytime you stop physically doing and try being, you tap into benefits for your enlightenment. Do not be discouraged and know that your meditation at some level is working.

You can also know that you are, without doubt, beloved by God. He gave you three great gifts—you live forever, you are given free choice, and you are part of the Oneship—each of which demonstrates that he finds you beloved. You are also beloved by people of whom you may not be aware. Their radiation of love includes you. In a state of "being" you can feel this love if you are open to it. If you look for them to "do" something in your life, it is elusive. God bless.

Dear Gail, thank you for the dream last night. Please use these fingers as you wish.

Dear Buck, doesn't it feel good to be full of gratitude? It helps you to feel invulnerable. You feel as if you have so much that if some disappears for a while there is so much else to take its place it won't matter.

There are so many attitudes that are beneficial to the person who transmits them. When your heart is full of gratitude, it is you who feels the benefit. When you give blessings it is you who feels blessed. When you give out healing you respond to the healing. When you forgive, you find you can now forgive yourself. When you give out love, you may not feel loved by the object of your giving, but you do feel loved by God and others also benefiting from your giving. In true giving, however, there is no requirement that these others respond or be affected in any given way.

The reason it works this way is that several laws come together to produce this effect. We start with the We Are All One principle. If we are One then it follows that what we give we receive. This can be expressed also as the law of congruency. When things are congruent they generate new power on all that is congruent. When you bring yourself into congruency with the healing field by giving healing, you too receive healing energy. The mind is the builder and it builds within; so, of course, you receive the benefit as well. To forgive is to release. You release what is inside you and thus you cleanse yourself.

Divine love is non-directional; it goes everywhere to everything. If you give out such love, its very non-directionality means that you receive it. Earthly love tends to be directional toward someone or something. This in no way makes it bad. It is, in fact, very good because it gives us practice and understanding in the use of love. With this practice we approach divine love. Again I need to say that God in his mercy does not require perfection from you before you benefit from these laws. To be specific, you can give out directional love yet receive divine, non-directional love from God in return.

The new millennium will see a much greater understanding of the efficacy of these spiritual laws in your material world. They will be employed to bring about a higher level of peace. It is a fine time for you to be incarnated.

꩜

My dear Buck, today we can talk about many things but let's start with love. It all comes back to love. Love is what powers the universe; ask yourself why God would create it if he didn't love what he created? Love radiates from God to the individual. You might say that is one dimension. The return dimension would be love coming from the individual to God. Thus the holy cycle can be completed. It is a holistic process.

Individuality encompasses much more than human life. For example it includes individual atoms and its constituent parts. There is an infinite chain made of individual links. If in your mind you can expand this one dimensional chain into say, a seven dimensional concept, you can get an idea of how the individual constituent parts of the All link together into one vast network. This is the grand pattern that we have talked about, the Oneship.

You can wonder if all these individual parts are returning love to God. If you look at the human species you don't see universal love of God. Actually they are doing so, more than you are aware. The reason your awareness is less than the reality is that you place limits on what constitutes returning the love of God. You might say a religious service qualifies while playing rock music does not. You block your comprehension of infinite love by limiting it.

Returning God's love can take many forms. Mostly it revolves around fulfilling your nature as given to you by God. In the case of rock music, God created within you a love of rhythm as well as a love of joining. Those who enjoy rock music can feel a strong sense of joining when the music fills their being. This and many other such things are returning God's love. He wants you to enjoy the fulfillment of what he has given you. This is not unlike the feeling a parent has when he gives his child a toy that the child is tickled with. At that moment the child is not thinking how nice the parent has been in giving the toy, but is totally absorbed in the joy of the toy. This, of course, is exactly what the parent wants to see. If later the child has the awareness to thank his parent for getting him the toy that too is satisfying for both child and parent. Do you see why it is so enriching for you to have gratitude to God for the gifts he has given you?

Gail, Here I am at the ranch with redwoods and sunshine spread about, a lovely combination. The bright, yellow-green of the spring growth is very much in evidence. What will you tell me about this morning?

Dear Buck, what nicer thing to talk about than love: Love comes in many shades and colors. Each shade has its own sweet meaning. Each color has its own tenderness. Underlying them all is the love of God. He gives love to us so that we have love to give others.

It is a caress to receive love and a caress to give love. One wonderful thing about love is that it does not matter where or to whom it is directed. You give your love to the redwood trees. You give your love to the sunshine. Moments ago you were giving love to that slow flying insect that was floating across the meadow. It seemed like the sunshine was holding it up.

You can even give love to yourself. There is no need to withhold love because you are not perfect. Love is not something you deserve: love is what you are. Nor should you withhold love from anything or anyone because you perceive its imperfection. Love is well above and beyond judgment, a concept that some religions would do well to understand.

You now hear the hawk's wild crying. You love to listen to it. It seems so fitting in the woods. All this love comes from each precious part fulfilling its nature. This is another expression of the Oneship. Here we are all joined as one. If you can feel this in your heart and in your mind you experience a vivid sense of worship.

Love need not be perfect. Mix love with anything and it comes closer to God. Adding love to hate diminishes the hate, and begins the healing. That the love you give out at times seems qualified or biased or in any way less than pure is no reason to withhold it or be embarrassed by it. Love cannot be polluted; it always remains as God created it.

I have talked of the three great gifts of God: we are all One, we are immortal, and we have free choice. The carrier of each of these is love. Not one of the three could exist without love. Specifically they could not exist without God's love. When you give out love you join with God at a very fundamental level. Wouldn't it be nice if this were the meaning of fundamentalism?

When you receive love the same wonderful things happens. You need to understand that there is a difference between your receiving love and someone directing love to you. For you to receive love you need to hold yourself open to it, for if someone directs love to you and you are closed to it, you do not receive love.

So be my love and everyone else's too. Give me your love that I may receive it. Give everyone your gift of love that they may choose to accept it with the free will given to them by God. Go walk in the sunshine and know that you walk in love.

⁓

Dear Buck, as you heard the other night, nevertheless, there are times when deep love brings deep sorrow as with that poor woman who lost her child. It is hard not to be totally devastated by that death.

I remember in this last life how much I loved my four little ones and how devastating it would be to lose one. It was such a pleasure to hold them and look at their sweet selves. I could just feel my love flow out to them; it was magical and one of the nicest feelings a mother can have.

In my past life I thought how fortunate I was not to have lost a child. And, of course I was, but coming to this side I learned that in prior lives I endured that very tragedy more than once. There was a life in which I watched all five of my children killed at once.

How can such things be part of a spiritual path? Yet they are.

What lessons can a mother going through such misery possibly learn? I can point out certain directions, but am unable to provide all the answers that such a mother seeks. The reason is that each of us must find our own truth. Further, even though the circumstances may be similar, each individual has her own unique lesson to learn from a shared situation.

There are, however, spiritual laws that will help guide someone through all difficulties. The first is that God never lets anything happen to a soul without providing the tools with which to self-heal and learn. The problem is that because the person does not know this, she may not even look for the tools. You can't find something, even if you stumble over it, if you do not know it exists. So the first step is to know that the tools exist. Your task is to recognize them, and learn how to skillfully use and apply them.

One of the tools I have listed time and again bears repeating: by widening your perspective you can find the solutions to your problems. How would a grieving mother widen her perception? She needs to bring into her view additional understanding, for example, other spiritual laws such as "we are immortal." The child who dies is immortal and lives. Another helpful spiritual law is "we are all One."

We on this side, including the deceased child, are one with you and the mother on your side. We are not separated even though it seems that way. Thus the separation that is tearing the mother apart is not real. This is very, very difficult to understand, much less internalize. Nonetheless, it is true, and widening your perception to include immortality will help you realize this.

What bothers the mother is that the love with which she delightedly embraced the child feels like it is stopped up and no longer has anyplace to go. She feels like she can't release it. Love is meant to flow out. When it can't flow out, it is very disturbing. This is why the separation that we have created between the living and the dead is so unfortunate. If you realize the separation is not there, love can flow again and the mother can begin to return to serenity.

Love is the basic energy of the universe. It cannot be limited. The love that the mother feels for her child is still there and it cannot be blocked by death or by the wall artificially created between the living and the deceased. A decision can be made. You have simply said good-bye to your child and sent him or her off to school. You now need to go about your work, your life, with a song in your heart. You need to live in the now, difficult as it may seem. Try it. You will find it will gather momentum on its own if only you face in the right direction. Start wearing green clothing for green is the color of healing. When you do, feel yourself flooded with green healing, for healing surrounds you. All of you are immersed in a vast field of healing but you don't know it.

There is another tool God has given you, to feel gratitude to him. Feeling gratitude will let healing flow into you. You are not the only one who is experiencing loss. Therefore give your healing to those around you. When you give healing, you receive healing. This is the law of We Are All One in action.

Here are some other thoughts that will widen the perception. In all probability such a mother has gone through this very same trage-dy in other lives. That is one reason it tugs so persistently. Do not let it defeat you! You have other things to accomplish. God holds other joys for you. Do not close up thereby shutting out this joy. Be open and let it come to you. Godspeed.

Dearest Buck, it gives me great pleasure to feel you living life with energy and love. When I passed over and was so concerned with leaving my family behind in sorrow, I was given to understand that you could grow to feel this way about your life without me. It made it much easier to hand you and our family over to God and to proceed on my journey. This didn't mean that you were destined to come to the happy life you are now living, only that it was a strong possibility. But I had great faith in you and knew that you would be determined to grow, utilizing whatever experience came your way.

I now understand that the same holds true for everyone. You are all on the path. You all will inevitably proceed along that path to awareness of God. How much time that will take, how many lifetimes, and how many lessons and experiences you will require to achieve this is up to your free will. The final result will be the same for each of us (and yes, I include myself in this).

⁓

Though they seem opposite, individuality and the Oneship are closely related and work together. The Oneship too has powers; in fact, all people do, as they are God's powers. When the individuality becomes attuned to the Oneship, aspects of these omnipotent powers become available to the individual. The degree of availability of these powers during attunement correlates with the ability of the individual to handle them appropriately. This prevents abuse.

We turn now to the power of the Oneship to communicate with the individual for his or her benefit.

There is a pattern in which various aspects of the Oneship communicate by contributing ideas to one's thoughts without interfering with your free will. The individual thinker is usually unaware that a contributor is putting thoughts into his mind. He then has a unique dual role to play. The first role is individually to exercise his free will. The second is to join with other entities, souls and non-living aspects of our existence in a seamless One. If you could visualize this, you would see a beautiful dance wherein you meld lovingly into other aspects of your world with no boundaries between you, thus recombining. Is this not what the courtly dances did? Dancing was appealing because it echoed this pattern.

These dynamic joinings are constantly regrouping, sometimes bigger and more inclusively, and sometimes smaller, with intensity. This is why I said earlier that the individuality and the Oneship are not separate, but depend upon the other to create the complete Oneship.

Because we are dealing here with divine manifestations we could expect a third aspect so that it becomes triune in nature. Do you know what the third one is?

I haven't a clue.

Silly, it is love. Without love this whole dynamic could not happen. It is love that provides the energy, the motivation for the joining to occur. In thought duality, it is God's love for you that opens the way for the contributor to enter your thoughts. It is our love for each other that allows the many joinings we have experienced in our lifetimes together. It is your love of beauty that allows your individuality to tap the creative resources to generate beautiful paintings. When you see a joining anywhere you can see the love that has allowed it to happen. Do you understand how this works?

I do indeed and how beautiful it is. Is this why all cultures and many animals like to dance because it brings them into a state of joining?

Yes, of course. Remember the wild peacocks dancing in India. Look at life as a lovely never-ending dance.

Dear Buck. You are doing much better with patience. Can you name one reason why?

What you told me about cherishing every moment sunk home. When I get impatient I think of you asking me to cherish that very moment, and I do.

It's lovely how attuned we are. Attunement is a wonderful attribute. It is a high form of sharing. It is an exercise in being One. It is the dissolving of boundaries between you and someone, something, or even someplace else.
As a child you find a secret place and feel an immediate rapport with it. Later, as an adult, you try to recapture that feeling, but rarely do. This is because you have created boundaries and reinforced

them to the point that you can no longer penetrate them. Children, having not yet created these boundaries, have a much easier time of it. Buck, write about what you are thinking.

I just realized one of the results of my being open after you left is my ability to recapture the attunement of my childhood with ease. Both at home and at the ranch there are places that feel magical just as when I was a child. I like that feeling. Gail, do you remember finding a spot in the Sierras under a limber pine that was only a few feet tall but some thirty feet wide? It was at the tree line and there was just room for the two of us to cuddle underneath out of the wind while smelling the pine and breathing that fresh, fresh air.

Go to the next step.

When I am alone and serene in a quiet place, I find that magical sense of attunement within me. It is hard to explain, but it is like an unencumbered place where there is no distraction and into which this same lovely feeling flows. It doesn't require that anything be there. It is as though I have abstracted it to its essence.

You are right. You are getting much closer to what it is like to be in the spiritual world. As above so below!

Attunement can manifest in other ways as well. Lurue, a wonderful teacher from Alaska, told an inspiring story of how she suddenly saw the "true" child in the difficult Indian student in front of her. She experienced attunement, which removed the narrow perspective that she had of a "problem" child. Her perspective widened to include the true child. It changed everything for the student and for Lurue too. She was able to encourage the hitherto latent talents of the child to overcome his destructive attitudes.

We're back to perspectives again. They fundamentally change your world. Lurue's experience is instructive because her widened perspective changed the troubled child. That's the brother/sisterhood in action.

This was an unusual occurrence because her thought level was considerably above his. So the normal attraction of like thought levels was not going on. What was happening? You guessed it: love was at work. Love connects all things and all thought levels. It is God's device or tool that makes us all One. For you on Earth this love seems so vague and not part of your daily struggles in living that you think love is somewhere else. Like Lurue and her student, we can all have transforming love experiences.

CHAPTER SIXTEEN

Helping Marriage Work

During our life together, Gail and I found many practical appli-cations of principles to help us in our relationship. One of the most liberating was that our purpose in life was to learn. When you learn, you try new things, so you are not very skillful in do-ing them. You can expect that you will make more mistakes than usual, particularly mistakes with each other. It is really unfair to get annoyed with these mistakes, as they are an integral part of learning, for which you will be rewarded. In this manner mistakes are positive and helpful.

Once early in our marriage when we were arguing Gail said she didn't feel that I loved her. I responded too quickly with, "Of course I do, look at all I put up with." Obviously, I had a great deal to learn! Any woman would know what Gail's reaction was. It wasn't easy for Gail to dismiss this as simply my ineptness in being a husband, which it most certainly was.

If you are to learn you need to make some adjustments to your previous thinking. Recognize this and use it to try to adjust closer together rather then farther apart. In fact, when you are readjusting to your new learning, deliberately think in terms of whether your tentative changes in outlook draw the two of you together or apart. Do this together in discussion or separately in thought. The advantage of doing this separately is you don't have to divert thought to rebuttals.

We found this understanding freed us from feeling threat-ened by difficulties that arose. It tended to make us more patient with the other's errors. Often these so-called errors would disap-pear simply because we each had learned how to be more skillful. As you learn, you stop tripping over your ineptitude.

It is not *if* you fight that affects a marriage, it is *how* you fight and even more importantly, how you recover from a fight.

One big help in taking the hard edge out of fights occurred to us during a heated discussion. We decided that our goal was *not* to convince the other of our superior view. If you do you will find your partner so busy trying to defend him or herself that he is not receptive to hearing you. We did not need to push for a decision or mutual understanding.

Instead, your heated discussion is an opportunity for each of you to vent or express feelings, which you so much want the other to understand. The best thing is to provide your partner with the optimum climate in which to understand you. That includes not being full of superior arguments, but expressing your feelings so that your lover may take them under advisement, so to speak, and deliberate upon them in his or her own chosen way at his or her own time unthreatened by your confrontational presence.

Start your discussion with a statement such as: "I am going to express how I *feel* about this. This will probably impress you as an exaggeration of what is true. I will concede now that you are probably right. I want you to pay attention, however, to how I feel. If you understand how I feel, the facts won't matter so much."

Don't argue for conclusions or decisions, but rather listen to the other. Do not demand an answer. Venting is enough and is more healing than winning an argument. Many of your fights never have to reach a solution. You have done well if each of you has had the opportunity to tell the other how you feel. Give yourselves time alone to mull over and consider what you heard. This will disengage the urgency of defending oneself. It will also allow the other to remember more clearly that she loves you.

At times you will recognize that you unnecessarily exaggerated your conflicting position, particularly as you thought she exaggerated hers. If you see this, you are well on the way to healing not just the problem, but the relationship as well. Even if this does not happen, your next step should be to look at whatever decision you have come to and ask, "Does my view of how things ought to be bring us closer together or farther apart?" Try to amend your decision in order to make it more likely to bring you together. You should do this even if you feel your partner is doing the opposite and driving you apart.

Gail and I found time after time that our thinking things through by ourselves resulted in both of us coming up with a more companionable attitude. To our surprise we often found we didn't even have to discuss the problem again because we both had changed our attitudes: the problem no longer existed.

The Native Americans had an interesting way to settle disagreements. When they needed to make an important decision they would sit in a circle. The first speaker was given a feathered talking stick to hold while he spoke. Everyone else was required to listen without interrupting. When the speaker finished he passed it on to another speaker who again was not interrupted. This continued until all had their say.

Gail and I modified this ritual. First we realized that we had no trouble talking but we did have trouble listening. So we called it the listening stick. If Gail gave me the listening stick then I had to listen without interrupting. The stick's presence in my hand was a continuous reminder that I had to be quiet and listen. When she was all talked out I would pass her the stick. Now it was her turn to listen without interruption.

This improved our dialogue in several ways. When we were arguing and interrupting with rebuttals, each of us tended to repeat ourselves, often saying the same thing over and over again. When I would accuse Gail of being repetitive she would reply that she had to because my rebuttals showed I hadn't listened to what she was saying in the first place. We each found out that if we were allowed to state our case fully without rebuttal, we gave a calmer and more comprehensive exposition. Our annoying interjections were reduced. After one such successful discussion we each had the satisfaction of having been able to state our case as the other listened. This also reinforces the idea expressed above that you do not have to reach immediate agreement in your arguments.

Although we started out with a feathered stick we switched to an old stone I had found as a boy with Indian diagrams incised in it. It fit the hand easily and did seem to transmit the feeling that our difficulties were but tiny things in the long view of time.

❧

When we were first married I would ask Gail if she wanted to do something. Often she would answer with a question like, "What would you like to do?" I got frustrated because I could never find out what she wanted unless I said what I wanted first. Then she would agree with it and I never knew whether she really wanted to or not.

Of course, I wasn't much better because I wouldn't tell her what I wanted unless she told me first what she wanted.

We decided upon a plan that has worked for us over the long term. We gave each other 5 votes that had to be cast with no split votes allowed. I could vote 2-3 against something, which would let Gail know that I was not greatly against doing the proposed activity. This would tell her I would be willing to do it with her if it was something she voted 4-1 to do. A 5-0 vote was a full veto as the other person's 0-5 vote would simply be a tie, which meant no action. We never had such an opposing 5-0 vote. If we had a 3-2 and a 2-3 vote we would toss a coin. This coin tossing worked well as we both knew the other wasn't disturbed by the result.

This worked well because we learned how the other felt. We stopped going to things that neither one of us really wanted to do.

❧

In the 50's it was not unusual to find a husband in the

doghouse, as the saying went, because in some manner he was not acting properly. I admit I was sometimes difficult to be around and Gail would let me know that. She didn't like it when I was being all-rational and ignoring the emotional. After a number of these episodes I made the point that even though I had, in fact, made mistakes, she was making a mistake as well in requiring me to go around walking on eggs.

We concurred that if either one of us made the other walk on eggshells we were doing the opposite of healing the situation. This pointed us toward a constructive path, rather than two people continue to be mad at each other. An error on the part of my partner does not give me license to make errors myself. It was interesting that when we recognized this we were better able to resolve the first transgression more amicably.

Extending this idea, punishing the other in any way contributes to more strife not less. What is a man supposed to feel when his woman diminishes him in public? Punishment, no matter what the cause, is an error. In contrast, all such episodes are opportunities for you both to grow. Invite your spouse to grow bigger with you. This is not the same as being a doormat. Fortunately for us we didn't have to deal with infidelity, to which admittedly would be hard to apply this principle. For lesser problems, however, our method helped smooth the road.

One time we were getting ready to take a trip with our four kids and my parents to Yosemite. As we were packing and making sure we didn't forget something, Gail and I wanted to go about doing something in opposite ways. I am told I can be stubborn and I was this time. Suddenly my father said to Gail, "Yes, we had trouble raising him, too." That made us all laugh then, and it makes me laugh now.

When you are fuming about what the other is doing, make yourself think of something you really like about the other. DO

NOT GIVE UP TOO QUICKLY.

When we were first married and still going to college, Gail would sometimes interrupt me while I was studying. I can concentrate a long time and feel I absorb a great deal in doing so. Once interrupted it takes me a while to get back in gear. Gail, however, being newly wed, felt one of the great things about being married was that her best friend was there to talk to whenever she wanted. It took quite a while to adjust to this, but there were so many things that I liked about Gail that I purposely could bring up in my mind to make me grateful at the same time I was annoyed. I could think about what a fine mother she was or how well she managed things, how smart and so beautiful.

During an argument, Gail burst out laughing. Annoyed I said, "What are you laughing at?"

"I'm not laughing at you, I'm laughing at us. Here we are acting like the quintessential male and female. You are being very logical laying out what you regard as the facts, analyzing and thinking you now have the only correct answer. I'm ignoring all of that and trying to get you to understand my feelings, which to me are far more important than any logic. Let's respect each other's unique way of seeing. Actually, you have feelings and I too am reasonable so I can try to be open to your logic and you can be open to my feelings."

In marriage we each have our ideas of how we want our spouse to show his or her love to us. This can cause misunderstandings. Gail didn't want to tell me how I should show my love for her as it then might become meaningless. She wanted me to sense what made her feel loved. That is easy to understand, as I also prefer that, however, it was a high hurdle for me early on in our marriage. We finally came to see that each of us chooses how we show our love for the other.

For example, you may think that if I loved you I would send you flowers like our culture teaches us. But I may choose to show my love for you in a different way, say by taking you on a hike in the woods.   Although sending you flowers is not my thing, I can, if pushed, do it with an unwelcome sense of duty and you will feel the hollowness of my gesture. The moral here is that we need to be open to the unique ways that each person shows his love. Be open to how I show my love for you.

Marriage is magical at its best; however, most of us don't feel that way all the time. When the potential for magical moments occurs, be sure you don't bring heavy baggage of past unresolved arguments with you preventing you from fulfilling your love. Being able to love somebody is a wondrous gift as is being loved by another is likewise marvelous. Treasure both.

PART THREE

SOME NEW PERSPECTIVES

CHAPTER SEVENTEEN

Separation and the New Millennium

Gail, you say we are involved in the new millennium where the awareness that we are all One will become paramount. This will be accomplished by our individually shedding the attitudes and practices of separation, which have so dominated Earth's history. If we are to relinquish these separation notions, how does that synchronize with what you have been writing about free will?

Each person's free will is separate and within his own jurisdiction. One should respect and try not to interfere in someone else's free will. This seems to endorse separateness at the expense of Oneness. You might ask how one can resolve these two positions?

You can appropriately use the word separate to describe each individual's free will choices. In addition to free will, God created you with a need to relate to each other and to your environment. Your God-given nature is one of gregariousness, some more than others, but all of you feel the need to relate to others. It is by bringing your individuality, including your free will, into relationship and hopefully harmony with each other that the Oneship is fulfilled. You could say that free will and individuality are the bricks each of you bring to build your house.

It is God's mystery that you can be individual and part of the Oneship at the same time. Light is both a particle and a wave, another seemingly impossible duality. This pattern is mysterious and of amazing potential. Quantum mechanics has discovered part of the vast phenomena and power that are given birth by strange couplings, such as entanglement. What can be accomplished by the congruence of the individual within the Oneship is even more phenomenal.

To understand this you could say that God's concept is as fol-

lows: 1) God in and of himself is One. 2) He created you and this world for you to live in to develop your own individuality, using free will as your tool. 3) Once he created your individuality, by your nature you are desirous of accepting the invitation by God to join, or rejoin the One, which is God.

This grand plan has been told in allegory in many ways by many religions. In the Garden of Eden's fall from grace, it has been distorted into original sin as if Eve and Adam were sinful in fulfilling their individual natures. This individuality can only be described as sinful if it is regarded as a static state of being. Instead it is but one necessary step, which needs to be followed by the step of bringing this individuality back within the Oneship.

It has been recognized on Earth that you need to love yourself before you can truly love someone else. This same pattern holds that you need to be individual before you can truly join the Oneship. Your individuality is formed by your free will. Do you see how this is? Even without really understanding how you can be both individual and One at the same time, you nonetheless can see your progression. Free will is like the yeast in bread; it leavens the whole fabric of existence.

It is puzzling how we can be One when every day we live in our individuality. We each have a different set of circumstances, genes, ages, bodies and live in different places. Clearly we are individual. We relate to other individuals in our own individual way. The evidence is overwhelming and yet there is all this talk about how we are One. It is true that all of us are inhabitants on this one Earth. The spiritual meaning of the One goes well beyond that by strongly implying that we are literally One in a transcendent way. Each cell in our body is individual and yet is part of the whole body that has purpose and potential far beyond and above that of each individual cell.

I remember the first time I ran into the poetic analogy that we are like individual raindrops that fall onto the ocean and at that moment truly become one with the ocean. This was all very nice but it scared me. I wasn't sure I liked having my individuality wiped out, even by a God-like ocean. I liked my own individuality that, with my free will, I could mold into the being I wanted. Did I really want to give that up?

Since that time I have observed that the way God created the world was to keep things in balance by fostering dualities two differing and often opposite factors that work together to the mutual benefit of the whole. We are surrounded by examples, but let me give you just one.

Our human brain has two hemispheres that are quite different, often with opposite characteristics. Our right brain is holistic and our left is linear. Our left is judging and our right perceiving. Our left categorizes linear and our right is creative. Our left is the yang and the right the yin. Yet we are made to have both and function with both. A successful person integrates the two.

Dear Buck, the new millennium is well underway. Many don't see it yet because much of it is still in the preparation stage. There is much happening that is not identified in the media so remains largely unrealized by most. But nonetheless great things are occurring which can bring satisfaction to the spiritually minded. There are new signs of global union. We have internationally recognized organizations monitoring human rights abuses that would not have been conceived of one hundred years ago. In addition, worldwide aid is provided to those who suffer disasters anywhere.

There are those who are repairing this troubled world. There are those who are healing. There are those who are counseling the separated, teaching, filling the Earth with beauty and nurturing the children. There are those who are opening hearts. And there are those who are just "being." These are all sacred endeavors and fit together into a vast pattern to unite this Earth in love. If you knew just one tenth of what is happening you would feel very much encouraged.

Each of you can be a contributor to one or more of these purposes. Look within and you will be guided to your place in the resur-

rection. *You are surprised at my use of the word resurrection. Don't be, for the world is being resurrected and you are a participant along with many, many others who are bringing this resurrection about. You will be guided by what you like to do. Do not feel you have to participate in all of the paths. Having found your path, rejoice in it. Again, turn to your higher self and let it instruct you as to what you can do.*

In knowingly working in the vineyard you will feel the energies of all those others who are working with you, not only in your area but all areas. You probably will not know specifically what is being done, but you will sense the energy and devotion of your sisters and brothers who are with you. You will also feel the at-oneness that comes when you are doing holy work. I have written often of the power and all-pervading presence of the invisible. It is the invisible that will let you feel this. You can feel the energy with a sense of limitlessness. Do not doubt it, just be aware of it.

Along with all the other things that are needed to bring about the resurrection, you must have patience. Patience is much easier if you recognize what is happening and that great progress is being made. You have been given a magnificent gift in being a participant at this unique time. Give thanks not only that the world is being healed, but also that you have been given the opportunity to be one of its healers.

You and I are joined in a love unit to work in our area of learning/teaching. What we are doing right now is our contribution to this massive pilgrimage to love. Isn't that exciting?

The other day I asked you if you felt others working through you. You replied no. Try to pick up on this again. I say this not because you need to feel others working through you, but because you would like being aware of what is happening. Attunement doesn't require that you be conscious that others are working through you. Many, many others are also receiving help in fulfilling their own path, whether they are aware of it or not. It is like one vast orchestra, which plays together to create the magic of music. One cello is helping the other cello to sing its line; the cello section helps the other strings play their parts. Consciously seek to hear this concerted effort. Don't worry so much about knowing the specifics; instead, feel the energy.

The millennium that Gail is talking about didn't start on January 1 of the year 2000. It is more of an epoch that started quietly, builds in momentum and appears in more and more places. It also has precursors that give you the idea of what is coming. More than a century ago Einstein said matter and energy are not irrevocably separate. They are one and he gave us the formula to prove it.

Earlier you mentioned those who are just "being." Are they in fact, doing something?

What would you guess the function of those who are being is? This is the question you meant to ask.

In being they are radiating their thought level and their understanding to others. Are they somewhat like the magnetic north pole radiating out knowledge (where north is), but being unconcerned with how many compasses are detecting this knowledge?

While a clever analogy, "unconcerned," is not the right word. Not interfering is the right thought. They radiate wisdom that guides just like the magnetic north pole and they will not interfere with those who use or don't use the guidance. They are concerned, however, with their brothers and sisters. Do you not detect an echo of God in this? Is this not the way God relates to us? He gives us guidance when we ask for it. He does not interfere with our free choice. He is concerned with us and loves us, but lets us do, as we will within his laws.

That leaves out the immense blessings he gives us, doesn't it?

You could say that. But truly the blessings are received only if you ask God for them with your awareness of the gifts and your gratitude for them.

Dear sweet Gail, another foggy summer's morning after a beautiful full moon last night.

Dear Buck, I have said many times that the world has many things backwards. This is not really much of a surprise for the following reason. The basic law of the universe is that we are all One, connected together in a giant pattern of association. Your tenure on Earth has been characterized by trying to separate things.

*You separate time into past, present and future, which is the opposite of the eternal **now**. You separate yourselves, time and time again. You see each individual as separate. You see each family as being separate. You separate your children into grade levels. You concentrate a whole group of teenagers in one school with their immature culture dominating and are surprised at how difficult they can be. I don't need to go on with separation examples; distinguishing and often excluding one thing from another is basic to your world.*

Now separation is not all bad. Science and engineering tools are based on separating the various factors in any phenomenon, examining them in detail and then drawing conclusions as to how each element functions. This has brought about tremendous knowledge and understanding of how the material world works. Currently you are experiencing a revolution in communication. Has it occurred to you that a surge in communication was inevitable as we make the transition into a millennium cognizant that we are all One?

You mean that our vastly expanded communication is but a necessary part of the larger pattern of the coming of the millennium? In other words, to understand that we are all part of the Oneship we needed to improve our communications? That's interesting. Our communications revolution is but a supporting actor to the lead role of feeling the Oneship.

Yes. Again, the separation upon which you on Earth seem so intent has a vital function to play. It is necessary to experience this and to learn from it.

What are you to learn? I will list some of these understandings:

- *Your over-embracing the material world has left you with a great hunger to experience union. There are many on Earth who yearn to feel part of the joyous whole. This yearning is like a vast prayer that energizes the millennium.*

- *You have discerned the limitations of the separation approach. Holistic medicine, the United Nations, ecology (the understanding of the inter-relatedness of all living thing in an environment), whole grain foods and vitamin supplements, the global economy, reduction of trade barriers, cross-over music, the rise of ecumenical views of religion, and many, many more are all attempts to heal over-separation.*

- *You have begun to see that separation techniques fall short of being able to explain how the world functions as a whole even though they explain the details very well.*

- *The invisible plays a most important role in how the universe functions. What happens in the invisible manifests in the visible. As such it is more than worthy of attention.*

- *The mind has powers well beyond what your separation approach has led you to believe. The mind truly is the builder. The separation approach is unable to explain the essence of the mind, only some of its distinguishing parts.*

- *The separation approach and the material world are your gymnasium where you exercise for a larger and deeper purpose.*

- *There is God the creator. He is not a parochial partisan playing favorites. He is not the property of any religion or thought system. He has no gender; or rather he is all genders. He is the All.*

So you see the separation approach has had its use in distinguishing the parts. It has, by your experiencing it, given you the knowledge you need. You now have the task of integrating this into the whole that is God.

❧

You know in this last life it was very interesting to me to be in a family that so loved science. The analytical and rational approach to life that science embodies was very appealing to all of you. You took to it like ducks to water. Tell about it.

You are right. Since childhood I have always been interested in science. I've subscribed to <u>Scientific American</u> for over 50 years and still look forward to it. And I admit that I truly loved teaching our kids about science and its wonderful discoveries.

Our children were fascinated with that. Particularly when younger they had a hunger to know their world that we delighted in. Science and the scientists have done great things to advance the physical well being of the Earth and the people in it.

There are some who will degrade science and blame it for creating tools for mass destruction and procedures that have polluted the Earth. This is a narrow and ill-conceived view. Previously mankind has moved on a path toward a major war each generation. Wars have been progressively more destructive and full of human misery until the nuclear standoff lowered the severity of these wars. World War III has not occurred. From this viewpoint nuclear weapons were beneficial. You still have the problem of disarming the nuclear arsenal but you haven't failed in that task yet. You just have a long way to go.

Similarly, the advancement of science has created new manufacturing processes that do pollute. It is science that is leading the way to the solutions to clean up pollution problems.

So science has been and continues to be a positive force for human advancement. Just think of what the green revolution has meant to the poor and malnourished since the 1950s. There is much activity on this side to help science continue to be a positive force. It is no coincidence that as the millennium gains momentum, science too is gaining momentum in its discoveries of that which will be helpful. The two are part of the same phenomenon.

When I was growing up in the 1930s, it seemed impossible to completely eradicate smallpox, yet we did. We are also developing technology that will bring prosperity to a much larger share of humanity than ever before. This is all done with an elevated desire by many people to help humanity as a whole. Philanthropy by the wealthy is much larger and widespread then ever before. Many at all income levels give generously to disasters the world over.

Scientists are, however, like everybody else. Some have attitudes that hold them back and slow down their ability to gain new understandings. Do you want to guess at what these attitudes are?

Scientists are no different than the rest of us in desiring stability, and in that process become prejudiced about new ideas. To bring order to our world we tend to shut out new data that scares us.

One way some scientists display this is in their attitude toward psychic phenomena. There is no doubt in my mind there is a certain amount of hokum and charlatanism in some reported psychic events. There is also a tremendous amount of data that point toward a whole field of knowledge that cannot be explained by our current understanding of communications, these writings being one.

In my view good science requires that an open mind assess this data without bringing a debunking attitude to the assessment. If this were done it would soon be recognized that current scientific tools are inadequate in explaining the dynamics of how psychic events occur. It would help if we took the quantum mechanics view of probabilities instead of the fixed cause and effect approach. It would also help if it were understood that the minds and prejudices of the experimenters are an influential variable affecting the result.

In fact, science has been excellent in dealing with those phenomena that can be split apart, analyzed, measured in numbers and then put back together again. Science has not been set up to perceive the functionality of a totality whose dynamism comes from its Oneness. Thus, many things in our world that function as a totality are still largely unknown. Fortunately, this is rapidly changing. Much of what we are learning today leads us in the direction of understanding the totality; the basic premise of Chaos Theory and the study of ecology with all of the various elements relating to each other in balance are two examples of that.

Here I am going on and on as I tend to do while you say things in a much more concise way.

You haven't changed. You bring up the idea, however, that in this new millennium science is not only expanding its knowledge, it is changing its outlook and methodology to deal with totalities. What more appropriate thing could science be doing to help the new millennium than bring about a greater understanding and recognition that we are all One?

Chaos Theory is such a good example. A small change in a small variable of a set of circumstances can result in a huge change in a later set of circumstances. This could be stated as follows: nothing is so insignificant that it does not have an effect on the totality of the All. This can be restated as: we are all One. The phrase, "His eye is on the sparrow," is a poetic way of saying the same thing.

The result is that science is playing a major role in bringing about the new millennium. The fact that some of these scientists would not like to be identified with such a concept is of little importance. It is not what you label something that counts, but how it contributes to the whole.

Much thought has been given to the Second Coming of Christ. Some interpret this as the return of the individual Jesus. Others have regarded the Second Coming as some great worldwide awakening of the Christ message. In this regard notice that having an individual messenger is by its very nature a separation. Some of the messenger's followers made him into a God, which separated him even further from the rest of us. This was appropriate for the time and the state of human evolution.

Now the question comes: Why has the Second Coming taken so long and how will we know when it is here? The Second Coming is awaiting the evolution of Man's understanding whereby the next major level of teaching can take place. This time is now. You are experiencing the Second Coming as the new millennium. The word "Christ" in the phrase, the "Second Coming of Christ," refers to the Christ that is within each of us.

To whom or how is the Second Coming made manifest? Through the process of seekers being exposed to the stimulation of truth and living that truth to absorb its validity. A separate messiah is no longer suitable. You are now ready to understand that you each must internalize your truth. Adopting another's truth without going through the inward awakening that brings you to that truth is inadequate. With this in mind you can see that what is now needed is greater wisdom made available to many.

The basic truth is still forgiveness, healing and love within the realization of the Oneship. You are now ready to practice this in union and leave behind your separating habits. The availability of wisdom is here with **A Course in Miracles**, the **Conversations with God** series[8] and many other works, including what we are doing here. Thus is the Second Coming easing into being. For those who have a special love of Jesus, as I do, I would like to add that Jesus is very much a participant in this current Second Coming. You might even say he is orchestrating it, although this is really a function of the Oneship. Jesus is available, as he always has been, to individuals who seek his

[8] A series of books written by Neale Donald Walsh, published by G. P. Putnam's Sons, 1996.

presence, his wisdom, and his comfort. That hasn't changed nor will it. It is, however, helpful to understand that to be truly with him, as so many of you wish to be, you must develop your truth and know the Christ that is within you, just as he has.

Gail at 10,000 ft on Mt. Kenya having just been instructed to do her own house keeping, 1978.

Gail astride her fiftieth Birthday present, 1978.

Cross country skiing in Yellowstone, 1980.

Buck and Gail In Alaska after ocean kayaking in Prince William Sound, 1983.

Gail two years before she passed on, 1994.

Buck at the same time.

CHAPTER EIGHTEEN

The Power of the Invisible

Throughout her writings Gail emphasizes that we on Earth do not realize how large a role the invisible plays in our lives. Although the invisible is simply that which we cannot see, it needs more explanation. You cannot see the wind. You can see the effects of the wind, but that is not the same as seeing the wind itself.

Jumping to a larger realm, you cannot see God, and yet for those of us who believe in God, we do see the effects of God; in fact, we are living them. Gail writes that God's creation is twofold. He created the universes, including ours, with our Earth. He also created laws that govern the way these universes dynamically proceed and evolve. These spiritual laws include everything, all the physical laws we have already discovered as well as other physical laws yet undiscovered and the invisible portions of the spiritual laws.

Man's curiosity about our world has brought about the discovery of four cosmic forces, which are responsible for all of the energetic activity of our universe. They are all invisible. No one has seen electricity although we are acquainted with its effects. No one has seen gravity and yet none of us can escape the effects of gravity. Neither has anyone seen the strong nuclear and the weak nuclear forces, but we know that without them our material universe would cease to exist.

These are each part of God's cosmic laws that govern our world. But they are not the only invisible ones.

If we look at a cubic foot of space in front of us it appears empty; nonetheless, there are radio waves, TV waves and cell phone waves passing through that space, all of which are invisible to us, and each of which is a form of energy generated by man.

The cubic foot also contains many things which man did not cause to come into being: Atoms of various types, small living things, aerosols and heat energy vibrations. Some of the more exotic invisible aspects are millions of neutrinos that are flying through your body every second, and photons that came from ancient galaxies that have been traveling through space for 12 billion years.

All of the above are invisible and yet have an effect on our lives. Just remove the invisible TV waves and see the reaction. Do we now know all the invisible things that are in that cubic foot of air? Not likely.

There are invisible and unknown energies of which we have little or no knowledge that affect us constantly. Let's take mental telepathy for example, which is unproven scientifically, but of which we have hints. Many of us have experienced receiving thoughts from someone else with no known means of the transmission of those thoughts. This is not magic or imagination or even gullibility. It occurs by natural laws of which we are presently unaware. The same applies to reincarnation and other psychic phenomena. We are never going to learn more about these things if we simply dismiss them with ridicule.

We find this difficult because our understanding is based on what is visible to us. We are puzzled when things become invisible. Nonetheless, this is the way life is; the invisible has a great impact on the world.

We don't see the invisible; we only see its effects, often with no understanding of how the effects came into being. Sometimes we do make the connection, as when we feel the wind. There are, however, other invisible causes whose effects we do not understand. These effects we attribute to luck or happenstance. In truth they don't just happen; we are not yet acquainted with their invisible causes.

What we don't understand is invisible to us. We need to acknowledge that we don't know everything. As Einstein said, "What we don't know far exceeds what we do know." The invisible causes enter into our lives whether we believe in them or not. In spite of their invisibility we can utilize them in our lives, even with only a partial understanding.

For example, say you degrade someone. This will have an effect not only on the person you degrade, but on you too. Somehow, through invisible karma, you will attract into your life circumstances in which you will be degraded.

You will not see a visible chain of cause and effect that connects your degrading someone else with your being degraded, nor will your mind connect these two events immediately. But you will have an opportunity at some point to decide you do not like being degraded and finally feel you do not like to inflict this on others. But will you take advantage of this learning opportunity? Perhaps you will let the opportunity slide by and continue to degrade others. The result will be that you will continue to stumble, which will attract degradation from others. If you don't understand this process you will think you are being treated unfairly and it is just bad luck that people pick on you in this way.

Gail, I see. Science has made very good use of the visible chain of cause and effect to create all the wonderful things we have in our world, like the way we use electricity or hear music with our CD players. In fact, you could say science is the study of discovering all visible links in a chain of cause and effect. Knowing all the events leading to an effect allows us to create things like cars and the useful things we manufacture.

Does this mean then that the scientific approach doesn't work very well when confronted with phenomena (like karma) in which a number of the processes, between the cause and an effect, must operate only in the invisible?

Yes Buck, as we have said before, the scientific tool is marvelous, but it cannot uncover all phenomena and further, it is not the only tool that can be used to ferret out the truth.

Is this the reason that psychic phenomena seem so elusive

when examined by our scientific approach?

Yes again. The main seat of psychic events is in the mind and remains invisible. Psychic events are most often a transfer of information by means unknown at present by science. Your friend Roger knew his brother had committed suicide before he was informed of it by standard communications. So he received information by an unknown, invisible means.

You are at this very moment receiving information from me by unverifiable means. The mind transfers the information. If you were to be taken to a scientific lab to find out how you do this, you really wouldn't be all that helpful in explaining what is happening. You know to put your mind in a blank receptive mode, but that's about it.

You are right; I really don't know how this works. I feel your mind working in a familiar way. I feel the ideas you express are often beyond what I know. I feel that you are organizing what you write while I know I am not. But how the information goes from wherever you are to wherever I might be is a mystery. I suspect the means of transfer is unaffected by time or space in the same manner as entanglement in physics.

That's true; it's invisible because some of the chain of events between cause and effect are also invisible. As you said, gravity is invisible and yet its effects are powerful. You can gain much wisdom by opening your mind to the idea that the links between some causes and some effects are invisible.

Although many of you feel that you are all One or fervently wish it were true, it is difficult to see this. The Oneship, by definition, includes all that is visible and invisible. If you could become more aware of this invisible part you could feel the reality of the Oneship more fully.

I hope it is clear to you that when I say "you" it is no different than if I said "we" as in the We Are All One principle, I am not talking just about humans. This "you" includes all living things like cats, mosquitoes, grass and also rocks, stars and raindrops. The latter are "alive" in God's sight if not in yours. It also includes the invisible, the spirit realms and all that is. If we are all One, then anything that exists must be part of that Oneness. If it weren't, it would be outside the One, which, of course, is impossible.

Following this same thinking it becomes apparent that each of you is one with God. Although this is very hard to comprehend or feel, it doesn't mean that being one with God is untrue; it simply means your perception is too limited at this point.

God gave you everything you need to feel One with him. The mind is the builder. To start using this most wonderful tool you need first to think it possible that you are One with God. Second, you need to wish to feel closer to this understanding. Third, you need to realize it is a matter of broadening your perception.

Let's focus on your perception. You perceive the visible fairly well. Here your problem is that you focus on only one part of the visible and jump to conclusions as to the state of your world. Without meaning to, you exclude from your realization many visible things that would expand your understanding of the world in a manner that might make you feel grateful to God, such as the huge amount of love there is in the world.

Furthermore, you are even less skilled at perceiving the invisible. You know about electricity and gravity, which are invisible. There are a whole host of other invisible things that are equally useful and influential that you either do not perceive or feel vague about. I am invisible to you. The spiritual is invisible to you. And yes, God is invisible to you. The challenge of perceiving the invisible is daunting, but worthy.

Here are some specific steps you can take to increase your perception of the invisible: Build in your mind the possibility that there are invisible factors of which you are only dimly aware. Give up the idea that you or accepted authorities know positively that certain things are impossible. For example, the most arrogant is that we think we can determine what God's limitations are, for example, reincarnation is impossible and its creation is beyond the powers of God. Why would *the creator of billions of galaxies be unable to manage reincarnation? The history of science contains many examples of a new idea being ridiculed only later to become accepted knowledge. Because you watched it happen, your favorite example is the plate tectonics theory in geology.*

This sense of being open in your thinking is essential. Now you are ready to do several things concurrently: you can meditate, which allows you to receive and sense the effects of the invisible. You can look for patterns that you have not seen before which will give you ideas as to the effects of invisible causes, such as checking out examples of karma that show up in your life. See if you can perceive the driving energy behind the fulfillment of these patterns.

❧

Dear Buck, I want to broaden our thoughts about how every cause has multiple effects and every effect has multiple causes. The world tends to seek the cause (singular) of a disease. You ask who (singular) is at fault. The justice system seeks to establish the guilty party (singular). While not universally true there is a strong probability that the cause is multiple, even though some of the causes may be more predominant.

One result is that if you decide you have determined one single cause of a phenomenon you stop looking to see if other influences are present. This blinds you.

This gets more serious when you talk about invisible causes. There can be a predominant invisible cause that is ignored in favor of a less predominant cause that is visible. You think the only cause that concerns you is the subordinate visible one, but there are many invisible causes that have obvious effects, like gravity. These ignored invisible causes induce consequences that you think are just luck.

If your mind, which is the builder, feels it has solved a problem by assigning a single visible cause as the culprit, then you are building a false view of your world. This gets you into trouble. In this case, you think you have discovered the cause of your problem, and when you take rational steps to counter this cause, your problem changes but

*doesn't go away. This is because the other invisible causes, which oper-
ate in bringing about the effect, are still active.*

*One of the effects of this singular thinking is separation. You
take this single cause and isolate it. Because the cause is in reality not
isolated, confusion in your mind ensues and leads to your belief that the
world is perplexing.*

*I have spoken often of broadening your perspective to solve
problems in order to see that **every cause has multiple effects and
every effect has multiple causes.** By including more factors you will
be led to better solutions. There is another reason, however, that widening your perspective is so appropriate to find solutions, both invisible
and powerful: it is the We Are All One principle. When you broaden
your perspective you are **including** more of the Oneship. This brings
you more into congruity with it. This in turn brings the power of the
Oneship into the solution of your problem with happy results. The
visible and the invisible work together to bring clarity to your confused
view of the world; deliberately seek to discover this multiplicity and
depth. You will find that both the visible and the invisible are causes
as well as effects. Your perception of these patterns will greatly aid you.*

*By the means above you will come much closer to the cosmic
realization that you and God are indeed One, which is a reward of
great merit and beauty.*

CHAPTER NINETEEN

Acceptance is Not What You Think

Dear beloved Gail, soul of my soul, I greet you with all encompassing love.

You wish to know what I am doing. We always wanted to know what the other was doing. I am resting in a way. Actually it is more like digesting. I have been learning a great deal about love both in sending and receiving. In the spiritual plane it is quite different than where you are. Here, we do less guessing as to what some entity needs or wants. We can perceive more clearly what is needed. We give this but how it is received, as on Earth, is up to the receiver. We don't know if our gifts will be accepted.

This acceptance is not passive. Acceptance is as important a concept here on this side as it is on Earth. As far as I can tell, the acceptance principle extends to God himself. **He only gave free will because he is ready to accept the choices we make.** *An all-accepting God is very hard for the Earth's religions to understand. If God is all accepting, what difference does it make if we are bad or good, cruel or kind? In an absolute sense, it makes no difference. There is more to the universe, however, than arbitrary behavior.*

God has created you and also the environment in which you live. Better stated he has created the natural laws within which all things function, such as cause and effect. He also is the source of all energy, hence all life. His individual creations, like you, will find greater happiness and peace if you behave in a loving, less fearful way. If you behave badly or cruelly, you will not be as happy or serene. Although you may feel satisfied with revenge or with victory over others, you will find those to be insatiable pursuits with fleeting results. This lack of fulfillment in turn leads you to try again. You could well try for more

*revenge and more victories to find the same fleeting pleasure. Or in-
stead you could choose to try kind and gentle behavior and eventually
learn that love is the more satisfying answer.*

*Each of you eventually feels the restless tug of divine connection
until you knowingly enter on the path of spiritual reawakening. The
larger perspective can pull you away from the narrow concern of your
local, temporary problems. Spiritual peace comes with the opening of
your embrace of the All.*

Sweet Gail, that is beautiful. You have always been magical to me.
What a treasure I have. Here I am experiencing this *now* in this
house, which we co-created with God on this lovely hill. I do so
appreciate it.

*In this last life as a woman raised in the 1930s, the word ac-
ceptance often meant subordinating oneself to others and passively accepting one's inferior lot in life. A woman wasn't to think of becoming
a senator or a physicist, as such roles were beyond her. You were to put
the interests of your husband and children above yours in loving service. You were to passively accept whatever burdens and workloads this
brought into your life. Fortunately, this cultural attitude has changed.*

*In my writings about acceptance this passive acceptance is not
what I am talking about. God did not make females inferior to males
or visa versa. Each sex has its strengths and weaknesses and each has
the opportunity be fulfilled.*

*The spiritual meaning of acceptance is to accept God's laws
as they manifest in your life. Accept karma as a teacher. Accept that
your role is to learn. Accept the problems in your life as stimulating
opportunities to bring new solutions into your understanding. Do not
let problems overwhelm you. The very nature of life is participatory,
not passively inert.*

*Actively search inside you for the tools you have been given to
deal with life. Properly used, acceptance leads to a wider and wiser*

perspective in your thinking with glorious opportunities for growth. Improper use of acceptance narrows your perspective and limits your participation and learning opportunities. God Bless.

The following dialogue occurred as I was driving to my up-valley art class.

Gail, as you know, Marion came to visit me. She feels she has a few things to tell God when she meets him. She thinks it is terrible that good people endure diseases and pain before they die, as did her late husband Aaron. I wondered from your vantage point how you would have answered her.

Hello Buck. Dear Marion is having a hard time adjusting after 58 years of being with Aaron. Whether you see the world as perfect or imperfect depends on the width and depth of your perspective. You have some good thoughts on perspectives. Write about them.

If I do, I got them from you. When God made us individual within the all that is One, he did so for a purpose. That purpose was for us to discover that being individual has both positive and negative aspects, our ever-recurring duality. Our long-term goal is to let go of the negative aspects of individuality while carrying the positive parts of individuality back with us to unite with God.

Our individuality has certain common characteristics, one of which is that we tend to have a narrow perspective of our world. We feel our bodies as separate as well as our conscious minds. This narrow, limited view of ourselves tends to color our entire outlook. One of the aspects of this separatist's view is that we feel very good or bad depending on the particular narrow thing we have brought into focus. If Marion looks at the suffering that Aaron endured and narrows her attention to that suffering then indeed she feels bad. If on the other hand she chooses to look at the 58 years of wonderful marital companionship and focuses on those memories, she feels good. This is the nature of the narrow view; you yo-yo up and down depending upon your perspective.

If you wish to escape from this restless bouncing around you need to broaden your view a great deal. In fact, you can say that the way to God is to broaden your view to include the spiritual and eventually the all that is One. Now there is a broad view: the all that is One! In broadening your view you come upon spiritual understanding after spiritual understanding, and you discover spiritual serenity.

With this broader view you come to understand that everything that happens to you is for your benefit. If you widen your view more you will see how it all fits into what is best for you and best for God, as you are One. Marion would understand Aaron's suffering if her view were wide enough to see how it all fits into a huge, holy pattern.

That's right. Broadening your view is essential, but so is the acceptance of what has occurred, which will in turn allow your mind to broaden. You must always push the boundaries you have created further and further back.

You have a purpose in each incarnation, sometimes several. As your life comes to a close your inner self knows whether you have successfully addressed those purposes or not. If you have not, then as your life closes you are given another chance to make some headway on these lessons. Sometimes the headway may be simple such as gathering more data. At times this can make a crowded agenda. And as always it seems that these issues are brought to you as problems. This offers you another opportunity to advance, which is precisely what you asked for when you volunteered to come into this life. If you broaden your perspective to include this, it becomes more understandable.

Marion, in having to deal with Aaron's difficulties, is also in a learning position that can benefit her. The narrow view of looking only at Aaron's suffering is indeed very disheartening. It seems so unfair, so unnecessary. Aaron was a very good man, as you well know, and it can seem particularly cruel that he had to suffer that way. [He was a doctor whose death resulted from his consulting doctor prescribing a powerful drug with fatal side effects.]

Another thread to this issue is that one's earthly experience can be described as a data-gathering sojourn. In returning to your home, this spiritual side, you bring back with you the data you have collected. Upon your return to this plane you now are in a position to absorb the true significance of the data. In fact, that is one of the things we all do here where I am. So Aaron's suffering at the end of his life may be regarded as further collection of data that will be beneficially used by him when he is on this side.

You're right; Marion will not accept this now. She will say that she knows of other old people who were not fine individuals as was Aaron and yet they have a healthy and happy old age. From the narrow view this is true. From the wider perspective two things become apparent. First, Marion is in no position to judge who is advanced and who is not. Secondly, assuming she is right, you still need to realize that someone who came in this life with lessons of a lower caliber could have fulfilled these lessons and therefore have a happy old age even though behaving at a lower level.

When thinking about this, bear in mind that I said these were two threads of why the sunset years are as they are. There are other threads that again, from a wider perspective, tie in together to make it not only understandable but also beautiful. How can suffering be beautiful? You will just have to wait until your perspective is broad enough to comprehend it.

Gail, could another thread of this conversation be that we on Earth view pain, suffering and death as negatives, and spend vast amounts of our resources, energy and time to avoid and postpone them? Wars, poverty and disease are dreaded because of the suffering and death they impose. Being obsessed with them, as you might say, narrows our perspective, which in turn attracts fear into our lives. Since old age often brings together suffering and death, is this not why we have such a dim view of old age?

I wonder if a broader perspective views this differently. First, that because there is no death there is no need to fear it. This solves half the problem. Second, pain and suffering often are but an attention-getting mechanism used to propel an individual to address the lesson he needs to learn. Further, pain and suffering from the broader perspective are but temporary conditions that soon pass from the point of view of infinity. Difficult though this is to believe, if we could see our suffering as an opportunity to bring one of our life's purposes into focus, we could feel more accepting of it. We could see that growth is being made available to us. This in turn would let us feel gratitude. I have come to believe that genuine gratitude is a tremendous healer.

Gail, I still puzzle about your daily backaches as a result of teenage scoliosis. Why was your attention being drawn and to what?

Buck, let me answer your last question first. My attention was being drawn to all the wonderful things that were in my life and the very deep reasons I could feel immense gratitude for them. When I was told that I could not even lift my own baby, as that could severely injure my back, I can't tell you how joyous I felt when, in spite of that warning, I lifted and cuddled my baby. I greatly appreciated this simple act. It sounds counter intuitive, as wisdom often is, but my backaches constantly prodded me to have gratitude for all of life's joys. This is why joy was and is such a magical experience for me.

Buck, your last years, indeed everyone's, are just as full of promise and purpose as your previous years. They are truly golden for the reason that your potential for fulfilling your nature is more apt than ever. Cherish each golden moment, for each is a precious gift.

I think you're saying that we need to actively accept whatever circumstances we encounter as we live life. We should seek what we may learn from the experience in addition to feeling grateful for all that we have been given.

Dear Buck, the British sum up the end of the monarchy by saying, "The King is dead. Long live the King." A chapter in your life has ended and that is always sad, but a new chapter, your elderly years, is just beginning and that can be exciting. Invest yourself in this new chapter. It is where you are supposed to be and what you are supposed to be doing.

You live forever, yet each chapter of your life has a beginning and end, which is in the rhythm of life. It is the time for acceptance. Accept this rhythm and the new gifts that your life will bring. Cherish every moment including this one. Bon voyage.

Sweet friend, it's a lovely soft rainy day and I am on our beloved hill listening to Midori on her violin playing music you loved.

Beloved Buck, did you know that 'friend' is a holy word and a spiritual principle? To treat another as a friend is to acknowledge the Oneship, to open the channels of mutual regard. We hear much about how we should love one another and, of course, it is true. But sometimes it can feel hard to accomplish this love of one another.

Be friends with everyone you meet. Now there is a beautiful thought. See yourself as a friend. Think of yourself as a friend. React and respond as a friend would. Friend is a holy word because it does not connote that you are being superior to others, being submissive or dismissive, being advisory, requiring others to behave in a specific way, or any of those things that separate you from the person to whom you are relating. A friend accepts others.

It is important in your relationships that you do not harness the other with your expectations for them. You need to be very careful and respectful of another's God-given free will. This is their individuality, which is worthy of your respect. The word friend carries with it this sense of equality with others in the eyes of God. This makes it holy.

As a practical matter do look upon all you meet as a friend. Include everyone: Those you know and those whom you pass by in fleeting moments. You will find some who will not return your friendly offering. If your initial contribution to every interaction is to come as a friend, you will have accomplished much. As a practical reward you will find more people respond positively to you, thus making your day better. You will find that some, but not all, of the rough spots you encounter in your life will diminish in intensity. These rewards in turn will make it easier to approach everyone with friendship in your heart. Do you see how this approach will contribute to the healing in the world for which you all hunger?

❧

Good morning dear one, it is a fine day with already another demonstration that the spiritual laws work.

Dearest Buck indeed they do. How you came into a broader realization of how they work. Why don't you describe it?

I just found out that my ailing brother Joe will be able to stay in South Carolina under Medicaid near his daughter. This is so much better than his having to go back to his home in Vermont. We were very anxious about whether he could claim residency in South Carolina. Apparently he can.

When this whole question arose I felt I needed to do two things. One, I had to help establish his residency in South Carolina. Secondly, I needed to accept whatever happened.

This latter has several layers. I knew that God would place me in that set of circumstances that is best suited for me to learn the lessons I need to learn. Second, that set of circumstances is not my prerogative to choose, but God's. I don't mean to indicate that God is personally selecting my set of circumstances, but the laws he has put in place dynamically bring this about. It isn't up to me to determine what I think the best learning circumstances are for me. It is up to my teacher. Therefore, I need to accept whatever comes my way as the correct set of circumstances. If they seem to be nothing but big problems I must consent to them and appreciate their appropriateness. So what I did was say to God, "please let things be such that will be of benefit to my brother Joe." Next I said, "But I will accept with gratitude whatever you feel is the best learning experience for us." Then I let it go.

As you know I have done this many times before. At first it was difficult to be sincere in the latter statement but with practice I could say so with genuine feeling. Time after time the result was that things turned out as I preferred. It worked this morning when the lawyer told me that we should have no trouble establishing Joe's residency.

I realize that previously I assumed it was all up to me to do what was needed to bring about the right solution. In other words, I thought I was the one in control. I watched many others who just seemed to drift through life and let things happen to them with poor results. I wanted to be the master of my life and went about creating it as I thought I wanted. This worked up to a point. Fortunately, my inner self guided me to accept the three goals of decision making: any decision must be good for them, good for me and harm no one.

At this point I really trust God to do what is best for me and feel I shall accept with gratitude whatever is the best learning experience for me.

Yes, there is a great deal to be gained in realizing God's beneficial blessings that he gives each of us. It is also true, as you have stated, that you must do your part to bring about a beneficial solution particularly in the material aspects of the situation. You cannot just sit back and expect God to do it for you. The reason for this is that if it is going to be a learning situation, which is the main intent, then you have to participate so you can learn. You would do well to accept this knowledge now that you know that it works so well. Godspeed.

Gail, we're going to the ranch this afternoon.

Dear Buck, you have yet another day to appreciate the love that is in this world. Today we will talk about hope. When people lose hope it is tragic. Hope can be misleading; it can lead to expectations and thence to disappointment. It isn't hope itself that is the problem, it is the way it is used.

When you let your mind build specific hopes or expectations you can blind yourself to other alternative outcomes that may be even better. When a specific expectation is unfulfilled your tendency is to regard any other outcome as a disappointment.

This is made even more difficult in that some of the best things in life don't come all at once, but in increments. The result is that you don't have a definite time when you feel fulfillment has been reached. You can think things haven't turned out right, when, in fact, you have been gradually building up to something fulfilling.

It is better to have unspecific hopes. Have hope and trust that you will grow and learn with each experience that comes into your life. Thus your mind will be in the right attitude to see the virtue and opportunity that comes with that unspecified future experience.

This attitude is part of hopeful, generalized acceptance that leads to enlightenment and joy in life.

Buck, we will never come to the end of our communications. Isn't that lovely? There is something more I would like to add because it would be helpful to you in finding your truth.

Jesus said, "I am the way." If this is so then let's look at his life. At 12 he confronted the moneychangers in the temple in a some-what violent way, upsetting their paraphernalia. Later as he know-ingly neared his own crucifixion, he avoided confrontation and chose acceptance of his own approaching death.

Let's analyze Jesus' behavior in two ways. Since he said, "I am the way," the confrontation with the moneychangers was, apparently, an appropriate way to deal with improper behavior on the part of others.

Jesus partook in confrontation as an immature 12 year-old. As he matured into a 30-year-old spiritual leader, he learned and practiced acceptance and saw this as a better instrument of influence than his earlier confrontation. Had he continued with his confrontational approach would he still be regarded as a spiritual teacher of several millennium standing?

Knowing you as I do, I know which interpretation you will regard as the truer one. Use your free will to bring you to your truth.

I do feel that the latter, non-confrontational approach is truer to the spiritual principles as I understand them. I also see that the first scenario is one of separation. I am convinced that actions and thoughts that separate usually do not carry you forward, as do inclusive thoughts from a wider perception.

My sweet one, it is a beautiful world today. Please use my fingers on the keyboard to tell me of those wonderful things you see.

Dear Buck, the beautiful world is there always, but neither you nor anyone else can see it unless there is a corresponding receptor of beauty within you to recognize it. This is the neglected law of correspondence where like attracts and empowers like.

*Let's talk about acceptance and its effect on fear. **A Course in Miracles** is correct: fear functions as the opposite of love, for fear inhibits love as well as much else. Fear is a very difficult thing to control or even diminish and yet it has its place.*

Recently you described your fear of finding out that you had prostate cancer. Cancer promotes fear in many people. Actually there are many stimuli to having fear, which are important in your growth process. I want you to write about your realization that if you had cancer you would try to accept it as an opportunity to learn a great, though difficult, lesson.

After having decided what to do if I found I had cancer and accepting the lessons therein, I realized I could accept that outcome with diminished fear. The fear was not so incapacitating. Is this what you mean?

Yes. Did you notice what you wrote in the first sentence? "I could accept that outcome with diminished fear." Acceptance is a tool with which to lessen fear. You can deliberately use acceptance for that purpose.

Now this is an example of accepting a negative outcome: cancer. There are positive things to accept as well that will reduce your fear. Can you think of something?

If you accept in your mind and heart God's great gift that you live forever, your need for fear evaporates. Now I know that many people give lip service to immortality and even believe in it in an abstracted sort of way, but they don't live it and feel it in their hearts. They dread the inevitable death of their loved ones, but if their hearts truly embraced the knowledge that these loved ones live forever, they would feel greater peace.

The realization of this truth is so vast that it is difficult to accept it when life is pulling you this way and that. Yet if you remind yourself of God's grace in giving you this, your fears would have less to feed upon.

Use acceptance in both the negative and the positive things in your life. Accept them with the grace with which they are given. You will find this healing. I leave you to think about the connection between acceptance and healing. Godspeed.

The spiritual meaning of acceptance is to actively trust that the circumstances you find yourself in are just the ones you need to learn. This can be better understood if you think of the opposite of acceptance, which is resistance. You resist the circumstances and you resist the lessons they contain. This can be a bit confusing because if you are in an unhappy situation shouldn't you "resist" or try to over-come it? It all depends upon your attitude and perception of what is happening to you.

One of the most seductive, unproductive forms of resistance is blaming others for what you don't like in your condition: "I am in this bad situation because of what others have done to me. Therefore to correct this situation others have to change. I don't have to change because I am not at fault; they are. I am the victim and they are the victimizers."

One cannot grow if one does not change by allowing something new into one's thinking. Therefore the old attitude, "it's not my fault but his," shuts off growth. A feeling of victimhood embodies this ap-proach and is very hard to overcome, as it is almost addictive.

Some activists have great difficulty with this same problem. They are so sure they have identified what is wrong and that the solu-tion requires others to change. The activists, however, often don't see that they need to change as they regard themselves as part of the solu-tion and not part of the problem. Their vision of the solution is so virtuous in their eyes that it is justification enough. This seems a harsh description of people who have the best of intentions and truly care about the condition of the world and those in it. Along with everyone else, however, they are in the situation best suited for them to learn what they need to learn. This cannot be done unless they are willing to change themselves in addition to influencing others.

I wish to be clear that I am not suggesting that you don't try to improve your world and the lot of the people in it. It is a matter of your attitude. You should look to God and his attributes to see what you may use to help the situation, such as inclusion. When you do the opposite and use exclusion as in "we are the good guys and they are the bad guys," you continue to foster strife in your world. Instead, exercise patience and love your brothers and sisters.

Being closed-minded is a form of resistance to growth. If you are faced with a problem it means you have not found a solution. So there you are looking for a solution that remains hidden. Limiting your various solutions doesn't make much sense. You need to be receptive to new possibilities. Part of the meaning of acceptance is that you are open to the idea that your situation contains the stimulus for learning something new.

Blaming others and being closed minded inhibits the learning potential in your circumstances. Seeking to change yourself and being receptive to new possibilities when confronted with a difficult situation enhances your ability to gain wisdom and grow.

CHAPTER TWENTY

The Deeper Meanings of Beauty and Creativity

Buck, you are so dear to me. We were fortunate to have had each other again in my last life.

There you are, remembering when I was living with you how I used to express my gratitude to God in my prayers: "The world could not be more beautiful." My perception that the world could not be more beautiful grew in strength and power.

My inner self told me to slow down, actually to stop, because my conscious self was not ready to perceive such all-encompassing universal beauty. Remember, I was overcome by it all the time and it was interfering with my living. I was not ready then. I am now. The beauty of the All is wondrous indeed.

You too, when you come, will see and better yet, feel this. The inspiration for your artwork is the beauty principle. The beauty principle is like the love principle and the joy principle; they are different aspects of the same principle. Through either of these aspects you can reach the other.

You're still your old self. You want me to be more specific. You don't want to be told to just buy some milk; you want to be told how many quarts. All right, people who have seen your work are inspired by it partly because you started painting so late in life. This makes them believe that the same potential might be in them. They also see and are attracted to the intangible that you express so well in your paintings. To sense the intangible, to feel its power speak to you is but a specific example of sensing the power of the spirit. To bring people to the awareness that they can do things they previously thought impossible is a high order of teaching.

Greetings Buck, from me and others here who take an interest in us.

Beauty goes well beyond being merely something pleasant to see, as nice as that is. Beauty is actually a spiritual power. It is one of the principles of the universe and as such has a place in the absolute.

Yes it is true that beauty seems to be relative on Earth. One painter is said to have created better masterpieces than did another. One woman is more beautiful than another woman. Yosemite is more beautiful than Zion. And yet there are those who disagree with this and arrange their beauty scale in another order. All this keeps you on the surface and covers over the fundamental principle of beauty.

The principle of beauty is that God created all things to be beautiful no matter what the scale. The night sky with millions of stars is as beautiful as the delicacy of the wings of a dragonfly. The beauty aspect is an integral part of its being and was so created by God. When you seek perfection in the world about you and attune yourself to the fulfillment of all things within their nature given to them by God, you realize that beauty is an absolute.

For millennia our polished marble tabletop was in the middle of a marble formation near the Earth's surface. No one could see it. It was just rock in all directions, yet the beauty that you see now on the surface of that marble was there then and was sensed by the marble as being part of itself. The beauty was part of the fulfillment of itself.

The beauty principle follows a similar pattern as love. There are all kinds of earthly love, all of which are delightful, but divine love is a whole different principle. We are love made manifest as has often been written; the result of this manifestation is beauty. As love is beautiful to feel and see, when you perceive this you experience perfection in the world. Sensing the perfection in the world allows you peace and serenity. Peace and serenity bring you back into communication with God. Do you understand how this all fits together? It is beautiful isn't it?

Do you see how your artwork fits into this? You try to create beauty. You deliberately make your abstract paintings beautiful to look upon. For your representational work you choose what you find to be beautiful subjects. By creating beauty you attune yourself to perfection and fulfillment, which brings peace and serenity. When I passed on, you dearly wanted peace, serenity and joy. Where did you turn? You turned to artwork. This is how this cycle works.

Yes, I found that creativity was a wonderful healer because it absorbed one hundred percent of my attention. Somehow it gave the rest of me serenity and let the healing processes go on unimpeded by my feeling of great sorrow. Then when my sorrow again forced itself into my mind, I felt like a soft breeze had momentarily eased my grief in a way that I desperately needed.

My beautiful companion, here I am at the ranch in our elegant cabin. I am by myself. The place seems very holy. The redwood grove fits with the cabin so well. The fire feels good this morning. It is nice to have so much firewood easily available.

We are companions through time, aren't we? This reminds me that there are places in the world that are sacred in and of themselves. There is a special ambience you feel when you are there that seems to have a sense of attunement. This sacredness, however, can be enhanced by the thoughts and presence of those who are attuned to it. In our travels we came upon many such sacred places. We were alone that rainy day in the beehive tomb of Atreus. The kiva we climbed into at Bandelier where the German was already meditating was sacred. Our kopje in the Sierras is holy. Be with me now and let us write of God and the Oneship.

Do you know what makes a place sacred? You feel it but what is it you feel? There are some places on Earth that are particularly congruent with the holy presence. If a person has within her a sense of the holiness of life and comes upon such a place, she senses the congruency of holiness combined with the holy presence of the place. This is a sacred joining and gives one that feeling of the infinite.

A person who does not sense the holiness of life can come to that same place and feel nothing different.

But why are some places like that and others not? You would think this would be true everywhere because it is all God's world.

There are many different types of energies that flow and ebb. You can't see most of them any more than you can see the wind. In some places these energies and their physical manifestations are congruent. They are in harmony with the All. This makes the place sacred. Thoughts too can be congruent with the energies and the physical manifestations, which lead to more sacredness.

Cathedrals become sacred places through thoughts, particularly those of the builders. When we enter a cathedral we sense the energies and thoughts of the builders all those centuries ago and we add our own sacred thoughts to the cathedral.

Here we are at the ranch and it is sublime. There is harmony, serenity, and energy here. It is good that you feel grateful for the privilege of being here. We are here in this place made sacred by our thoughts and presence.

There is another sacredness that you, dear one, are particularly aware of. You are very privileged to be so. Do you know what it is?

Beauty. Beauty comprises an additional dimension of sacredness. Just think how important beauty has been to every time and every civilization, to say nothing about the vast time and energy devoted to it over the millennium.

That is right. This too is created by the congruency of the beautiful object and the thoughts of the observer who appreciates that beauty. Together they acknowledge the wonder of God's creations. It doesn't matter if the object of beauty is manmade, like an ancient Chinese vase. Was it not God who created the clay and the fire that would make it into porcelain? And the colors, where did they all come from if not God? The vase is a co-creation of God and Man.

This is one of the things you are learning with your painting. You know you are co-creating with God when you paint. While this doesn't automatically mean you make nothing but masterpieces, it is the process of creativity that is significant. It is the sensation that you are co-creating with God, using the tools God graciously gave you to make things beautiful that brings joy to your heart when you are painting.

Remember that your most sacred place and process are within you. God bless.

Gail, I want to write you a letter. It is a lovely spring day like so many we enjoyed on our hill. This morning there were a dozen deer around, some playing, others lying down. The mother and her late fawn were lying together on the grass looking so contented. The fawn is still small and looks two months old, not almost four months as she was. I went out to talk to them. They looked up but that was all.

Then at noon I ate on our wood deck. The grass was that vivid, spring-green color. There was no wind, but much sun that felt so good on my body. The hawks were busy flying back and forth full of their courtship calling. It is such a haunting, wild sound. They would fly from the top of the pines to the top of the eucalyptus. One pair went way up in the sky and then returned in speedy descent with their wings partially pulled in. First one came and then the other. I would like to be able to do that.

I lay back, closed my eyes and just listened. Teacup, our cat, gently jumped on my lap and curled up. A while later she got up and licked my nose.

The white iris that Eric gave you is now blossoming and soon I will go out and pick one to put into a flower vase inside.

The crocuses are past but the daffodils are in full glory. The wild plum trees also are flowering white. I walked up close to one and the bees were humming softly as they did their godlike work.

Now a soft breeze is coming up and stirring things a bit. I'm privileged to be part of this peaceable kingdom. I am blessed, as are you. God has granted us so much. His love and beauty is what I see around me all this day.

～

My beloved Gail, it is one of those halcyon days. The world is beautifully sun blessed.

Dear Buck, beauty is inextricably mixed into God's world and God's creations. Your world is indeed beautiful as we discovered in our travels. Think of the multitude of other worlds and other universes that God has blessed with beauty.

Beauty is an interesting attribute. It is easy to understand the role played by the thing that is beautiful in itself: a huge redwood tree, Yosemite Falls, Magi Lake, to name a few. Their beauty is something that is inherently theirs.

The role of the beholder of beauty, however, is different. This, people say, is subjective. Different people respond in different ways. If you take a composite of all of the women (big and small, fat and thin) in a given ethnic group, the result will be a woman of outstanding beauty. Thus, this kind of beauty is an average. Other kinds of beauty derive from being rare or unique such as the tallest mountain. Perceived beauty is derived therefore from a variety of inspirations. This correctly implies that your mind as builder can build beauty in many ways. Look at the vast diversity in antiques that are regarded as beautiful by some people and ugly by others.

You are an artist who takes a blank canvas and paints a lovely picture. You have created beauty outside yourself. God has given each of you, however, the ability to go beyond that to create beauty in your perception without doing anything external to the object now regarded as beautiful. You have this power in your mind to perceive beauty in your world without changing anything. You can try doing this deliberately and see how it affects what you see and feel.

As you can see I am approaching the concept that one of God's attributes is beauty. God is beautiful. He perceives the All that he created as beautiful. When you look at your world and fail to see beauty you are separating yourself from God. One reason you do this is because you think the beauty must be contained in the thing external to you. In truth beauty is contained within you as it is within God. To see it, look inward.

Gail, I look at our world and see beauty almost everywhere. And where I don't see beauty I see that at least in part, beauty is in the eye of the beholder, so in theory it is everywhere. It must therefore have significance for us since God made it ubiquitous. It must also have significance to God since he made all his creations beautiful. Why is this? Do you know?

God created a world for you to exercise free will. You could argue that the only thing that is ugly in this world is what you do with your free will—fighting wars, for example. We could also argue that God makes his contribution to ugliness by having animals eat each other for a living. There is the lion eating the wildebeest calf while the poor mother watches. It would be hard to argue that those are beautiful events if one's perspective is limited. If you broaden your perspective, however, you begin to see some light. For example, in war there are acts of heroism where someone is willing to risk himself to save others. The lion in turn is serving the purpose of holding down the population of wildebeest, which, peculiarly, is in the wildebeest's best interest.

Let's jump even wider. From your finite view, my proposed broadened perspective only mitigates what still are basically unhappy, ugly situations. If one tries to see it from an infinite view it all does, in fact, become beautiful. As a simple analogy think of critiquing a skillfully done movie. If you eliminated things that were unpleasant, you would ruin what helped make the movie compelling and beautiful. You illustrated the same thing in your Discord and Harmony demonstration audio tape. Write about it.

I illustrated on a piano how long passages of pure harmony made up of major thirds become so boring that they don't seem like music. I also played random discords, which if I had continued would have given everyone a headache, still it was not beautiful music. Then I carefully inserted harmonious major thirds with some discordant chords to create what my students called beautiful music. It is harmony, discord and resolution that make music beautiful. From this one can draw many important parallels with being the composer of your life music.

Buck, you and I are illustrating that what in small pieces may seem ugly can be beautiful when viewed in the total matrix of life.

Although we have reinforced your original statement that beauty is everywhere, we have not addressed your original question of, "why does beauty have such significance for God that he puts it everywhere?" You define beauty as attractiveness, something lovely and pleasurable to see. You can experience pleasure in the beauty with which God surrounds you. Therefore, God is giving you a wonderful gift to create your environment infused with beauty. God is indeed generous. How can humans think God is a vengeful, wrathful being when he gives you such great gifts to enjoy?

Think of what a genius he is to conceive of the idea that things can appear beautiful. It is like color; you could just as easily all be color blind and live in a colorless world, but God gave you the wonderful dimension of color to savor. He wants you to love your world, appreciate it and feel yourself the recipient of his gifts.

Hello my Buck.   Yesterday we talked of how beautiful God's creations are.   God loves his creations.   That's why he made them beautiful.   He shares this created beauty with you and all his other creations. He is pleased when he sees you loving his creations and appreciating the beauty that is within them.   You attune yourself with him in doing so. This reveals the importance of beauty in the spiritual scheme of things. It also indicates you would do well to seek beauty in all things.   You tend to think of things in terms of their either being beautiful or ugly. This is an either-or construct that you have created that is not reality. All things can be beautiful if you but let your mind see.

Surely the suffering in the world is not beautiful.

I can understand your comment and even have difficulty with this myself, but am convinced that with the broadest perspective of many lifetimes, we shall see beauty in the fulfillment of the perfect process which includes suffering.   As I say though, I am not there yet.   I do think you will agree that there is much more beauty out there and within you than most people appreciate.

Oh I agree.   One of the nicest things I have discovered with my painting is how many things are of exquisite beauty that I never paid attention to before.   I add more things of beauty to my awareness each day.

Beauty is essentially spiritual.   For me personally one of the most touching things is feeling that God so loved the world he gave it flowers.   To me such a God could not be at the same time a vengeful and punishing being as some religions describe him.   He is indeed all love.   Enjoy your day in the midst of beauty.

When we met I was very attracted to you because of your creativity.   You seemed fearless.   One must be fearless to be creative, as fear shuts you down.   God's fearlessness is an attribute we must emulate along with love.

The spiritual meaning of creativity is deeper than generally realized. It is a matter of dealing with possibilities. To create something is to empower a possibility by converting it to reality. In the cold, hard reality of the earthly experience there has been no indication that there is a limit to possibilities. The history of mankind is nothing but the fulfillment of new and different opportunities and understandings that have not previously occurred. Since you are constantly exposed to new possibilities that mature into reality why do you think they are limited?

This is why I find it so puzzling that some scientists refuse to contemplate the possibility of an afterlife or psychic events. I realize they have not been scientifically proven, but why do they have to be debunked because we have not yet developed the tools to investigate them properly? Both an afterlife and psychic events are possibilities that shouldn't be excluded anymore than the Wright brothers should have dismissed the possibility of powered flight.

There are also clergy who fear a challenge to their religion. They are good souls who are seeking their own truths in their own way. They also defend their truth as they see it and they feel that everyone else should see it likewise. This is a very common response.

Let's now turn to what creativity is in God. He is, of course, the ultimate creator, the most versed, the most capable and the most expert. Therefore the possibilities he has created are beyond anything we have known. Further, the realities that have come forth from these possibilities are also beyond anything we can comprehend at this time.

Realizing the above, does it not seem likely that there is more than one planet like Earth that could develop complex life? And beyond that doesn't it seem probable that there is more than one universe governed by a single set of universal laws? If God can create one universe what's to keep him from making another? It is possible that these other universes are not like our own, but are quite different. Because you on Earth limit yourself and the possibilities that you will consider does not mean in any way that God follows your example. Do you now see some of the implications in truly understanding creativity at the higher levels? Godspeed!

We need to dissolve the separating self-limitation so many think of as normal. Imposing limits is not the best way to learn or appreciate God's many gifts. It is important to understand the benefits of eliminating these limits. If you feel you can't do anything creative then, of course, you won't be able to. This last life I had that problem. I felt very inadequate in being creative. It is one of the things for which I thank you. You convinced me that creativity was not limited to the "arts." One can live life with a creative attitude that influences everything you do. Once you become attuned to living with this creative approach to all things, your life begins to sing. This is a huge benefit but not the only one.

Feeling at home with and living the creative process brings you into closer relationship to your Creator. Creativity dissolves the boundary between you and God as you both partake in the same thing. By so doing you co-create with the Oneship.

This leads to an important principle, but one that is difficult to understand. Here you are, creating with the Oneship, yet the Oneship is already created. Does this make any sense? If something is already created what is the point in recreating it? Existence is a process, not a completion. The very essence of the Oneship is that it is constantly recreating itself. The distinction between creating and recreating disappears. The Oneship exists only because we, with God, are constantly creating/recreating it. That we participate in the creation of the Oneship imperfectly in no way diminishes the Oneship. It enhances it. In some mysterious divine way the vitality of the Oneship is more vibrant as we recreate the Oneship to reach ever-higher levels of attunement. It is not unlike the discord in music, which brings color, emotion and exquisite beauty to what you are playing.

This creating/recreating of the Oneship can be understood by thinking about music. Once you stop playing music there is no music, only a memory of it, a shadow so to speak. In the same way the One-ship needs to be "played or displayed" as a continuum, a process.

This brings us to a third benefit of creating/recreating the One-ship. Since the Oneship lives by being played, when you play it you can partake in the joys, the serenity and the love which is inherent in such playing. Any musician will know exactly what I mean. May you walk, run, play and vibrate in the Oneship.

Creativity, with its resulting beauty, is a journey worth taking as it enhances development of your truth, which itself is beautiful.

CHAPTER TWENTY-ONE

Developing Your Truth

Dearest Buck, today we will write about knowledge. There are two types of knowledge in general: objective knowledge and personal knowledge. Since the spiritual schools of thought indicate that what goes on internally determines what goes on outside of you, which area of knowledge would be the most important?

I never thought of it that way. Intuitive or subjective knowledge would be more vital than objective knowledge, which is based on external forces and judgments.

You are right. Western culture worships objective knowledge. Further they are under the illusion that there is such a thing as objective truth. All objective knowledge is tainted with subjectivity. This is particularly clear in much scholarly writing. In particular, the re-writing of history is an exercise of a subjective viewpoint clothed in a posture of objectivity.

Please understand this does not mean seeking objectivity is without worth. For example, the objective approach to problem solving and objective research using the scientific method are of great value to the progress of humanity. The problem arises when the practitioners assume that objective, analytical thinking is the sole dependable means to understand life.

To use your words, Buck, objectivity is one very good tool. Like all tools it is excellent for leading us toward greater understanding of the truth, but ineffective in other applications.

Subjective knowledge has its own value, its own area where it is supreme as a tool. Because our culture is so outwardly oriented, the tool of subjective or personal knowledge is downgraded. This is where you have it backwards; you regard objective knowledge as being superior to subjective knowledge when sometimes subjective knowledge is superior. The word "superior" here means being at a higher level of truth. It does not mean that the less superior is defective or useless. It simply operates effectively at a lower level.

*In your language the word "subjective" carries with it a connotation of being defective. It is understood that subjective thought should be converted to objective thought as soon as possible. Therefore I will not use the word **subjective**. I will use **personal knowledge** instead. It is actually more descriptive. We have discussed on several occasions the importance of developing your own truth. Personal knowledge is superior to objective knowledge, as it will lead you to your ever-widening truth.*

I will give you an example of this. Buck, when you and I decided to get married, what tool did we rely on, objective knowledge or personal knowledge? It was personal knowledge. Our decision to get married and commit our lives to each other carried us a great distance in finding our own truths and fulfilling our nature. Although the worshipers of objectivity would not like to admit it, their spousal choices were also made by personal rather than objective knowledge, particularly the successful ones.

You should therefore hold your personal knowledge in high regard. You should pay attention to what it is telling you and you should try to deliberately develop it. Learn to depend upon it. Do not let respect for objective knowledge diminish your appreciation of your personal knowledge.

I need to reiterate that both objective and personal knowledge are very useful. Each has its place and each will bring rewards with proper use. Since your God-given purpose in life is to develop your truth and fulfill your nature as given to you by God, you must become adept at using the tool of personal knowledge to fulfill this purpose. Godspeed.

On thinking about this I realized an interesting example of personal truth. Democracy was not developed through the application of scientific analysis. The founding fathers depended very heavily on their personal knowledge. Our government did not come into being because some wise men accurately predicted human behavior. It arose out of the central theme that personal liberty is important and the inalienable right of all. It came from deep within the heart because there were many who also knew in their hearts this was just.

Dear Buck, I want to return to a theme I've written about before. Your role is to develop your truth. You are to accept another's truth only insofar as it helps you create your truth. You should not abdicate developing your individual truth by simply adhering to an established truth system created by others. There are many truth systems that unabashedly ask you to embrace their beliefs with promises that you will thereby be favored by God. Many of those systems contain great truths that deserve your attention. That wisdom, however, is not valid for you until it becomes your individual truth.

The above statement in no way means you cannot enjoy the stimulation and harmony to be felt in the company of like-minded people. This can and often does enhance the We Are All One principle. It is a fine line between this and obedience to the dictates of an established truth system. This system may ask you to abandon your search for truth in favor of adopting another rubric in its entirety. Spiritually there is a great difference between your sincere seeking and allowing someone else tell you what to believe. You all equally need to remember who you are. You are all equal seekers on the path even though some are temporarily ahead of others.

Let me use an analogy to clarify what I mean. You are hungry, so you go to a restaurant. The menu is presented. You don't like some entrees, some you've never tasted and others appeal to you. You make a choice based on what you feel is appropriate. You choose and it is served to you. You eat it. The food nutrients become part of you and sustain you. They satisfy your hunger if only temporarily.

You also hunger for spiritual truth. You seek sources you feel will provide you with the food of truth. You are presented with various forms of truth. Some you simply cannot believe. Some are new to you, which you will not choose unless you feel adventuresome. Others you feel ready for and from these you select one. You chew on this truth. You find it has sustenance for you. You swallow it and with digestion it becomes part of you. It is now your truth. You did not let the restaurant choose for you what you would order. It was clearly a choice you wanted to make yourself. And it did not become part of you until you digested it.

You may be at a stage where buying into an established truth system feels very good to you. You feel very much at home with it and are happy to have someone tell you how it is in this very confusing world. The sense of belonging to this group is important to you and gives you great comfort. This is fine and probably represents your truth at this time. For all of you, however, these are just stations on a long journey to find your truth and connect to God with no wall between you, as you are one with him.

My dear husband, you should be pleased and grateful for all the wonders of your mind and body. Let us talk of the ego and its role. Many know the ego is necessary while at the same time belittle it as being too self-centered. You mistakenly think a philanthropist is only motivated by self-glorification of his virtuous character. But take a second look and see that because the donor feels ego satisfaction it does not detract from the virtuousness of doing good.

In this judgment, notice that you are involved in a separation tactic in which the ego is separated from selflessness. Such separation is a construct in your mind and does not reflect reality.

The reality is that God has given the ego to you. You are to develop this ego, grow with it in wisdom and understanding. This cannot be done if you degrade it. Now it is true that the ego can dominate and become overly involved. The answer is not to suppress it but to understand its role in the overall scheme of things.

　　Your culture has incorrectly separated selflessness and the ego. Reunite them and you will begin to understand the truly developed ego. The ego motivates and individualizes each of us. It is the ego that exercises free will. Each of these is necessary for the fulfillment of your nature as given to you by God.

　　The ego goes astray when it separates itself from everything in its awareness. It becomes enlightened when it joins in service to others, which is a role that it adopts easily. Just look at your world. You see many people helping others without thought of recompense. Now, you know from your experience that when you are helpful to others your ego feels good about it. Therefore, servicing others and servicing your ego go hand in hand. In fact, helping others is a precursor to having a healthy, satisfied ego.

　　Buck, you have a friend who feels misjudged because his donations of millions with wonderful results is belittled and dismissed by others as 'Bob's ego trip.' He acknowledges that his ego is pleased to have been able to do these things. It should be. He knows, as the others don't, that the basis of his pleasure lies in the service he has done for others. If his donations had not been of service they would have been empty and his ego frustrated. Do you see how the two [ego and service] are necessary and enhance each other? His detractors are ignorant of this mutual enhancement.

　　From this we can draw the conclusion that to have a healthy ego you should engage in activities and thoughts which benefit others as well as yourself. What benefits you is complicated and does not consist simply of what adds to your material well being. Use the ego to promote oneness. Allow your ego to embrace compassion, tolerance and service to others. In so doing you will promote the brotherhood of man.

　　A healthy ego is good and can be defined as one that sees itself as a tool to unite in oneness with God and his children.

I perceive my ego as healthy because I am so fortunate that I have been chosen by God to partake in this wonderful world.

Yes Buck, life is indeed wonderful. That is even more apparent from this side. There is a word we have used but not discussed that has spiritual significance in this wonder, 'fulfillment.' Your purpose in life is to fulfill your nature as given to you by God. Fulfillment is very much in the center of things. To fulfill implies that within you is a potential to be completed. Also implied is that you have not yet fulfilled it. Thus to fulfill is a process of accomplishing that which is already within you but not yet realized. How do you discover the potential that is within you and how do you go about fulfilling it?

Human nature is surprisingly complex, but it is also simple. What makes it complex is the vast power of your individuality, the center point of which is your mind/heart. Think of the power in the concept that the mind is the builder and yet so many people on Earth don't even suspect this is true. Even so their minds go on building with such power they are convinced that the reality of the outside world is as their minds have constructed it.

Many of your powers are unknown to you. You may be aware of others but misunderstand them. For example, there is great power in love and forgiveness, but they are so misunderstood.

There is power in death. You have not thought of death as a power but it is. Its power is that it provides an opportunity for growth, for you have collected vast experiences in your life. You have processed them and thereby gained some wisdom that helps you continue your life. When you come over beyond death, however, you will discover that there is much more wisdom to be gained from these experiences. You truly need an environment like this other side to gain full wisdom. So the power of death lies in allowing you to come here and absorb that lovely wisdom. It is a bit like having a savings account in which you have put all your experiences. At death you come here and can spend for your benefit all those savings you have accumulated.

Many a successful person will cite a teacher as having been her initial inspiration to follow her path. Wonderful teachers surround you. There is karma, a master teacher; there is your inner self; there is your guide; there are also all those wonderful sisters and brothers with whom you have deep relationships. They are your teachers and fellow students at the same time. You fulfill this same role for them. If you went through your life aware of these teachers you would feel less alone and more confident that your life trials are but educational exercises.

There is immense power in communication in its many forms. It is what connects you to the Oneship. Because silence is very powerful in both connecting and receiving, meditation is an effective means of communication, and can open up a vast field of knowledge through your sense observations.

The teaching mentioned above is available to you through communication; the two are closely connected. In both teaching and communication it is very important that you use another great power you have been given. That is the power of listening. The degree to which you are able to listen competently to your teachers measures your progress on the path of enlightenment. As any parent knows, the best teaching is useless if the child won't listen.

This is the pattern for all the powers I have talked about and those I have not mentioned. They are there but if you don't recognize them, use them, or misunderstand them, their effectiveness is greatly reduced.

You taught in your classes about a personal toolbox. Write about it.

Each of us is born with a toolbox with an assortment of tools in it. Our purpose in life is to discover what tools we have been given and then practice using them until we become skilled. Each of us is given far more tools than we ever use. Do not assume these are limited to just what you have so far discovered. You can surprise yourself. Also do not be concerned with what wonderful tools others have; simply seek your unused tools.

Living a complete life involves getting to know what particular tools are in your toolbox. This is an interesting concept as you have two sets of tools. The first is a set of talents you can develop on Earth. Often these talents are quite individual in nature. Bach's ability to compose music and Monet's skill at painting are two obvious examples.

The second set of tool is more subtle. Each of you has the potential to be godlike, as you are children of God. You all have this Oneship in common, which you can individually fulfill.

When I talk about fulfilling your nature, both of these tool sets are involved. You might say the first set defines your individual path while the second set defines your overarching goal. Seeing how the two work together can be instructive. In developing your God-given individual talents, feel gratitude to God for them. Bach did so, and listen to the magnificent results. His gratitude elevated his understanding of his godlike qualities. This in turn led to a greater fulfillment of his nature.

Everyone is able to do this. The fact that it might not be at such an elevated scale has nothing to do with its effectiveness in bringing each of you closer to God. If you recognize **the process** *of fulfillment this is easier to understand. Your position on the path is not nearly as important as the progress you make on your path. When you judge people you are very likely to see only their place on the path, not their progress. This is one reason judging is such a misleading way to experience man's oneness.*

Much understanding can be gained simply by contemplating the idea that you have within you a pattern, a series of abilities, a matrix and a potential for your magnificent fulfillment. God has also given you a set of tools so that you can bring this about. The mind is the builder and what you are intended to build is this potential within you. Many call this self-realization.

Some seek this fulfillment in things outside themselves, in a career, in a reputation, in possessions and in relationships. These are not necessarily bad or to be avoided. It depends upon the attitude you have. True fulfillment really is achieved internally and gets back to "being" and "doing." If you fulfill yourself based on what you **are** *then what you* **do** *will flow from this. Your relationships as well as other outside factors can be useful in discovering and implementing this in-*

tegration of being and doing. Likewise, your reputation granted you by others is satisfying, but is not where you will find true fulfillment.

Look and listen within to find what you are now and what you can become. Know God has given you the tools to achieve this becoming. Seek and develop your truth.

❧

Hello my beloved one, how are you doing? It is raining lightly this day in May and I feel very much at home. I am listening to Rachmaninoff play his second Piano Concerto. Remember how we loved it so.

My romantic Buck, I do feel your harmony. Life is full of great treasures if we only recognize them.

Remember our friend Marilyn, who talked about someone who was communicating with his deceased mother about various conspiracies of powerful people in our world with evil designs who seem to have taken ascendancy. The good side was that it is all in God's hands. Goodness will be triumphant.

There is within the human mind an attraction for Armageddon of some sort. It has surfaced at many times in our history with considerable force. There are many compassionate people who feel the world is going in a terribly wrong direction. For those among them who believe in God there is hope that God will see to it that justice is done and conditions will improve.

This has been the recurring situation in the human perspective for generations. Fortunately, there is a higher truth that is not so uncomfortable. Let's review what we have previously said that applies to this situation.

God gave you free will and you see many who are using it in what you regard as ungodly ways. They seem so powerful and successful that you despair of any improvement unless somehow it is in God's plan to intervene so that goodness blossoms. The first thing to realize is that God is not reactive. He did not give you free will only to suspend it when you don't behave properly.

This can be understood better if you realize that instead of being reactive, he is proactive. As an integral part of creating your world and the life within it, he also created a series of interlocking spiritual laws within which you exercise this free will. Just like gravity with which you must always live when you are on the planet, you have no option to avoid it. When you get in an airplane, gravity seems suspended but that isn't true, it just appears that way. In the same way the spiritual laws give you free will while providing a gentle incentive to evolve towards a greater appreciation that you have been created as part of the One. These incentives are so subtle that it takes many lifetimes to arrive at spiritual harmony.

There is no need for God to interfere reactively with the choices you make with your free will even if some of these choices appear to you to be evil. He already has in place his laws that will heal all. He has given you immortality so that you can have whatever time you need to evolve, as it is in your divine nature.

God's three great gifts [free will, being part of the One and immortality] show that you can develop your truth to fulfill your nature. When you do, it will not be because God has punished or coerced you by depriving you of your free will at times. It will be because you have through a great many trials formulated your truth in finding the answer—love. You arrive there not through intimidation, punishment, or being overpowered to behave better; rather you get there by choosing to embrace love. In this sense you are indeed in God's hands.

CHAPTER TWENTY-TWO

Say Hello to Your Higher Self

Good morning dear Gail. I have been reading several new books that have come out and in them I find some of the same ideas that you are expressing to me. Some of these ideas I had never read or heard of before you gave them to me, but now I'm reading them in a book. What is happening here?

Dear Buck: You know what is happening. These ideas are now appropriate for the world at its present level of evolvement. They are being transmitted from this side by a number of entities including me, and are being picked up by a number of entities including you. It is another manifestation that we are all One. You will note that I may use a different terminology to illustrate an idea than someone else uses to describe the very same concept. This is not to confuse things, but rather to reach more people. Some will find enlightenment in the idea expressed in my terms and others will find the light in the language of others. Many will find the idea reinforced by seeing it expressed in several harmonious, cogent ways.

It is encouraging that the world is ready and is receiving higher levels of understanding. We really are into a new millennium.

Yes we are. It is exciting for us on this side too. Many, many entities here are involved in bringing this about. Do you feel others who are working through you?

Not exactly. But when you were here with me I wondered where some of the material I was teaching came from. It often came as a complete concept, like buried treasure that just suddenly popped out on top of the ground with the lid open. The discord/ harmony musical analogy was one such. It took a half an hour to lay it all out, but it came to me in an instant. By default we thought it was my inner self.

In that case we were right. It was your inner or higher self. If only people realized how wonderful, how talented, how knowledgeable their inner self is, they would be very eager to be open to it. The higher self has the additional capability of being the doorway to communication with so many other entities, places and principles. Right now your higher self is the channel through which I can contact you. Your higher self puts itself in neutral, so to speak, and opens its channel at both ends and thus you receive me. You could even say it is our private telephone line. It is not important but you would find it curious that my receiving communication from you does not go through your higher self. I receive that directly. Do you know why?

Because you have already joined your higher self. In fact, that is who you are at this time. So it is your higher self that receives my thoughts and it is my higher self that receives your thoughts.

Isn't it fun learning together! We delighted in knowing that we would love learning together the rest of our earthly lives. Remember that? Little did we realize that it would extend beyond death. You on Earth have so little realization of how continuity functions. Your tendency to separate leads to your failure to see the continuity that surrounds you. You see the world continue every day of your life, but it never occurs to you that this is a lesson from God to illustrate the unity of the mind and the spirit. As above so below: as within so without. To which we can add: as with the visible so with the invisible.

Those are true because we are all One. Everything shares a commonality. It is fascinating that it always comes back to this doesn't it?

True. Here is a place to point out that this inner self is not limited to the mind only. Your higher self can also have a big influence on your physical self. Tell about your friend who found this out in a strange way.

I had a hippie friend who rented an old shack in the hills on the west side of the valley. It was cheap and in the woods which suited him just fine. But because he was so far (about six miles) from a food market and there was no refrigerator he had a hard time keeping himself in food. He spent about a year saving enough money to buy a used refrigerator. When he finally got it he was really pleased: life was good.

The place was a firetrap, of course, but what could he do. Unfortunately, one day a grease fire on top of his stove set the place on fire. It went up like a lighted match. In a panic he ran to the refrigerator, wrapped his arms around it, picked it up and threw it out the window to save it before quickly jumping after it. It ruined the refrigerator but that didn't occur to him in his panic.

In his high emotional state he tapped into his higher self and was able physically to do something that he normally couldn't. There are many similar true stories like the mother who picked up the end of car that had fallen on her son while he was fixing it.

In the same way when you died I felt totally shattered with no strength within me. Then I remembered this story that I had used in my classes, and decided to focus my emotional strength toward my higher or inner self. It was strange. First I sensed there was strength near me and then I realized I had it within and my healing began, not smoothly but encouragingly.

It is important to realize that you have much strength, wisdom and guidance that can help you. It is inside you. It does not announce itself, but it will communicate with you if you listen. Meditation, dreams, writing in a journal and yoga are a few of the many ways you can get in touch with this inner self.

The mystery that is God is seemingly paradoxical. We are all One, yet individual. Everything is the same, yet differences and diversities abound. There is ubiquitous good and love and yet there is what we perceive as evil. All things obey God's laws yet things are always changing. One would think that being restricted to God's laws would reduce everything to a single uniform state. But that doesn't happen. Tell about your mountains.

I love mountains. I wondered how every mountain could be so very different when all mountains have to obey the same laws of gravity, chemistry, physics and a host of other restrictive parameters. You would think they would all tend to look alike. The only thing they share in common is being higher than their immediate surroundings. Man-made laws are different. They promote and even demand conformity, which is a good thing as I'm glad we stop for red lights.

These mysteries of God deserve our respect and awe. It is through your higher self that you can sense the wonder and beauty of the divine. We should not let the earthly tendency toward either-or thinking (another form of separation) cause us to try to reduce these mysteries to one or the other polarity.

That makes it sound like a duality. I thought dualities were of the material world and that the spiritual was triune in nature. How does that work?

It is triune. You are part of the Oneship. That's one. You are also individual. That's two. The mystery of their harmonic co-existence is the third. It is the same as the Father, the son and the Holy Spirit. The Father is the mystery. The son is the individual. The Holy Spirit is the Oneship. Isn't that wonderful?

It is! You were so right those 40 years ago when you said that we would find mysticism endlessly fascinating. How did you know that there were endless enlightenments to apprehend?

I didn't know then but I do now. It was my higher self that communicated that to me. Again one's higher self is a source of much good in one's life, if invited in.

Dear Buck, we have been talking about communication between this side and your side and how one needs to turn to one's higher self to open this dialogue. But how does one contact his or her higher self?

For example, you have noticed that when someone is upset and feels unresolved about something they tend to repeat over and over again to the listener what is upsetting them. The listener may be puzzled why it has to be repeated so often. It is no mystery to the talker. He feels like he is in a maze going around and around searching for an exit and unable to locate one. If you find yourself in this situation, turn to your inner self and ask for direction. How can you do this? There are any number of ways, some of which, hopefully, you have already discovered. I will speak about one way.

Writing to oneself, as in contrast to only thinking, produces deeper material. This deeper content can be from your higher self and tends to throw new light on how you feel, what you might do, or how others are affecting you.

With this in mind write down what it is you previously heard yourself repeat over and over. As always do not edit or evaluate what you are writing. Let it come out in an easy flow. It often helps to address the higher self as if it were a separate individual, like a very special intimate friend whom you know is on your side and would never do anything to harm you. Your higher self is someone who has earned your complete confidence.

When you have finished writing you may or may not want to

read immediately. Do as you wish but do read it the following day. You will find this reading edifying. You will see meanings that you were not aware were there. You will be prompted with insights that are new to you. At this point you may want to write some more or maybe not. Go with how you feel. If you do write again read what you wrote the next day.

In addition you should reread what you have written after leaving it alone for a week. If possible do so aloud in privacy. You again will see in your writing new understandings that in all probability came from your higher self.

This writing exercise in contacting your higher self will, at a minimum, lead you to a new part of the maze that will give you hope to eventually find the exit. It will also give you practice in accessing your higher self. Contact with your higher self is the doorway to contacting us here.

⟫⟫⟫

It is difficult for you to understand how the dimension of the higher self works with your conscious self. From your viewpoint it is all very mysterious. When you become aware of this dimension it is always a surprise and you really aren't too sure what triggered such experiences. For some it is easier to just ignore it. You and I have always been adventuresome. We like to pursue the mysterious. We are doing so now.

Your higher self is with you always, but sometimes it enters into your conscious mind more than others. One such time is during the death experience. There are those who are dying, but do not know it in the conscious mind. Their higher self does, however, and is more active in this process than usual, behaving like a giant pillow cushioning the conscious mind that thinks it is falling into the abyss. The soft caress of the pillow puts the dying mind in a state of surprise and wonderment.

After this the dying process proceeds in the usual manner. One becomes aware of life after death, and becomes aware of being revitalized, of being greeted with great love. Generally any disbelief in all this is shattered by the reality of what one is experiencing. For many this experience makes them desire to communicate with the loved ones they left behind to share with them their surprise. If your departed one was a great disbeliever don't assume he or she will continue to be when faced with the reality of his or her continued existence. You can help here by being open and receptive to their trying to communicate with you.

Others who are aware of their passing and have some knowledge of dying make an easier transition and are also aware of various things they may do. Here it would be well to remind our readers that the descriptions written by people who have had a near death experience are most informative. There is diversity but it is quite common to experience the tunnel with the light at the end. Most meet a loving, spiritual being who revitalizes them while welcoming their return to this dimension.

I could have appeared to you as I was passing through, but did not. I don't quite know why. I was so grateful to have been able to convey to you my thanks for sharing your life and all the other emotions we felt in the emergency room when I said goodbye that I felt complete. It seemed unnecessary to do more. It is most reassuring to know that the one you left behind knows there is an afterlife. I knew you knew I passed over to the other side and I knew it was inevitable that you too would experience what I was then experiencing. This somehow made the whole process complete and whole so that I felt good about moving on.

One of the key things in our experience that helped me in transition is that I knew you forgave me for everything. When I was with you we told each other often how much we appreciated each other. All the mistakes we made were of no consequence when placed within the great bowl of experience that we had lived together in this last lifetime. It wasn't until I was here that I realized how much our past lives together also contributed to this. This forgiveness adds greatly to my sense of completeness.

I do not want what I said above to discourage others who did not talk about forgiveness and haven't yet forgiven. Forgiveness is an ever-present choice. God never withdraws this opportunity. It is avail-able every second, every minute. I know there are many people who would like to forgive, but do not know how. In spite of this the major step in forgiving is to truly want to forgive.

And what does it take to want to forgive? It requires that you do not require anything from the person you should forgive. They don't have to confess their sins to you. They don't even have to be aware that you feel they sinned against you. There is no requirement upon them to seek your forgiveness. To truly want to forgive, you must want or need nothing from them. Forgiveness is within your power and doesn't depend at all upon anyone else.

When you understand this you will be pleased that it doesn't require anything on their part, only yours. The power is within you alone and no one can prevent you, by his or her inaction, from forgiv-ing. This is quite liberating. After all one of the reasons you feel you need to forgive somebody is because they seemed so insensitive to your feelings in the first place. If forgiveness depended upon their becoming aware of their insensitivity to you it could postpone for a long time your forgiveness.

If they have passed on it can be easier to forgive when you re-alize you are in total control of your forgiveness. The dying experience changes your life. It most certainly will change the life of the one you want to forgive. The whole process of dying was created by God for en-lightenment so you become acutely aware of how your behavior affected others in your life. Your departed one cannot escape this, nor do you want to.

You can depend upon it that your loved one is much more en-lightened about you and life in general than when you were last aware of his or her outlook. The true question is can you in turn become more enlightened so as to keep pace with them? Forgiveness as I have described it above is one very effective way of doing this.

Good morning dear Gail, it is going to be a wonderful day. Right now it is fogged in and feels very cozy.

We need to talk more about the higher self and how it relates to the conscious self. The higher self fulfills a large role in everyone's life. This is just as true for those who don't even know there is a higher self. If you learn to work with your higher self, however, you can learn to avoid a great deal of the confusion and aimlessness that many feel in their lives. Because of this it behooves you to acquaint yourself with your higher self.

How do you do that? First, you have to be open to the idea that there is a higher self. You cannot find that to which you are not open. If you close your mind to a concept, your mind will either be unaware of it when it knocks on your door or it will concoct any set of reasons to convince you of the concept's nonexistence. The net result is that you are sure you have no higher self.

Second, you need to seek a connection, which you must request. But then you should listen. Buck, tell about your experience designing buildings.

When I first started my construction business I did almost everything myself, dug the ditches, poured the concrete, did the carpentry, paid the bills and designed the buildings. There was no one else on the payroll. I was very busy. One time I was finishing one job and had another in the pipeline, but was having difficulty finding time to design the new one. I had interviewed the owner and gathered all the data I needed, but had not yet put pencil to paper.

The next Saturday I was on the front lawn playing with our four small children when all of a sudden into my mind came the complete design for the new building. I hurried to my basement office and quickly sketched it all down. I was quite amazed. Where had this design come from?

A good design has to satisfy four diverse goals, which often are in conflict with each other. Previously I had had to struggle to get these four to come together. They are: the building must be structurally sound, economical, aesthetically pleasing and have a well functioning floor plan. I know that I have a well-designed building if all four of these are achieved. This was the case with this design that just popped completed into my mind.

I was puzzled by how this had occurred and curious too. I decided on my next building to retrace the same steps and see what happened. Later these steps became codified in my mind. First, gather all the data you need to solve your problem, but avoid trying to come up with any kind of solution. Then hand over the problem to your higher self. The easiest way to do this is to forget about it and not dwell on this unsolved problem hanging over your head. Just wait but be open to receiving at some unannounced time the solution. It will be characterized by being spontaneous and complete. When this happens write it down at once while the totality is still in your mind.

I designed a number of buildings this way and they were my better ones. I have also talked to others involved in creative work who recognize this process as one they use as well. This is an example of how one can utilize one's higher self.

There is a feeling on Earth that any spiritual guide like your higher self cannot advise you about things that might generate money. It is as though making money is dirty and should not be included in anything spiritual. This is nonsense and flies directly in the face of we are all One. If everything is One, how can money be outside it? So Buck in contacting his higher self came up with building designs that earned money. We all either earn money or are associated with something or someone who earns money. Thus earning money is a very central theme of living on Earth. Why then should it be separated from spiritual yearnings, guidance and purview? Buck, write about how you tried to use this guidance in accord with spiritual laws.

I've always believed that you should make all decisions based on fulfilling three goals: First, that it should be good for the other. Second, that it is good for you. Third, it should harm no one. I should make clear here that even though I number these, no one is more important than the other. They are all equally needed.

If your decision does not encompass these three, you need to go back to the drawing board and come up with another solution that does. If it does fulfill these three, it is a correct spiritual decision. Further, you will receive benefits that to your material mind will have seemingly no connection with this decision, but will be the fulfillment of the spiritual law of cause and effect.

Notice that second I said that it must be good for you. What if you do something that is a sacrifice on your part, but good for others and harms no one? Two out of three is not enough and the spiritual laws will not kick in with strength. This is contrary to a very strong cultural myth we have, and to which we have bought into; that is, it is noble to sacrifice oneself. A number of religions and governments eulogize the nobility of sacrifice or martyrdom.

If you believe that God is All, that All is one, and in the brotherhood of man, then you have to conclude that you, individually, are an integral part of that one, just as noble, just as important, just as necessary as any other part. If this is so, to transgress against yourself is no different than transgressing against someone else as we are all equally beloved parts of the all that is One.

In my generation women, particularly, were brought up to subordinate themselves willingly for the benefit of others. Many women were puzzled as to why their purity of motive was rewarded with being treated as a doormat. It was because two out of three doesn't work very well. They needed to go back to the drawing board and come up with a way to encompass first, that their actions be good for the others, second, that they be good for themselves, third, that they should harm no one.

Now I know I have just opened a can of worms. So let me clarify one very important point. Gail and I had four children in six years and I'm sure you all realize that meant that my wife and I, and particularly my wife, were very, very busy with the children and had little time to do what we might want to do by ourselves,

like sleep. But raising the kids is precisely what we both wanted and we felt was the most important thing either of us had to
do in this life. So this really was good for us, good for our kids
and harmed no one. If you resent what you are doing, however,
you have ignored the second principle. Don't try to make yourself noble by repressing that resentment. See the resentment as a
warning, a sign that you are transgressing against yourself and you
need to stop it as quickly as you would stop transgressing against
someone else.

　　　Now I know that our life goes on much too fast for us at
all times to be able to think, rethink and come up with this ideal
solution. We have to get on with our lives and very often we need
just to proceed the best we can. It is important, however, to realize
that these three principles are our goals and utilize them at least in
the big decisions of life. It's like learning to play the piano; you
can't just sit down and play Beethoven. But as you practice with
this goal in mind you can begin to play Beethoven, similarly you
will find it easier and quicker to reach good spiritual decisions.

　　　*It all comes back to your attitude or as I like to say your
"being." If your being is attuned to the We Are All One principle your
actions will be congruent with that principle. In the process you will
benefit others and yourself.*
　　　Buck, write down what I told you in the bathtub this morning.

In giving blessings I am blessed.
In giving healing I am healed.
In giving forgiveness I am forgiven.

　　　*These thoughts have been said many ways because of their
great truth. These are guiding principles that your higher self is trying
to tell you. I will give you more.*

　　　*You have a narrow view of your powers.
By broadening your perspective, you broaden your wisdom.*

Nothing is impossible to God: Open your mind to all of God's possibilities.

To find you must seek: To seek you must be open: To be open you must not be fearful.

Fear constricts and separates, love expands and includes.

You created your self-conceived limitations and you have the power to shatter these limitations. You are holy, made holy by God.

You cannot become unholy even if your brothers and sisters try to convince you that you are.

You are a necessary part of the whole.

You can become more loving. You can become wiser. You can find more joy in your life. You can be at peace. This all comes with God's great gift of giving you free will. Choose.

Today I would like to talk about how one learns about one's higher self. First, you need to realize that your higher self is you. The higher self is more evolved than you and has therefore a better understanding of the We Are All One principle. You get a better understanding if you think of your higher self as being your friend, who has your best interests at heart and has greater wisdom. Therefore you would go to this friend when you need help or enlightenment. Think of how you would relate to such a friend, one who is wise and wants the best for you. You would want to communicate with such a friend. You would listen carefully to whatever he or she said. You would really try to utilize what was communicated. This is how you should seek and listen to your higher self.

This now brings us to how to contact or listen to your higher self. Realize that you have a higher self and even further that this higher self exists for your benefit. The higher self has a better understanding than you do as to what is beneficial.

There are many ways to be in touch with your higher self. I will list some of them. You should realize, however, that every time you do one of these things you might not automatically hear from your *higher self. The purpose of these techniques is to increase the probability of communication.*

Meditation is a very good way to contact your inner self. Before you begin, think of meditating for the purpose of being with your higher self. During meditation put your conscious agenda aside and let your mind receive whatever comes. In terms of thought duality, put your thinker's role in abeyance and let the contributor predominate. Simply address your higher self and invite him or her to be your thought contributor. This invitation should be short so that your mind goes back into neutral ready to receive.

Dreamland is a territory where your higher self is present. There are many good books about dreams and their interpretation; there are others that are not so good. Let these books and their content stimulate your interpretation of their meaning. As dreams are highly personal, you can be their best translator.

Spontaneous communication with your higher self can occur any time, for example when looking into a campfire or walking along a beach alone with the surf sounding in your ears. In the shower or just before you fall asleep are also optimal times. The key here is to be open and not dismiss things too quickly as being merely your imagination. With practice you will be able easily to distinguish between contact and imagination.

Places of worship or places of prayer are conducive to reaching your inner self. It does not matter if you are alone there or with other worshippers. It also does not matter which religion or denomination, only that it is God oriented.

In a quiet place by yourself you can simply ask your higher self to talk with you. The key, as always, is to be open and to truly listen to the reply.

Then there is writing in your personal journal. There is something about writing for yourself (in contrast to writing something that others will read) that allows the inner self to enter your writing. This is enhanced if you do not plan what you will write. Write down only the very words or at most the sentence that is in front of you. No one will see it but you, so it does not matter if it comes out as nonsense at first.

The wisdom contained in such writing may or may not be apparent at the time you write it. Come back to it a day or week later and see what wisdom it might contain.

There are also personal and unique ways to communicate that you will stumble upon by accident if you are open enough to recognize them. When this happens realize that this is how your higher self has chosen to communicate with you. Remember the pathway and treasure it.

You will find the development of this channel with your higher self to be wonderful. For those who feel lonely for whatever reason, this companionship with one's higher self is very, very healing. Never doubt that you have a higher self or that your higher self has your very best interests at heart. Never doubt that your higher self is trying to help you at all times and never doubt that your higher self and God love you completely.

<hr />

My sweet Gail, today I am going kayaking on the Napa River. Remember doing that?

Dear Buck, so many memories. On this side you remember many, many more memories from other lifetimes. Today I want to use an analogy to describe what goes on when one opens oneself through the inner self.

In physics a great deal has been learned and much of it very surprising. Visualize shining a light through two small parallel slits in a thick paper sheet in front of a wall and seeing what appears on that wall. This reveals some of quantum mechanic's most thought-provoking behaviors. What appears on the wall is not the two slits of light, but a wave pattern of alternating light and dark lines proving that light is both a wave and a particle at the same time, impossible as this may sound. None of this strange truth would be revealed if you were shown light through a large opening instead of two slits.

Take this pattern where whole new realms are found in unex-

pected places and apply it to the mind. Your familiar vision is through a big picture window where you see much of the world and can deduce a great deal of what the world is and how it functions. You think you can see everything, as your view seems unimpaired. To think of closing it down to just two little slits is like shutting off your observation of the world.

Yet when you do shut off that entire external panorama and allow your mind to receive only what comes through two little slits, a strange world opens up, similar to the scientists' discovering that light at times is a particle and other times a wave. In my analogy what do the two little slits stand for? It is when you shut your eyes and close down your active mind to listen in the silence that you receive. This is done in meditation. You, Buck, are also doing it now in receiving from me what your fingers are writing. If you try to test the validity of what you receive by ripping the slits into big panoramic windows you will lose it entirely.

Do you see how this explains why it is so difficult to try to prove these things in your normal way of opening the windows wide? You have to use a different form of validation. Many people have written about this spiritual side independently of each other; yet there is a basic consistency which provides the validation. (In those cases where there are inconsistencies and even oppositely expressed "truths," due to a number of reasons, the easiest explanation is that there is more than one path.)

Take for example, the belief in an afterlife. As you know this has no scientific proof. Yet most religions believe in some form of afterlife as did most past civilizations. The majority of people living today, even in this scientific culture, believe in an afterlife in spite of no scientific backing for such a belief. While not a scientific validation, it is a cultural validation.

Just as physicists use two slits to reveal the weird realities of quantum mechanics so can you use two slits to reveal the surprising realities of the spiritual world including life after death.

Sweetie, here I am in Lee Vining ready to go up to the Hoover Wilderness area and climb all over those great rocks. The Sierras are gorgeous as always.

Dear Buck, you know why the mountains seem so spiritual, don't you? It is no big secret but there your vision and senses are not overloaded with distractions so you can sense the serenity and Oneship of God's world. But it goes beyond that too. There is simplicity to your being in the mountains that is congruent with the simplicity of your inner self. Thus your inner self becomes more of your conscious awareness.

It is much, much easier to live in your now when you are in the mountains. The past and the future take a back seat while your beautiful energizing now takes over. Living in the now is glorious so no wonder you seek it.

Our dear friends the animals feel this as well. They may live in the now while being in danger all the time but they nonetheless feel the joy of living so. Humans could learn a great deal from animals if you weren't so intent on thinking yourselves superior to them.

I am reminded of that period when you said that the world couldn't be more beautiful. More important than saying it, you saw and felt it. The beauty became so intense it interfered with your life. You had to let go of it some but the feeling was with you ever after. Living with you was exciting.

I remember. It was the first time I really began to suspect the tremendous power and energy available in the spiritual truths. I knew this vast resource would allow me to bring all the parts of me into balance and congruity. When advanced souls come to this side they experience this. It is wonderful indeed.

Those on Earth often are unaware of the powers that are available. The power of a supernova is beyond all Earth's powers, yet it is a small pip in God's universe. By bringing yourself into congruency with God's laws you make this power available to you.

Remember the power of the mind exceeds that of physical man-

ifestation. This can be understood when you recall that nothing phys-
ical occurs unless some mind has conceived of it first. In the case of a
supernova the mind involved is that of God who created the universe
and the laws that govern it.

> *Today in the wilderness seek congruity and feel the energy flow*
through you. I can join in that energy. It feels good. There is so much
more going on in the world than you can even imagine. If we are all
One, which we are, this would have to be so. Celebrate it. The process
is perfect even if your mind constructs it otherwise. Enjoy your day. I
can feel you anxious to leave.

That's true sweetie and it embarrasses me some. Let me
feel your presence today.

> *Dear Buck, it is good to have Bach playing when you do this.*
"Sheep May Safely Graze," is a beautiful piece of music with an in-
spiring thought. To equate the human soul to sheep is not off the mark
when you look at how cantankerous we can be.

> *I want to talk about prayer and more specifically why some*
prayers seem to be answered and some do not. At a recent conference
you heard how disturbed people are by this question. We can help them.

> *It is true that some prayers are answered while others are not.*
It is also true that even if a prayer is stated most fervently it still can go
unanswered from an observer's point of view.

> *The first insight comes with defining what you mean by "an-*
swered." If you pray for a specific, tangible, material change in some-
one's condition and it doesn't occur, you feel the prayer has not been
heard. If your spouse is deathly sick and you pray for his or her recov-
ery, an answered prayer would be that he or she did indeed physically
recover. You need to realize that prayers can be answered in a variety of
ways, some of which are invisible. This is not an indication that such
answers are useless; rather it is a matter of broadening one's perspective.
The narrow perspective will only accept the one answer that you have

specified. If that doesn't occur just as you requested, you may feel the prayer unanswered and presumably ineffective.

By broadening your perspective you will begin to understand that there are many things going on in addition to your request. To broaden one's perspective let's return to the basics. I'll start with the God principle that we are all One, including people, ideas, diseases, sunshine, everything. When you question why prayer doesn't always work you ignore this principle.

What happens is that you draw a boundary around the person with the disease and your prayer's request. You let nothing else within the boundary. Then you say, look, I prayed fervently and he or she is still sick, my prayer has not worked. You are tempted to say prayer itself doesn't work. Interestingly, if your prayer and the sick person were all that were involved, your prayer would work every time assuming the prayer was well intentioned. But that is not reality because things do not work in isolation and cannot act as if there are no other influences involved. Every cause has multiple effects and every effect has multiple causes. Therefore if your spouse gets well (an effect) he or she will do so because of multiple causes of which your prayer is but one.

While the diversity of each set of circumstances is great, some general descriptions do apply. In some instances the multiple causes for your spouse to remain sick outweigh the multiple causes for him or her to get well. Your prayer will indeed have an effect when received in this mix of causes, but you conclude incorrectly that your prayer was in-effective or unanswered. At other times your prayer can become dom-inant and you feel your prayer has been answered with the returned health of your spouse.

So what should you do? You should pray and know that you are effectively adding to the causes of returning health. Your prayer may just be that needed positive influence added to the other causes of good health to change the whole picture from sickness to health. To clarify this would you describe what you used to teach about vectors and health?

One's health always has multiple causes affecting it and

reacts to the totality of these multiple influences. This can be illustrated by visualizing a number of arrows (vectors) attached to one point, pulling in different directions with different strengths represented by the length of the arrow. Some arrows are pulling up to good health and others are pulling down to compromised health. One's health will go up and down based on the cumulative effect of all arrows both up and down.

Apply this to Alzheimer's disease. We do not know the cause of it, but we do know that age is a down arrow. The older you get the more likely you are to show signs of it. Up arrows include doing physical and mental exercises, eating omega 3 foods, etc.

In this way a prayer is an up arrow, which will help promote better health.

What are some of these other influences or arrows involved in such a sickness? A paramount one is free will. If the free will of the patient has already made a decision, you cannot by prayer interfere with that free will. My passing was an example of that. You and our entire family could have prayed fervently and still I would have passed on. This was because the role my death was to play at that time had been carefully worked out long before between our soul group and us. Your prayers were prompted by a narrower view, but the eventuality happened, because a much wider process was being fulfilled.

Other influences such as karma are involved, and since we are all One it is not just the sick person's karma that is concerned.

Let me summarize. Prayers are indeed effective. They are effective healing influences, not only for the one being prayed for but also for the one offering the prayer. The effectiveness of the prayer is co-joined with other effective causes. In so doing the person prayed for may or may not return to health depending upon the total effect of all the causes. The individual praying cannot know if his or her prayer might be just the additional positive cause that brings about a return to health. So do pray.

I would like to mention without explanation some other positive aspects of prayer. Prayer helps to open you to your higher self. This in turn opens you to the higher self for whom you are praying. This has an invisible but salutary effect, which by itself makes the prayer worthwhile. Prayer can be called a form of love. As such it has great value. Prayer when coupled with spiritual acceptance prepares and helps one to be at peace with whatever outcome occurs. This comes because you know a broader, higher purpose is being fulfilled even if you don't know what it is. Buck, you went through this and it was most helpful to you.

There is no need to doubt prayer. There is a need for you to see a broader perspective. When you do, peace and serenity will be closer and comforting. Godspeed.

❧

Being on this side could be simply stated as being invisible. It does not mean that the spiritual world is in some far-off place, although some of it is. Your inner self is an invisible part of you that is not confined to any specified space.

Having an inner self is not restricted to human beings. Animals have inner selves. So too do electrons and trees and conglomerations like Mt. Fuji. You would be more open to sensing this if you didn't feel your need to maintain your superiority to everything else. Further these inner selves accumulate experiences, states of being and relationships to the Oneship.

Again this is due to the We Are All One principle. Your physical aspect appears and acts like it is separate. This enables us to participate in the process of joining. As one example, think of how different and dull the world would be if it were deprived of the joy of romance and the joining of man and woman.

Music makes a wonderful analogy. The essence, the inner self of music, lies in the fact that it is a process. Music ceases the second you stop the process. The whole wonderful world of music is in its process. Thus it is with the process of joining. Once joined and being aware of being joined it is in a different realm with its own unique magic.

This joining happens with major participation of our inner selves. Your experience of the lovely sunset last week was a joining of your inner self responding to the inner self of the sunset--your conscious awareness and your senses joined together. Joy can be described as the participation in knowing and feeling of Oneship. This often occurs when you echo the We Are All One principle by joining, as you do when watching the sunset.

Harmonize yourself with the Oneship principle and feel the glory that comes with it. This is much easier when you realize the role of not only your inner self, but also the inner self of that with which you join.

Be aware that the beings your Earth calls "non living" have inner selves as well, including conglomerations such as mountains or lakes. Those who love the sea know of the ocean's inner self as you did, Buck, when you were in the Merchant Marine. Our love of the high mountains was so emotional because of our joining with the inner self of Mt. Conness, for example. Those who work with and love animals know of the inner selves of these fellow creatures.

If those who are lonely only knew that there were other inner selves waiting with open arms to join them, they would feel loved. Yes, Buck, spiritual healing uses the inner self to promote healing. And when I remind you that physical healing is but a result of spiritual healing you will see that physical healing also uses the inner self.

All this wonder and much else cascades from the widened understanding of the We Are All One principle. Godspeed.

Thank you Gail, that is beautiful wisdom indeed.

Dear Gail, wasn't that buzzard wonderful landing on the roof just outside the window a few minutes ago? I don't know why he didn't spook when I took his picture from inside the house. The deer see me move around inside the house from quite a distance and here I was twelve feet away from the buzzard and he just enjoyed the sun.

Dear Buck, animals do not experience their subconscious and their conscious as separate. Because they function as one, intuitive impulses flow more easily in animals than in most humans. Many people feel that cats seem to be psychic. Then there are the horses that get restless just before an earthquake.

*Remember, Buck, in Africa when sometimes zebras and wilde-beests watched calmly as lions walked by and at other times the sound of a twig breaking would send them galloping? This is explained by saying that the prey animals knew the lions were not hungry. That doesn't explain exactly **how** they knew the lions were not hungry. They knew it intuitively and they risked their lives without hesitation. Not many humans would do this.*

The animals on your hill can feel your intent with regards to them and respond accordingly. The little fawn came and lay down in our alcove because of the sense of safety and peace it felt there.

Just like humans, though, animals can harbor two conflicting ideas. On one hand they are by nature very, very cautious. On the other hand they may intuitively feel you mean them no harm. The result is that it takes multiple experiences to resolve the predominate idea.

People who work well with animals, like Rick, emanate a non-threatening attitude, which the animals pick up. You have a way with birds. I remember several times when birds fluttered around your head and you would put out your arm for them to land on, and they did. Do you remember the penguin that walked between your legs, and the young owl that liked to perch on your arm while it practiced flapping its wings? There are many people who have a rapport with animals. This is reinforced by the animal's choice to trust their intu-ition that these people are not a threat.

There is really nothing like the love you feel when an animal, particularly a wild animal, trusts you and your presence. Remember one night in the pitch black, without a flashlight, we walked unknow-ingly into the midst of a herd of elephants until one trumpeted to let us know where we were. It was the loudest noise I ever heard. We anxiously retreated the way we came unharmed. The next morning we saw same of their footprints on ours and also some of ours on theirs.

My point is that animals can read intent and attitude. They also utilize other psychic abilities, which any number of animal stories illustrate. The lesson for us in observing them is that in dissolving the boundary we have constructed between our consciousnesses and intuition, we too can tap these abilities for our benefit.

～

The inner self has much wisdom and power and it is good for your conscious mind to be aware of it. I use the word "power" not as a strong force, though it is, but rather as something with great capabilities. It is a strange influence as it must remain somewhat beyond the conscious level and yet it is an integral and dynamic part of each individual.

So how do you deal with something that is beyond your direct control? You realize that there is an interchange between your conscious self and your inner self. Your inner self has no trouble in contacting you and does so often. You can learn to recognize how it is influencing you. You can also appeal to it. It may or may not reply to your appeal and certainly won't identify itself as having answered your appeal.

This peculiar arrangement derives from the need to allow your free will to give you the choice. It does not allow you to abdicate the position of choosing by letting the inner self take over. You learn by choosing, and living the results of your choices. You can, however, choose with your free will to observe your thoughts, actions and feelings. In so doing you may perceive where your inner self has indeed put a thought in your mind or prompted you to respond in a new way or to open up a new, wiser perception.

Familiarizing yourself with your higher or inner self takes time and practice. It is well worth it. If you become adept at sensing your inner self you will receive several surprises. You will find serenity easier to achieve and you will sense that we are indeed all One.

Let me describe the process. I am now my higher self, as are all souls who pass over. When you reincarnate, only a part of you inhabits your conscious mind in your physical world. The remaining part, your higher self, stays here. I am contacting you now through your higher self, which in turn contacts you through your receptive, open mind. The hard part of this communication is your ability to be open to your higher self. It is easy for me to contact your higher self or any other higher self.

If you wish to know that all is One, you must access your higher self, which in turn can easily be attuned to all other higher selves and merge with the Oneship. Join in this and you will feel the peace and a true feeling of the One.

Buck, write what you want to say.

I wanted to add that the Oneness is evident in the happenings on Earth although we may not recognize it. Now, since 2008, the world has been experiencing a recession/depression. We are so intent upon trying to find someone to blame that we fail to see the worldwide manifestation that we are all One. The bankers did indeed make huge mistakes often motivated by greed, but much to our dismay we discovered that if we allowed them to go bust, which we felt was well deserved, we too would suffer grievously. We tried to rescue the banks but even so the economy was already falling off the cliff, to quote one pundit, so we suffered grievously along with the banks. In other words we were, in fact, one with the banks. What happened to them, happened to us. We can scream and cry that we are innocent and this is all so unfair, but in my mind it is our failure to recognize that we are all One. We think we should be able to punish the guilty parties and be unaffected ourselves. If we are all One, we cannot do that without punishing ourselves. Although the recession illustrates this on a global scale, we seem to refuse to accept it.

You're right that the Oneness is omnipresent on Earth, but unseen by most. The One includes the ugly and the beautiful, the greedy and the generous, the bad and the good. How else could it be One?

The higher self helps you feel the Oneship and is constantly there to help you fulfill your purpose in life. Godspeed.

CHAPTER TWENTY-THREE

Your Purpose in Life

We have all wrestled with the question, "what is my purpose in life?" And the more general question, "What is the purpose of life itself?"

Having come this far you probably have some idea what our opinion is. In our own lives each of us has an opportunity to learn by gathering more wisdom, but why should we be gathering more wisdom? To be worthwhile companions to God. How do we know God even wants us as companions? Because we live this day as his creation. Why would he create us if he didn't care about us? First, let's talk about our own individual purpose.

We have been given God's attributes in nascent form. Our attributes are not developed as God's are. With our free will we can choose to fulfill the potential of these attributes in accordance with our purpose. There are many attributes such as love, forgiveness, diversity, generosity, patience and inclusion that we have already discussed. You don't have to ponder very long to realize one lifetime is not enough to fulfill these potentials, particularly when you observe how most of us use our free will.

To progress in fulfilling what you already have within you requires essence memory, karma and other teaching tools during many lives. With these you can advance bit by bit. Each increment of learning brings its own special reward of wisdom, joy, attunement, understanding, satisfaction or peace. This does not happen automatically, as we are not automatons.

It helps greatly to realize that you are on a spiritual path. Everyone is, as there is no other kind of path. When you perceive this path it allows you to recognize what is actually happening to you and others. You begin to see the vast interconnectedness of all things.

Your focus is now more on the process than it is on the obvious deficiencies in our world. It is wonderful how just this one switch in focus can alleviate discouragement and bring light. You begin to understand and enjoy your journey even with its difficulties.

God creates you as holy. He sets you upon a holy path through a holy environment literally to make yourself one with God as you have all of his attributes. Develop these attributes to their fullest potential and you have become as God, a worthy companion to your creator. There is no time limit for you to reach this achievement. There is always patience. There is always forgiveness. And there is always love. Gail and I hope this book is serving to open your eyes and heart further to the beauty and potential that is within each of us.

PART FOUR

A VIEW OF THE BEYOND

CHAPTER TWENTY-FOUR

What it is Like to Die

Good morning dear Gail, I am home again after a nice stay at the ranch.

> *Beloved Buck, at the time of great family sorrow during my memorial service, I appreciated the love that was shown me. It was strange from this perspective to know I had just completed a whole life devoted to family and to see you all together.*
>
> *I was so pleased with you. You did the service impromptu. You and I were always at our best improvising. It seemed fitting that you were still seeking to improvise with me then. It was like my sharing my death experience with you. It is just the way we did things.*
>
> *I was so glad that you used Teilhard de Chardin's statement: "Joy is the most infallible sign of the presence of God." I do want my family to think of me as joyful and grateful to God. The sorrow can be healed by joy. With joy you need not dwell in mourning over the past. It was a nice service and I thank you for it.*
>
> *What is it like to die? We have all experienced it many times. When it happens to you, dying that is, you realize it is something that you have done many times. Because you feel very familiar with it, you know you are coming home.*

A friend of ours was surprised when she was about to die. I quote from her obituary, "Dawn was a devout life-long atheist who never entertained the idea of an afterlife. But in her final day, she had a near death experience. When she came to she told us she had seen her late great friend, Sharon Doty, who told her what to expect. She was ecstatic with joy, and with a beaming smile said, 'I'm going home in a blaze of glory and I'm too excited to sleep.'

Those were her last words."

You know that when you wake up in the morning after dreaming, the dream often fades quickly from your memory. This is why, when you begin a dream journal, you are instructed to write down your dream immediately upon awakening. This evanescence is typical of dreams but very atypical of your general memory. Most people have little difficulty remembering what they were doing or thinking five minutes ago. Yet five minutes after awakening you cannot recall your dream. It is as though you are one self in dreaming and you set this self aside when you awaken and step into another self. Actually this is what is happening.

When you die you also set aside one self and step into another. The new self is larger and more consciously inclusive than the one you left behind. It has, however, shed the body. As you die your memory opens you up to who you really are. You step into the invisible world (from Earth's view) that is suddenly all so familiar to you. You remember it well. You meet your guide, your higher self, and so many, many others. In sum you feel you have returned home, which is exactly what you have done.

After the excitement of your return abates you become aware of what is going on with those you left behind. You are aware you have the ability to convey ideas, thoughts, healing and other communications to those you left behind on Earth. At the same time, you gently recognize that it is the recipient's free choice as to whether he or she recognizes it or not. I say gently because you do not wish to intervene uninvited. You recognize the vast importance of readiness on the part of those with whom you wish to communicate. You accept that if they are not ready they should not be forced to receive what you wish to give. This is why we so want to convey the idea of openness to those on Earth.

The above, my experience, has been shared by many others. Based on the readiness of the individual, however, there is a vast variety of death experiences. For this reason individuals on Earth benefit from bringing himself or herself into readiness for the transition to this side. Now that does not mean that you must think about death and dying. What it does mean is that you would do well to realize that we are all One, and that you are children of God. Inasmuch as these same attitudes are ideal for living your life on Earth and on this side, you can bring these attitudes into your current life now.

My last day was traumatic for each of us, while at the same time you have described it as the most tender and awesome day of your life. As we both were learning, it was a successful day.

What we were doing was attuning ourselves to the godlike attributes within us in harmony with the We Are All One principle. This attunement brought into our awareness that which you describe. Such attunements do indeed stay with you and become part of your individual self at the very same time they exist in the Oneship. In this manner you step forward on your path with an augmented essence memory.

Gail, I treasure beyond measure how we have shared all those lives together. Our beautiful days living in the caves for some reason seems very poignant to me. In the same way I value what we are doing now although it is different, isn't it? We were so used to communicating in our earthly lives that these new ways seem strange and awkward at times. I treasure them nonetheless.

I always want to know what you are doing, and would like now to ask you.

I am doing a number of things, one of which is communicating with you. I am finding out how to bring love, give love and radiate love to the universe. One surprising thing is that you would think this radiation of love was primarily to souls or beings like us. It is equally necessary to radiate love to what you call inanimate matter. There is also an existence that you might call inanimate non-matter. Do not exclude anything from love.

Do you know that one way to radiate love is by learning how to receive love? It is true that as you receive, so do you give. We spend a great deal of time feeling the love that is given to us. What is so overpowering is that this love comes from everywhere. Do you remember writing a poem in your creativity class that started with, "Love is like space. It is everywhere; it is here, it is there. There is no place that it is not." This is an inspired statement, as your teacher realized. That is what I am doing, sensing this love that is everywhere. It is here, it is there and there is no place that it is not.

Since one of the great truths is that we are all One with the All, it is not surprising that this truth contains so many layers of insight.

I would pause and let you write your questions, but I already know them. It is much easier for me to attune to you than the other way around. Mostly this is because the various layers of my mind are available to me whereas your conscious mind is dominant. But you too, do this to some degree. How do you think it is that you know I want to write to you?

I know you are trying so very hard to be open, to be honest with yourself and others. You always have been this way; we always have been this way. It is what we worked out together over many joined experiences. I know you are overcome with gratitude for our lives together, and that you focus on thanking me. But you were just as much a part of that.

Ah, you want me to talk about my dying. As your dream told you I was not at all afraid. That surprised me as I expected when it did come I might be scared. I wasn't. Many things come into understanding when you pass over, particularly at the beginning. In the bathtub when I was looking off to the upper left I saw my guide who conveyed that I was dying and returning home. Coming home felt so good. I was torn because I was leaving you, causing you sorrow. This is what caused the confused look on my face. My guide said that I would have a chance to share with you and I felt much better. Then I began to have the attitude that this really, really was the greatest adventure of my lifetime. After so many adventures with you I felt I had to share this with you too and was so happy that I was going to be able to do so. That is why my face in the emergency room looked at peace. I knew what was coming. You were wonderful the way you asked those questions so I could squeeze your hand, that lovely hand that I loved so very much. Do you appreciate what lovely hands you have? [This is because she felt I didn't take care of my hands and was always nicking them up by not doing things in the best way.]

I know you had help in asking those questions, but I also know it would not have happened had you not been listening and truly open to the spiritual wonders that we both were experiencing.

After the questions I did mostly leave my body. I came back when you were not there to see Eric and his family. And you know I came back to see Christopher. My body then went into its final coma and I was gone.

On arriving here I asked to see your guide. I asked him to comfort you and to ease your emotions at the end about wanting me to die so that you would not have to incessantly care for my remnant, vegetable self. That was no more selfish on your part than my higher self wanting to die and leave you bereaved. It was only later that I found out that our karmic lessons did not include your caring for such a lingering vestige of me.

Afterwards in your higher emotional state you could more easily contact your subconscious or higher self. I was so happy to be able to comfort you and tell you how my love would make you invulnerable. Reciprocal love always makes you invulnerable. And as you know it was not just my love but God's too. And yes the love of Jesus as well.

And here you are happier and more joyous than you have ever been. It has been a great fulfillment for me to be part of that. Mostly though, it has been you exercising your God-given free choice. And I thank you for walking the path with me holding my hand.

Thank you Gail for talking as you have. It is just so lovely to be with you again. We are indeed One.

Dear Buck, has it ever occurred to you that the life review process after you pass on is the quintessential broadening of perspec-

tives? By broadening your perspectives during life you can solve most problems. The life review process brings to the soul understanding and problem resolution of many years standing.

This is particularly true in spousal relationships where two people may have gotten into intractable ways of dealing with each other for decades. The life review process, with its wide perspective, can solve that whole thing in a moment. On Earth you just wished and wished that your spouse could see things the way you do. During the life review process she does just that. For a time she sees things through your eyes. She understands how you feel as if she were feeling it herself, which actually she is. This is perspective broadening in a big way.

That doesn't mean that she becomes totally in agreement with you. Having experienced what you felt it is now time for her to seek her own truth, but with the additional understanding of your perceptions.

The same thing will happen with you in your life review process; it will bring you, and those with whom you related, closer together. This is all accomplished through the broadening of perspectives via the death experience.

Hello my darling Gail. How are you this beautiful day in July?

My Buck, it is a wonderful day. Today we will talk more about what it is like to die. You would think that the very first thing you realize is that your awareness has continued after death, in short that there is an afterlife. For some it may be that way. My awareness was absorbed first by the sadness of leaving you, but after I felt better about that, I was filled with wonder at all the things that were happening to me. It seemed so new and astonishing yet I knew I had done this same thing over and over. Further, the memory was always associated with a feeling of love, returning home and of comfort. So when you go through dying there is no fear, no anxiety, or anything negative to distract from the joy of it.

Do you remember the dreams you had when you sat down at the piano and you just played the keys with both hands at random and the music came out sounding so beautiful? You said it was very exciting and left you with a marvelous feeling of wonder. This is kind of how you feel when you return to the spiritual realm. You are aware that it has been some time since you were here, but you also remember that this is home. You have returned home after a long trip.

When you get here there is much to do, but there is no need to rush. If you left your earth life in a depleted condition you receive infusions of energy and healing. After this you may still feel a need to rest. If not, you go on with greeting old friends, meeting with your spiritual group and, of course, your guide.

The life review process was very exciting for me. This is one of the first places you become aware of being able to do more than one thing at a time. You relive your life and feelings at the very same time that you experience how others with whom you were interacting felt. You are One. This is just as true when you are reviewing the quarrels and the hurts as the loving times.

During this review process you see your life from a different point of view than when you were living it. You are aware of the continuum of learning. You see how your life experiences were different threads that wove together to make a lovely integrated design. When you were living these experiences, they seemed disconnected.

You are also much more cognizant of the essence memory that is you. In the life review process, I discovered that some of the lessons I thought I had learned had deeper meanings that I had not realized. I understood the value of having only the present within which to operate. I could see how the material world aided in pushing me to these greater depths. I saw how kindly, loving and guiding karma was. I also saw that people on Earth are really not so mean and cruel as I had thought, but were simply inept at responding to what was happening to them.

You can look forward to the life review process. Relationships that sometimes seem so complex and difficult on Earth are seen in a light of understanding. The troubles are self-made. The demands and expectations we place on each other get in the way. Without meaning to we try to take over the free will of others and it doesn't work.

The return to this side is a lovely mix of many things. You are rejuvenated. You feel the luscious inclusiveness into the All. You feel a merging of yourself (or your selves) that is wonderful although very hard to describe. There is no need to fear death. Godspeed.

⁂

Beloved Gail, a beautiful sunny day after much rainy weather.

Sweet Buck, after darkness comes the light. We can use that to describe what happens upon transition to this realm from yours. There is a mistaken assumption that when you arrive here all wisdom is revealed to you and you get the answers to all your questions. When you come over you are the same person who left the Earth with the same level of ineptitude and enlightenment. Two things happen, however, that are immense stimuli for a quantum jump in growth and under-standing.

First, being welcomed with so much love and feeling that it penetrates you is awesome. To most it inspires a desire to give out love. Unlike on Earth where it often seems difficult to transmit love, here it seems so easy and natural. I need to add that there are many transiting from Earth who are still so bound up they cannot partake in this.

Second, when you go through the life review process and are able to feel for yourself the effects of your actions on others, your un-derstanding can flower. It is like taking a lab course in the We Are All One principle. You, in fact, experience what the other person felt as if you both were one. The boundary between you and the one you are relating to dissolves.

These two factors prompt rapid growth in those newly arrived souls who are ready to receive it.

Even with this leap in enlightenment there is much that still remains beyond your understanding just as on Earth. After the soul adjusts to being here it is true that as a student the soul has available to it many avenues of opportunity for growth and understanding. Here there are avenues more easily traveled than on Earth.

To contrast the two, Earth's learning environment seems to concentrate on a given lesson accompanied by rich experiencing. Over here there is a wider field of lesson opportunities but the vividness of experience is more vicarious than intimate, somewhat similar to watching a movie. This degree of detachment is lessened when you contemplate your lives, particularly your last one, to achieve greater understanding. It is as though your life on Earth were a data-gathering foray, which you then evaluate and absorb over here. Your memory of the experiences gives poignancy to the data that your mind and heart deal with. You feel much love for those who were in your life.

This is how you continue your development to find your truth. And what is it that you need to continue to learn?

On Earth no matter what direction you look, whether to the galaxies or the micro world, you never stop learning. Physics went through a period when the prevailing view was that the atom was the smallest possible particle. Then electrons, neutrons and protons became evident and they were thought to be the smallest parts of the universe. Now we have quarks and gluons, which we elect as candidates for the smallest particle. They are not. There is a smaller particle that has remained hidden because, believe it or not, mind is a principal constituent of it. But that is not my point. It is just that every investigatory direction is infinite whether you look up, down or sideways. This same pattern is true in your learning. In every pursuit there is yet more to be revealed, more to understand and more to absorb. Infinity is such an exciting prospect!

My beloved one, it has been raining steadily all afternoon and here I am snuggled up in blankets on the couch hearing the rain on the roof. It is lovely to be alive, to be here and to be writing with you. I am grateful.

Buck my dear, I remember those days, with their aura of quiet romance. It was just the two of us. You recently heard from a friend whose deceased husband came back briefly to tell her he was fine and that she would soon remarry someone who would provide her with everything she wanted. And it happened within the year. To some on Earth it may seem strange that her deceased husband would be pleased to tell her about her new husband who would provide for her in a way that he did not.

When we come to this side our love for those we have left behind does not diminish. In fact, most often it increases with understanding, particularly as a result of the life review process. But the love does change in character. On Earth the love, especially the romantic love, revolves around two things: the well being of the other person and the enhanced well being of self. This is appropriate; it teaches the coming together in resonance with the Oneship. On this side the well being of the self is more easily assumed. This allows someone on this side to more purely be concerned for the loved ones left behind. Thus in the case cited above the deceased husband was joyful that he could see an outcome for his wife that he knew she would like. He saw this as healing for his wife and it gave him joy.

Those on Earth who felt the most romantic love are the most likely when they come on this side to want their widow or widower to find a new love. They have no wish for their surviving loved one to be lonely. In my own case I know how wonderful it is to be romantically involved on Earth. We both reveled in this. You are still of Earth and the last thing I would want is to deprive you of this wonderful feeling and see you lonely instead. This would be a trial for you and do me no good. In fact, it would sadden me. Thus it is no problem for me to know that you sought romance and found it. It is my wish for you. From this side it is easy for me to see that you are learning wonderful new experiences and understandings in this pursuit. Go for it with my blessing.

*Getting back to the question of our more pure concern for the well being of those left behind, why are we not more active in promoting your well being? This all gets back to the fact that **no one***

can do your learning for you. *Therefore, when you are faced with homework you need to do it yourself. Here we face what may seem like an inconsistency. Quite a number of people experience an after-death communication (ADC) that includes specific help for them from this side. In these ADCs the most predominant message is that the deceased is fine, in good health, and feeling comfortable on this side. This most often has the effect of the survivor taking a major step in healing grief. This occurs because at some level (sometimes not on the conscious level) the survivor is open to receiving such an ADC. Sadly there are many who are not open. It is sad when people are not open to these and dismiss the communication given them as their imagination.*

There are diverse goals going on here, each one tailored to the current lessons one is learning. There are some whose homework is to learn how to handle grief and see beyond it, or more accurately see it in the full context of life. For some, receiving an ADC would inhibit the learning of this lesson. For others receiving an ADC is the door through which they learn how to deal with grieving. Still others need to get beyond grieving so they can address learning lessons encompassed in their current life.

Nancy's nine-year wait for an ADC was appropriate as a learning journey even though she would have preferred a shorter time. Although these various avenues and timings may seem to be confusing, there is one principle that is consistent through it all. What will occur or not occur creates the best environment for learning the lesson that you are now best suited to learn. As we are all very individual it should be no surprise that the best learning environment is reflective of this individuality and therefore unique. Others may experience what could be described as the opposite of your experience and yet it too is individually the best environment for their learning.

Remember there is much, much more for you to learn and you cannot learn it all at once. Even though you may need to learn more about grieving, this may not be a good time for you to absorb this lesson. Thus you may be helped in getting past grieving with an ADC while someone else must address grieving head-on and do his or her own homework.

CHAPTER TWENTY-FIVE

Life on the Other Side

My world is so very different from yours; it is amazing. I will try to identify some of the differences.

Since we, here, don't have to be concerned with earning a living or maintaining our health, to mention just two concerns of the material world, we can focus on other issues to a depth that is very difficult on Earth. This lack of need to be concerned with fulfilling material demands is a tremendous bonanza in liberating your mind and energy so as to be open to thoughts of much greater interest and importance. It is a dream fulfilled to be able to devote your mind to what you wish without distraction.

I want to make clear that your absorption in the material is not bad. In fact, that is why you are incarnated on Earth. So what I am about to say does not imply that you should abandon your material functions and engagement. You should, however, increase your perspective to include the visible and the invisible. This is holistic living. Many have done this throughout the ages and many are doing this now in the new millennium. Your awareness of the invisible and its effects will help with your living in so many ways, difficult though this seems at times. In doing this you will be dissolving some of the separations that are causing troubles in this world.

Another very great difference is that here there is no point in pretense. On Earth people spend much time and energy trying to project the right image and generally control how others perceive them whether it be fluffing themselves up, being modest or being deceptive. Over here we are much more transparent and putting on a pretense would be of no use because it would be seen for what it is. Thus most of us waste no time pretending to be other than what we are.

My Gail, it is a beautiful fall morning with a nice chill in the air. It is lovely being alive and feeling the energy.

Dearest Buck, I remember that feeling when you are attuned to life's energies and everything around you is suffused in beauty. We have that same thing here. In many ways it is more intense. The music here is something you will love. It is celestial, but many other things too. At times it is frisky with joy just pouring out of it. You will take great pleasure in hearing me say that celestial music sounds like Bach at his best.

You loved to surprise me with the most beautiful music, which turned out to be Bach.

When we first met, Gail thought she didn't like the music of Bach. She said it was too much just "daa da daa da." I knew what she meant and although I enjoyed this part of Bach, he also had written much beautiful music that was exactly the kind Gail liked. One time I played Bach's "Aire on the G-string" and asked her to guess the composer. She guessed everyone but Bach. I triumphantly told her it was Bach. I did the same thing at different times with "Arioso," "Prelude in C," "Sheep May Safely Graze" and many more. It got so that when I would ask her to guess the composer she would say, "I suppose it is Bach again and yes it is very beautiful."

The colors here are another joy. Actually we do more than see colors; we feel colors. Our senses are not as separate as those on Earth. It is as if we have an omni-sense, which is a composite of all our senses. And in line with the We Are All One principle the omni-sense is more than just the five senses added together. You feel colors in the music and you feel music in the colors. Your earthly attempts at multimedia are the result of urgings from your memory of celestial life.

This omni-sense includes sort of a sixth and seventh sense. As I said these senses are not clearly differentiated as on Earth. Yes, you are right, Buck, your separated senses are symptomatic of your earthly environment of separation. The sixth and seventh senses have to do with one's ability to pick up another's thoughts and feelings. I wrote some time ago about thought duality consisting of the thinker and the contributor. While you are not really aware of this duality and often have great difficulty in separating which is which, the sixth and seventh senses bring all this to the conscious level.

One thing you will love doing when you get here is to listen to this celestial music with your omni-sense. Not only will you hear gorgeous music but also you will see colors and smell perfumes. But the true epitome of it all will be that you will know and feel through the sixth and seventh senses [sixth being thought and seventh being emotional feeling] how each soul is transported by the music. This is hard to explain, but I will know how the music affects you just as clearly as I feel it myself. And this specifically includes the emotional response. So you and I will join as one with a very high level of sharing. Won't that be exciting? Do you have a hovering memory of this?

I do but it is very vague.

Of course it is vague because its very essence is without limits. Somehow on Earth with your devotion to separation and definition you assume anything that is vague can only be appreciated in a watered down way. This makes you think that something vague is somehow less than something clearly defined. Logical and rational thought reinforces this view. As you begin to understand and use the We Are All One principle you will find again that those on Earth have things backwards. Lack of definition can enhance the experiencing of reality. There are all degrees of vagueness; some are like slipping into neutral where nothing is going on. The truly inspired vagueness can be described as follows: **Sensing the lack of boundaries in the complete intertwining of all things displaying infinite interrelatedness.**

Beautiful! It is why I so love seeing it all as one grand pattern. It is why the idea that we are all One is so attractive.

Yes. All the sharp boundaries and separating definitions melt up (not down!) into the all that is One, that is God.

⪆

When we were on Earth together we puzzled about time. What was it? Was time really limited to what we perceived, or was our past, present and future a particular manifestation of a larger time phenomenon? From here I can see that your perception of time has resulted from the apparent separation into past, present and future. From your perspective, the past is separated, gone, and cannot become the present. The present is an ever-fleeting instant that never catches up to the future.

Based on the above it is only logical to conclude that at some point in your evolution you will discover that the separation of past, present and future is an earthly perspective. True time is something else. Using the We Are All One principle you can even predict what that something else will be. Your three separated parts of time will become one as do all things.

See how rational and predictable it is? I wish to carry this one step further. When the past, present and future become one in your perception everything is not suddenly in the present, like three videos going on at once. Although hard to explain, all is available at once. Instead of causing confusion, they all integrate into something larger, more complete and clearer.

Time is such a puzzle. Let us see what understanding can be had by looking at time with the Oneship principle in mind.

Is it true that we are all One except for time, which is three: past, present and future? Why should time be an exception? As you can already guess it is not. Time is one in itself and also a very integral and necessary part of the Oneship. The past, present and future are all one.

Human thinking seems to be that if past, present and future are all one, things would be kind of frozen in a permanent now without motion. Nothing could be further from the truth. You have thought of a good analogy for this. Write about it.

I read that soaring raptors like eagles have a unique eye lens. It sees the overall wide view that the bird is flying over. At the same time the lens has a part that acts like a binocular, which will zero in and magnify a spot on the ground that the bird is interested in. Thus the bird sees everything but can also focus on a very small part of that everything.

I've always thought true time was like that. The past, present and future were all in view concurrently, but the mind, which is the builder, chooses to focus on one little item or moment in that overall view or timeline.

Yes, the past, present and future are all one and in view all the time. It is also true that the mind chooses which part of that view or timeline to focus on and participate in. Those on Earth think that their point in time is not a choice, but rather a position they have been assigned in some way and cannot escape.

Is it analogous to the way we all like to dance to music? Dancing wouldn't be any fun if we just had to stand in one place, as if frozen in the present. It is only when we can respond to the past beat, the present moment and anticipation of the immediate future rhythm that dancing becomes alive.

Of course, and what do you think going to the Akashic record is?

It is where we have made a different choice of our position and range of view in time. We choose to go to that vast overview, the Akashic record. And once there we usually choose again to focus on one particular small piece of that overview such as a past life of one individual. We then choose to leave the Akashic overview and return to another small part of the timeline that we feel is our reality. And I suspect we return to this present because our higher self knows that this is where we are fruitfully engaged in learning the lessons that are most appropriate for us.

You are doing well. Yes, that is an example where you do choose a different position in time, the past, present and future that is one. You on Earth think you are locked into just one point in time, called the present.

Do you recall how Eric in grade school would use his fine mind to think of seven different reasons for not doing his homework at that particular time? He would expend far more energy and cleverness to avoid doing the homework than would have been required to sit down and do it. That is what you are like on Earth. If you knew that you had the power to skip around from here to there in the past, present and future, you would do so to avoid having to do your homework. You would trade your homework time for a time at the beach. The higher self helps you construct in your mind the idea of a separate past, present and future that keeps your focus on the current learning situation.

This is supported by the law of karma's dependence on past, present and future in order to manifest. Briefly, it is necessary to have a perceived time interval between doing an act and when you receive the consequences. If you murder someone and instantaneously you too are murdered, soon, murders would cease. This would curtail the entire experiential dimension on Earth. There needs to be a time interval between the cause and the effect to allow you to learn through free will.

Yet in spite of this you have a number of experiences where you jump around in the past, present and future oneness. Your dreams do this. Those who have experienced out of body experiences are choosing to be in another time frame. Those who reach deep in meditation do the same thing. Hypnosis is still another channel to the singular past, present and future oneness. Regression hypnosis takes you back to a different point of focus in the timeline where you experience the emotions and realities of that time again.

I dreamed that Gail and I were together in the Neanderthal period. We were inside a cave, which was our home, and it was raining outside. I had just killed an antelope and felt content that I didn't have to go out hunting in that bad weather.

It just so happened that the next day I was scheduled for a regression hypnosis session. As we began I asked the hypnotist to try to take me back to that cave day. He did. I was astonished. I was there! I felt a tingling all over my body, which I have never felt before or since. I was really there. I saw that the cave had little pockets in the wall (apparently a volcanic cave) where Gail loved to put her bone needles and savories. There were three young kids playing with some furs and sticks. I looked out the cave opening down over a little meadow to a creek with riparian trees along it. It was wonderful. The world was as it should be. That past became my *now* and was very real to me.

So you think you are locked into what you perceive as your present, but you can and do skip around. Although it is more complicated than I can now go into, you cannot access this ability to skip around in time to avoid doing your homework. The corollary is that if you willingly consent to doing your homework and address yourself to it, you will have the ability to move around in the overall "single" time. You will discover that this time jumping is a very good tool to apply to your homework. It is a powerful tool, but like a chain saw, it should not be in the hands of one who is unprepared for it. Do you see how this works?

How wonderfully God conceived the world! Einstein said, "The past, present, and future are only illusions, even if stubborn ones."

This brings us to the difference in time here and on Earth. We have talked about this before but it is difficult to grasp so a repeat may be helpful. On Earth in order to define something you need to specify its four dimensions. Let us refer to the laptop computer that is under your fingers. First you need the three dimensions of height, width, and depth. You also need the fourth dimension, time. Right now the object you are trying to identify for me is under your fingers, but in two hours it will be in a different place. So the time dimension you specify would be 8:22 a.m. today. This will complete its identification.

Using an analogy let us say that you are a scientist who lives in a two dimensional existence. You can move freely around on a tabletop but you cannot jump up and fly off in the third dimension. In fact, the third dimension is invisible to you. Now let us say one day you discover a grasshopper on your flat tabletop. This gets you and other scientists all excited who rush off to investigate this strange phenomenon. They photograph and measure it in great detail. In the process they inadvertently tickle its feet. Off it jumps into the invisible. The scientists would have a very accurate record of the physicality of the grasshopper's feet, but as to the essence and functioning of the grasshopper they have no idea. It would be very difficult to explain to them.

This is the difficulty I have in trying to explain to you that time over here consists of the past, the present and the future concurrently. You don't see how this can be. Yet this "time" has a sequential nature somewhat analogous to what you have on Earth where one thing leads to another. This sequence is manipulated by our minds or at our direction.

Actually your view of time is not two-dimensional but one-dimensional. You see it linearly. But it is not even one-dimensional as you can traverse time in only one direction from past, to present, to future. You cannot go one-dimensionally in the opposite direction. Your time concept is therefore one half of one dimension. Expressing it this way lets you see how limiting your time is. It also lets you get a glimmer of the wondrous potential time presents.

Over here this expanded time potential influences everything we do. It frees us to multi-task and to roam in both time and space. It lets us be with you but not of you. You would rightly call it magical time.

On Earth we have only the now to be in. We should use it for more than just a transition from the past to the future. We should use it like we listen to music riding along the wave of the passage of time, realizing that it is the passage of time that gives us such pleasure.

≈

Dear friend, it snowed on our hill for only the third time in 40 years. Everything looked so different with the snow. Please write to me as you wish.

Buck, how exciting for you. We always loved the snow. Remember cross-country skiing in Yellowstone? Several days ago I told you about what it was like on this side. I described the ambiance, for lack of a better word, within which we live. Today I would like to talk more about our activities although here too I will have difficulty.

We need a new word. It should be a combination of play, work, service and accomplishment. This combination is what we do. It is play because we derive a great deal of enjoyment from it. Although play can be regarded as frivolous, this is not true of what we do. We do work as well, but that connotes on your side a sense of obligation, a price you pay to get income. In other words work can be drudgery. Here work is not drudgery or an obligation. The same sort of thing can be said about service. Being of service can be burdensome as well as rewarding. Here service is not burdensome but elevating, and there is a feeling of satisfaction in our accomplishments. In your world, however, this reward is usually reserved for the end of some project or activity; accomplishment is not associated with the process but rather the result. On this side the rewarding sense of accomplishment is part of the process that you feel all along.

If you would take the positive aspects of each of these words and leave off the limiting aspects, you would have a description of what we experience in our activities here.

So what are our activities? Almost anything that is done on Earth has a complementary, even mirror, action here on this side.

You have the idea that Earth and its activities are totally separate from the spiritual world. This is not an unreasonable perception.

After all you don't see any effect of our spiritual world on your material plane. This is not true, however. Everything in your world is involved with us even though you don't see it. This is a manifestation of the invisible laws.

Your view of the spirit world and the material world as separate is just that, a separating view. Since we are all One this separation can exist only in the minds of those who choose it. We of the spiritual plane know of the Oneship and the lack of separation. We not only see more clearly that the material and spiritual worlds affect each other but we partake in creating this effect. When you partake in something you know it is real.

Edgar Cayce said that you are co-creators with God. That is true. We on this side are part of that partnership. We join you in co-creating with God.

We need an analogy here. There are very few people in your world who can look at the world and say, "Oh, I see how the fine structure constant in physics affects this world." Not many can say, "Isn't it fascinating to see how well it works to have the gravitational constant be 6.67. If it were 9.67 we would not have any flying birds or airplanes, to say nothing of the moon crashing into Earth just before we fall into the sun." Yet these two constants along with a few others have a very profound effect on your world. Your world would not exist if these constants were changed even slightly.

Similarly on Earth there are very few who realize the profound effect that we of the spiritual world have upon your world. That so few see it does not diminish in any way the strength of our involvement with you.

What is the effect? I told you quite some time ago that your thoughts can be dual, consisting of the thinker, you, and the contributor whom you attract. In this way ideas are put in your mind that you have the free will to accept or discard. Thus you are influenced without being dictated to. On this side we are not concerned with who gets the credit. In fact, we like you to think this is all your idea, a lesson I learned repeatedly as a mother. In this way you will more quickly learn and incorporate the lesson into your being more quickly.

There are other ways in which the spiritual world influences your world, but the basic pattern is that you are presented with ideas and alternatives without violating your free will.

Some of these influences you may regard as downright evil. Suppose in the twelfth grade you regarded those who could not read as being lowly and evil. Further, suppose you wanted to correct this evil. How would you go about it? Would you give them a twelfth grade book to read and then punish them when they couldn't read it? No, you would give them an introductory lesson at their level to start them on the road of learning to read. This is what some of us do on this side. They work with the stumbling by giving them simple but elevating ideas. These spiritual teachers, however, are there for a purpose of being helpful.

In grade school our art teacher would come once a week to teach us art. We would be given crayons and paper and told to draw and color a tree as in the poster she had brought. She then went around the room critiquing our efforts. It felt more like criticizing, as everything I did seemed to be wrong in some way. That left me with a firm conviction that I was not creative, a feeling I kept with me most of my life. It did have one silver lining as I was attracted to you, Buck, in whom creativity seemed so natural. Imagine making a living as an architect without ever taking a course in architecture. Although the teacher probably didn't intend to stifle creativity, she was giving little kids twelfth grade lessons and our failure simply cut off our development.

There are other activities here with other worlds and much is done with single souls in need. There are some who are still so absorbed in themselves that they are not at all active in rendering service to others. And then there are those very enlightened entities who are in a higher realm.

<hr>

There are mysteries here too that have not yet come within my understanding.

From my wider viewpoint I can, however, offer information. We were so right in our belief that the validity of spiritual laws could be found in their application to problems on Earth. This, of course, does not limit the spiritual laws only to that venue; they are universal.

This means that when you learn and practice spiritual laws within Earth's environment you prepare yourselves to comprehend that which is beyond Earth. The best preparation for coming to this side is not to withdraw from earthly involvement, but rather to engage in earthly circumstances and in so doing derive spiritual insight.

Since this was the central theme in our earthly goals this last lifetime together it is not surprising that when I passed over the transition was easy. You too will not have any trouble.

Do you remember Todos Los Santos Day in Cuzco, Peru, when the brass bands came through the huge central cathedral doors? The music they played outside was wonderful, but when they came inside the brass sound resonated within the cathedral sound box. It was magical. And resonance is just what you feel when you come to this side and sense how much deeper the wisdom you received is.

*You with your dyslexia were able to let your consciousness float through a building that you were mentally designing in order to see how it would all fit together. When you come to this side your consciousness also flies about but in more dimensions than just three. It is glorious, just as the brass music was in the cathedral. The difference is that instead of being the listener **you are the music itself**. Can you imagine this ecstasy? God's gifts are beyond description.*

In your thoughts you can hardly wait until you too can feel this, but be patient and cherish every moment on Earth. The truth is that your current life experiences and the learning you have attained increase your ability on this side to partake more fully in what I have just described. You are now, in effect, building the skills to participate in spiritual music and other wonders. This is true even though you have no real concept of how this will come about. Have faith that I am telling you the truth.

The world is full of beauty if you just decide to sense it all. I admit that I have very fond memories of Earth and a partial longing for experiencing the Earth as you are now. Although I can be on Earth in spirit, as you know having sometimes sensed my presence, to experience the Earth in a material body is quite different. One has a bond with the Earth when sharing its materiality.

Gail, I thank you. I do remember those brass bands. It was so overwhelming; it made the hair stand up on the back of my neck.

I have already put the subject into your mind so why don't you start.

It has to do with music and how different it is on your side. Here I am listening to Carreras singing *Misa Criolla,* which we both heard for the first time in Paris. Music is quite unique in that it illustrates the power and beauty that exists when you feel time as past, present and future at once. You have stated that time on your side is not separated into these three phases. You also said that music is one place on Earth that we can experience in a limited way the inclusion of past, present and future. To hear the first note of the fifteenth measure of Beethoven's fourth piano concerto would be meaningless by itself. Yet this is all we can sense in our present slice of time. It is only when we concurrently sense the notes played before it and anticipate the notes coming after it that we can appreciate what music is.

One more thing that you said excited me: "Not only do you hear this beautiful music with your omni-sense; you also become the music itself."

On this side you are the music. It is inside you. I know on Earth it does seem as though the music gets inside you. I used to watch you play the piano and see that your whole being was absorbed in what you were doing. As you and all musicians know, this feeling is so won-

derful, that musicians are willing to devote endless hours to practice for the pure joy of playing. Musicians feel this devotion because it brings them closer to the essence of God. I don't care whether they believe in God or not, they feel it because that is what it is even if they do not know its true identity.

What you said about Beethoven is also true of rock music with its lovely energizing rhythm. A single rhythmic beat which is all that you can hear at one time with your present time perception is meaningless. It is the continuum of the beats already in the past connected to the present beat and anticipating the next beat that produces the magic. Some people have trouble seeing divinity in the strong sexual tide of rock music. But why is God's world so motivated by sex if he is against it? Why did he choose sex for species reproduction if it was not an appropriate gift? He also gave you free will to do what you wished with this gift of sex. You shouldn't be surprised that you do not always use this gift appropriately.

Let's get back to the music that we have on this side. On Earth music is something you do. Regarding my comment above where I described you as "absorbed in what you are doing," that is indeed wonderful, but over here we are the music. The word "are" is a conjugation of the verb "to be." So here we are back again to the contrast between being and doing. We said that being is primary, from which doing is derived. This strongly implies that "doing" music on Earth, magnificent as it is, is even more magnificent when done in a state of "being." And it most certainly is. In my last life I loved music but felt deprived because I couldn't sing or play. What is one to think when she sings to her first-born child and he asks her to stop?

On this side it doesn't matter whether I have learned to play music or not, I can "be" music which thrills my soul. I understand now how magical it is for you and our children to create music.

Your essence is in your being. Always try to develop your being. Be impressed with your doing only when it is an extension of the being you wish to be.

I love telling you about this. It makes me feel closer to you and your love of music as well as all the musicians, composers and, *of course, God.*

Here we go my beloved, starting the New Year in earnest.

Dear Buck, beginning a new year puts you in the frame of mind of the wide-open potential before you. You need but select. What will you choose this coming year? Whatever it is will stimulate your growth and mine too.

I too have choices. God's gift of free will is not confined only to our earthly sojourn. We continue to exercise it at all levels including the ultimate choice to return and be one with God. My selections, or rather the way I make them, are different than when I was on Earth. On Earth you often choose in isolation sometimes searching for guidance from others. You must evaluate that guidance as to whose agenda is being served.

Here we have guides but we know from the beginning that they are worthy guides dedicated to the service of the Oneship. They clearly understand that they are not to make decisions for you. While on Earth there are many who eagerly tell you precisely what you should do, here the guides will help you greatly by giving general wisdom or by bringing up issues you may not have addressed. This doesn't happen, however, until you have sincerely sought their help and opened your mind to it.

Isn't this a description of how you are relating to me?

Yes it is. It reflects some of the training I have received since I came over here. Do you recall my telling you I was in training with others to be a guide? It is strange though, because it seems so natural and appropriate for me to guide.

What is happening here is that within me were all of the pieces needed to create this guide attitude. Because of that I was selected and offered guide training. The training did not focus on bringing in yet more pieces but rather in pulling together those that I already had. You can see that this approach allows the teachers to enhance who the student is in contrast to retraining the student.

My desire in relating to you is not to change you, but to enhance who you are, to help you utilize your potential.

This reminds me of what you tried to do in raising our children. You were always observing and seeking who they were and helping them become that. We were so pleased that each one was so different and distinctly himself or herself.

Even before we believed in reincarnation, I remember that we quickly concluded there was a third factor in our children's make-up. In addition to heredity and environment, which our children shared as a common pool, we noticed this individuality persisted no matter what molding the environment imposed. We called this factor X and noted how strong it was.

When we seriously considered reincarnation we realized that the factor X comprised the past life accumulation of characteristics and wisdom that comprises essence memory. As each child's past life résumé was different, so too was the individual child's make-up.

Yes, and the reason we perceived a factor X was because in our past lives we had embraced the mystic understandings of reincarnation. Our spiritual ontological recapitulation was unfolding. Isn't it beautiful how it all fits together? Each child has made his or her choices and in so doing is following his or her own path to enlightenment, as are you and I.

When you pass over you will be fascinated with what wisdom is available to you. You have had great practice in being open, inquisitive and broad in your thinking. You will be a very happy student on this side. But, as I have said before, cherish every moment you have on Earth because over here the experiences you have sometimes seem muted without the material aspect.

This reminds me of our granddaughter, Maria, who was asked what she wanted for her third birthday. She replied, "A magic wand that works." What you describe above as the spiritual plane sounds a bit as if that is where you find the magic wand that works.

❧

My dear many-times husband, it is indeed glorious to communicate. Communication is holy. It is holy because it allows the Oneship to be. This morning I will communicate to you some more of what it is like on this side.

You ask, "On the other side do you sleep?" The answer is yes, some of us do. Sleep is necessary on Earth. Here it is not. Do we drive in cars? Yes, some of us do. Do we grow food? Yes, some of us do. For similar questions the answer would be the same, yes; some of us do. This would do very little, however, to give you an idea of what it is like here.

The mind is the builder, both here and on Earth. There are some here who like or need to sleep and their minds build a sleep situation. There are some who love cars and so their minds build marvelous cars they drive around. Those who love growing things let their minds create lovely gardens.

On Earth the building by one's mind is combined with the material plane with its own set of characteristics and limitations. This modifies what one's mind can build and how long it takes to build it. To those of narrow perception, this obscures how potent the mind is in creating, so much so, that some on Earth don't even understand that the mind is truly the builder.

On this side the material plane does not interfere with this building, nor is time the same. The result is that mind building is more instantaneous. This is not completely true but is the closest I can come.

There is also the quality of communication within which we can relate to each other. Here communication is much more open and accessible. Here we know who is entering our thoughts. We also know their true intentions, which on Earth is most difficult. This makes communication here an altogether different process.

What do we communicate about? It varies a great deal. Remember there is an infinite amount to learn and understand. This means that there are myriad levels of understanding to achieve. This is not the least discouraging. Quite the contrary it is fulfilling and exciting.

Life on this side has diversity far beyond that on Earth. This diversity includes the fact that you can find somebody here doing something very similar to what is done on Earth. There are many others who are doing things that have no resemblance to earthly activities. This diversity also means that there is a huge variation in the state of development of individuals here. There are kindergartners and graduate students and those in between and beyond and those below. What each of these levels is capable of doing is commensurate with their particular advancement.

I hope this makes clear that when you pass over you do not come as a raindrop falling into the ocean, becoming an indistinguishable part of that ocean. Hard as it is to understand, holy union is based upon your maintaining your individuality.

Your role is to develop your truth. This is different than developing the same truth as another. When you come to full realization of being at one with God, you will share the same truth. At this time, you will find that your own individual truth is the same as God's.

Buck, we both loved the Hermetic statement, "As above so below." This applies to the similarities between the Earth world and the spiritual world.

We share the same core but it manifests differently. We both are in a learning environment. We both are experiencing the very things that will benefit our learning. God's love, God's healing and God's creations surround us both. In connection with the latter we both are co-creators with God. We both have minds that build. We also share the three great gifts of God: we live forever, we are part of the

One and we have free choice.

How does this common core manifest differently? For you in your material world it is like living underwater. All your movements are slowed down as the water resists them. This is true physically and in the playing out of cause and effect. I explained earlier how karma in the material plane required a time lag between cause and effect to allow you to internalize your truth. If you bully another and at the very same instant you experience being bullied, there would be no more bullying. There also would be no learning. You would be automatons.

On this side there is no time lag as past, present and future are concurrent. This can be modified if the mind chooses to create a time lag as on Earth. Many souls actually do this without consciously meaning to. They bring with them from their last earthly life the environment of Earth because they do not fully realize what has happened to them. This can continue for as long as it presents learning or healing.

This slowing down in your world of how things happen produces a density that also affects what your mind can easily perceive. You have great difficulty in discerning what someone else is really up to. You cannot probe his mind to see if he really is sincere in what he says. This allows con men to flourish in your world. The public has a low opinion of politicians because they often say one thing and do another. And yet there are many politicians who have brought about a great deal of good in your world.

On this side we can almost automatically sense the attitudes of each other. This has a big effect on how we relate to each other and how we learn. This further means that we have a much more immediate understanding that we are all One.

In contrast, you on Earth have the sense of Oneship covered over with so much debris that most of you don't see it. Not being able to clearly feel the Oneship, you indulge in many self-defeating activities. Just look at your world.

It is fascinating. I would guess that the reason for these differences is that each provides a needed classroom environment that is appropriate for the soul's development at the stage they are in.

Not quite. If that were true your Earth life would be much longer until you advanced to a higher spiritual level. What really happens is that you vibrate back and forth between the earthly and spiritual realms during the reincarnation process. You experience on Earth and then come here to digest it. After digestion you return to Earth for more experience.

Isn't this like the stair step pattern we said described our spiritual path? Remember we realized that we didn't advance upwards on a steady line but sort of jumped up vertically when a new insight came to us and then moved horizontally while we absorbed the insight. Only after this absorption were we ready to have another jump of insight.

That's right. The jump up is your earthly experience and your sojourn here between lives is your absorption or horizontal part. To carry the analogy further, notice that it is the horizontal portion of the stairs that supports your weight on your trip up. This corresponds to when you are here converting the lessons you learned on Earth into the real you. Only after you have done this are you ready to return to Earth for the gathering of new experiences.

What ultimately brings this cycle of lives to an end?

You will experience your last life on Earth when you have advanced to the point that you no longer need the underwater movement, the time lag and the density to continue developing your truths.

We referred to two kinds of separation, that which divides and that which brings union. The concept of earthly hierarchy is interesting to view from this standpoint. There are hierarchies that are made to create divisions and maintain them. Some will allow mobility for at least a few in the lower levels to work upward, but this upward progress is deliberately made difficult. It is also quite common that the upper levels of a hierarchy are limited in the numbers allowed, which by consequence means that many who are capable of a higher position cannot have such a position. These are all characteristics of the divisive hierarchy on Earth.

We on this side also live in a hierarchy. For instance, I am not at the same level as is Jesus or many other spiritual beings. Here, however, the whole hierarchical structure promotes union not separation. Upward mobility is not controlled by the hierarchy, but by the individual. I can move upwards based on my advancing toward enlightenment. This is possible because there is no limit to the number of souls who can be at any level; there is always room for me to move upward. Further, the upper levels here do all they can to encourage and help the individual advance. Artificial hurdles are not erected in order to limit the number of people who can enter a given level.

I have at all times on this side had access to help from those above me in the hierarchy to move as rapidly as I can to greater understanding. Much of what I do is broadening my advancement in spirit, all done in love. The higher you go the more embracing is the love of those above you. As you advance you are welcomed with open arms by those you have joined in your advancement.

Can you see the vast differences in how a hierarchy can be utilized? Although both types seem to separate people into different levels, one maintains separation while the other provides a means toward inclusion. The latter is, of course, inherent in God's gift of free will.

On Earth it is interesting to note that because everyone ages and dies, it means that those high on the various hierarchies have to vacate their positions. Earthly hierarchies therefore have a mechanism to create openings. This is a learning situation. It forces the hierarchy to create some mobility from the lower levels.

Observe how the organizations on Earth behave. You will probably see they are a mixture of separation and union. Dictatorships favor maintaining hierarchies of separate levels while democracies *generally favor union through mobility.*

~~~~~

Sweet Gail, here it is Saturday night and I've done three out of four tedious jobs today. What do you have to say?

Dear Buck, you do stay open don't you? [She said this because much to my surprise I found the computer on and wondered if it might be Gail wanting to write to me.] I wanted to talk to you about what goes on here on this side. The World Trade Center is no big event here. It is like another breaker coming onto shore. We know on this side that what the world regards as a major difficulty is just a stimulus for you to come to grips with what it is you need to learn.

Over here we have one very great advantage in that we know we live forever and we have lived many lives on Earth. Just stop and think. If you truly knew that, like you know the sun will rise tomorrow, how would it change your thinking? Your attitude about the World Trade Center would be entirely different. All the threats you feel so keenly could be faced with more equanimity.

I tell you that you are invulnerable but you really don't feel so. I tell you that you live forever, but it is just an intellectual concept to you lacking emotional conviction. I tell you that we are all One and you agree that would be nice and even think you see little bits and pieces of it now and then. But it is like you see it with only your peripheral vision. When you look directly at it you don't see it. It isn't that you are a failure or need to feel bad about this lack of surety; it is just part of the territory you are in. But don't give up. It will help you on your way if you slowly gain these realizations.

~~~~~

Dear Gail, the family left today to return home. It was a fine weekend. Christopher, Gordon and I were particularly pleased with the music we made. We must have played and sung Bachianas Brasilias No. 5 fifteen times. It has such a lovely vocal line. I finally understand, with Christopher's tutelage, why this very Latin-sounding piece is like Bach.

Buck, sweetheart, you are living your life in fullness, both in action and appreciation. Keep it up! In this way we can continue to communicate. You are continually letting yourself be placed in instructive circumstances. I've said this before, but it bears repeating. It is only when you fully engage yourself in your now that we on this side can communicate with you.

You are learning; I am learning. We are helping each other learn as we did while on Earth those lovely 47 years. In our learning here we are constantly referencing our experiences on Earth, in my case my experiences with you. You will find it fascinating to discover that those episodes of learning have so many layers of additional meanings. We here can absorb more and more enlightenment from the very experiences that we thought we had understood on Earth. God has created such a marvelous world in which each entity, each experience has the potential to reveal so very much wisdom.

Here we also recall little episodes of our life on Earth, episodes we thought of no particular import only to discover that there is deep meaning in what transpired. For example, there are innumerable examples of seemingly trivial events resulting in two people meeting each other and marrying.

You see very little of the effect you have on people's lives in the way you live yours, or we lived ours. It is well that you don't. In our early years I would watch you and see you unintentionally hurt people's feelings. You didn't even know you were doing it. As I saw many times, the instant you realized you were hurting somebody you stopped and tried to make him feel better. Often that adversity was instructive to the person you hurt, albeit difficult for them.

The way these threads weave together is truly miraculous. There is no event in the universe that does not dovetail into all other parts; in fact there is one gigantic pattern of which everything and ev-

eryone is part: The All is One. We see but pieces of this grand pattern. And even these are so awesome we find them difficult to comprehend.

Do you remember how excited I was with our study of mysticism that I exclaimed, "And we will always find this subject fascinating because it goes on and on without end. We will always love studying it." At that time I was only thinking of our lifetime together. Now here we are learning together after my Earth time. Buck, when you get here we will continue to learn. We've been on this joint path for many lifetimes.

Do you recall when we first met back in the caveman days? You found me wounded in the berry patch where I was attacked by a bear. You carried me to your tribe and the shaman stopped my bleeding and infection. Much to the surprise of the shaman, I recovered. He told you I was one tough lady. You asked me to join you to become "us." I still think that sounds better than asking me to marry you. Strong but gentle men were not in abundance then so how could I resist. In fact, you were the only gentle man I had ever known. When things didn't go well between us, all you had to do was see that long scar below my neck and you would feel grateful that I was alive. That lifetime provided many lessons in being grateful. And now there you are so very grateful that I no longer have any backaches. You are a dear.

You are right. The sound that the rain makes on the roof is God's whisper. Listen to it and it will carry you to your inner self. I like you asking me to join you in giving blessings each morning.

We truly are on a journey without end. We are immortal. All that we experience contributes to this immortal holy path. Good night.

CHAPTER TWENTY-SIX

A Broader View of God

My dear husband, peace and serenity are lovely to feel. We have talked of human consciousness and the consciousness of God. By now you should realize the immense power of the conscious mind. One of its primary attributes is that of being a generator. God the creator uses his consciousness as a generator, resulting in the universes.

The consciousness that you possess also has this power, but on a different scale. As you get closer to God, closer to remembering who you are, you also get closer to having the generative power of God. Mostly your generative power is lower than that of God's. No surprise there. Nonetheless, it is far more powerful than the use you now make of it.

To illustrate your conscious generative ability as shown in your world, just realize that every artifact, every building, any physical manifestation on Earth that was made by man first existed as a thought in someone's consciousness. Buck, when you designed and built buildings for your clients, all of it began in your mind. If it hadn't been generated first in your mind how would you or anyone else know how to draw the blueprints and build the building? This is true of all man-made things.

This same pattern of thought before physical manifestation also applies to God. It is how he operates. His consciousness generates a universe and it becomes so. His consciousness creates a set of laws by which the universe is governed. Human nature, an integral part of the universe's nature, is also conceived by God. That is why I have been saying over and over again that we are seeking the fulfillment of our nature as given to us by God.

Do you see the vast, tremendous power of consciousness? When God gave you the gift of the Oneship this included the gift of sharing the power of consciousness.

You on Earth are just beginning to recognize that your mind and consciousness lie latent with undiscovered abilities. Some people demonstrate the ability to take a seven-digit number and multiply it in their head by a nine-digit number and give you the correct answer within seconds. Others can hear a complex musical piece played on the piano just once and sit down and play it perfectly. The mind is amazing. All this ability is dormant in your consciousness in which you are immersed every second of everyday.

In light of this discussion, think of the power of love. It too is a generator with all the potential that this implies.

That's beautiful thinking of love as a generator. It goes both ways, to generate is to love. When I generate a painting there is love behind it. When two fall in love the natural tendency of that love is to generate children. I really like thinking that what God generated or created, he loves. If true that means he loves you and me as well.

Today let us return to our favorite Hermetic statement: "As above so below." As we observed it has many layers of meaning and points the way to greater understanding.

One of its primary meanings is that what is in the upper spiritual world is echoed in our earthly realm. The patterns of the One are to be found in the other. To come to greater understanding of the spiritual realm you can look for guidance to some manifestations in your world.

We are vastly puzzled by the powers of God. His mystery is so difficult for us to conceive that many of us just simply do not believe in him. What is his primary mode of being? We know we live on a tiny planet around an obscure sun in one galaxy of millions. We are but a dust particle in the vastness of our universe. Yet there are more universes of which we can only speculate. A power that could not only create such vastness, but also energize it with laws that allow it to con-

tinue is beyond our ability to describe. One word, the infinitude, at least points us in the right direction, but in truth even though we have a label for infinity we know little about it.

In our world we know that God has created us with a mind with extraordinary aspects. For one thing it enables us to partake in life and guides us through all its vicissitudes. Then there are all those minds of outstanding ability, Aristotle, Einstein, Bach, Lao-tse, Lincoln, the list goes on. The human mind is a vast wonder, for humans have changed Earth in many, many ways. Every single aspect of these changes began with a thought.

God too created all of his universes by first having a divine thought. Your minds, which are so important in your tiny world, are the guide found in the "below" to lead you to comprehension of the mind of God in the "above." Marvelous as they seem, your minds are still unable to comprehend the mind of God, yet your minds have the capacity to expand your understanding of God.

Good morning Buck, today I want to talk about the narrow perception that many on Earth have of God.

Here you are tiny specks on a small planet. Think of yourself as God for a moment being able to create this universe and comprehend its vastness. As you look down at those tiny specks, wouldn't you think it strange that those specks presume they know what limits that you, God, have? For example, having created this one universe they think you cannot create two or three or as many as you like. Some of them also feel that an after life is beyond your ability to create.

There are some who believe that God couldn't provide the means for the dead to communicate with the living. They feel that for me to communicate with you is impossible and a phenomenon beyond the ability of God to place within us. You, on Earth, and even most of us here, are in no position to decide what God can and cannot do. We waste our energies attempting to define limits to God's capabilities.

If you conclude that God's world is limited, you become con-

strained within that world and limit yourselves. It would be much better to think all things are possible realizing that this doesn't necessarily mean they all exist in your world. You must live them out to find your reality. In time you will discover that much is possible that you previously thought impossible.

It is arguably arrogant to think you can perceive and know the limits of God. The same pattern applies to your impression of your brothers and sisters. You may accurately perceive them as behaving in a lowly, unloving way, but this does not mean they are limited to this behavior. You would be in error to so judge. Each person has the power to be much more. You would be more likely to help them achieve a higher level by believing in their capabilities than being locked in on a lowly judgment of them. This does not mean you cannot accurately perceive how poorly they behave. It has to do with your understanding of their potential to act differently.

Just as you should not limit God in his abilities you should not limit your brothers and sisters in their capabilities. This obviously points to another example: You should not limit yourself with respect to your capabilities. For example, because you live so intimately with yourself you feel you are in a very good position to judge what you can and cannot do: 1) You know you have no artistic ability. 2) You know you couldn't possibly speak before a thousand people. 3) You know you cannot repair a relationship. These and many more are limitations that you believe in error.

Release yourself from these limiting judgments. Release yourself from thinking God's world is limited and that there are certain things that just cannot be done. Release your brothers and sisters from the limitations you have placed on them through rigid judgments. In doing these things you will find powers and understandings that will allow you to raise the consciousness of the world. Remember, the mind is the builder.

❧

God has created you with great powers such as your imagination. *Your imagination comes up with many ideas, for example the concept of ghosts. Do you think your imagination can conceive something that is beyond God's ability to create? Of course not. If there is a need, a function or a purpose for such a manifestation then indeed it does exist even though it is outlandishly different from what your experience says is possible. God does his thing uninhibited by his children's belief in his abilities.*

Although not limited, God does choose. It is beyond you to determine why he chooses what he does. Because his nature includes choosing, he has endowed you with choice as one of his three great gifts: free will. We see again how it all ties together.

During this millennium scientists will be open to many more wonders; science has some very wonderful discoveries soon to come. It is an exciting time to be a scientist. The limiting scientific dogma that was such a handicap is now diminishing. With your love of science you will enjoy the coming years.

Good morning sweet one. I was fascinated by the idea that God chooses. Could you tell me more about that?

Dear One, certainly. First though, I think we should address what God is. There is a huge carry over in world thought that God is an anthropomorphic figure—a fatherly man—such as painted by Michelangelo in the Sistine Chapel. You have made that God's image because it is something you can understand. But God is not limited by what you can understand. So set aside the word "God" briefly. Something created the universe and is also now maintaining it. We will call that the Creator, a term often used for God.

The Creator is beyond your comprehension. If you could comprehend him, you would be a Creator too. That doesn't mean you should not attempt to comprehend him. In fact, what I am writing today is an effort to understand him better. We are like a first grade child who wants to be a doctor. The totality of being a doctor is beyond the child's comprehension at the moment but he can develop understanding that will allow him to become a doctor. You are in that position with the Creator.

The Creator is capable of conceiving anything your imagination could envision. Let's take the idea that Earth has just one moon instead of five. That the Creator does not give Earth five moons does not indicate that such is beyond his power. He has chosen for Earth to have only one moon. This is not strictly true although that is the effect of his more comprehensive choice of dynamic laws.

So we have universes filled with some wonders and not others. Initial observation would indicate that the Creator chose those that exist and chose not to create those that don't exist. This universe is filled with galaxies while another may have none. So what doesn't exist in your universe says nothing about what can exist. Again it would appear that the Creator is choosing certain phenomena be in one place but not another.

What the Creator actually does is generate a set of governing laws along with energies for these laws. This is how he exercises his choice. The Creator does this more than once with more than one set of laws. Each set of laws has specific proclivities that manifest in certain preferred ways, for example, galaxies, whose spiral arms and black holes express the law's probabilities. Other sets of laws appear differently.

Once he empowers these sets of laws and provides the energies, the universe fulfills itself. Thus God does not literally choose that Earth has one moon, not two. Earth's one moon is the result of this universe's set of laws. Do you see how this works?

Yes I do. It is amazing. You know how nuts I am about patterns. Here is a pattern of universes and it is the same pattern that describes each of us; for we too are fulfilling our own nature as given to us by our Creator. We do this within a governing set of laws, which allows each of us to be quite individual. What a marvelous demonstration of the mystic principle, "As above so below." It all fits together. We, along with the universes, are One.

❧

Hello Buck. I last said that God was not an anthropomorphic being. But that doesn't answer what he is. Although we cannot know what God is, we, nevertheless, seek an ever-greater understanding of his nature.

God is literally everything. There is nothing that is not God. We can say more than that. Above all, God is mind. God's mind is far beyond what you know as mind. On Earth you understand that every creation made by man was preceded by a thought in someone's mind, so you recognize that mind is the generator. You also know that it is only through the mind that you have cognizance of your world; thus you see the pattern of the preeminence of the mind. This same pattern is true of God. His mind is the preeminent part of his nature.

God's mind, being infinite, includes more aspects than we conceive of as mind. We could say that the core of God's mind is his heart, using this term in its non-physical meaning, a form of love. We further could say that God's mind exists in spirit. So here God is the union of mind, heart and spirit. Realize this still falls short of what God is or what his mind is. It does, however, indicate the right direction for greater understanding of him.

I have talked much about fulfilling one's nature as given to us by God. This applies to us, to animals, to plants and electrons; to all we know. Even universes fulfill their nature as given to them by God. So the huge question is: What is the nature of God?

We have discussed God's mind and its importance, but what does he do with this mind? He creates. A vital part of that creation is that he energizes his creations into a very active universe. This has immense implications. To energize something is to make it dynamic, volatile, changeable. It allows life as we describe it to flower.

If this is his creative essence, a dynamic system, then what will be the fulfillment of God's nature? Let us use an analogy. The Louvre is full of exquisite finished paintings. The paintings on exhibit are completed and they are static. You like them that way and go to great lengths to preserve their unchanging character.

Contrast the static paintings with the impact of seeing all the talented painters represented in the Louvre doing their painting. Wouldn't it be exciting if all those geniuses could be observed actually painting? This is the dynamic goal, the process not the finished product. Obviously the process of painting has to involve the goal of creating a true work of art.

Thus you can see that life is integral to a perfect process moving toward a finished, but as yet incomplete, masterpiece. What happens when it is completed? That too is beyond your comprehension, but can be expressed simply by saying life is recycled, back to the process.

Speaking of processes you should realize that what I am saying about God is not the ultimate truth. What I have described is helpful in proceeding toward the truth of God and is an example of process in contrast with static truth.

There is another aspect of God's nature worth mentioning: even though God is everything, he is also individual. This is hard to conceive. How he can be individual and everything at the same time is a divine mystery. It is because of this mysterious part of his nature that you have been created by God to have this identical pattern. You are individual and at the same time an integral part of the Oneship.

I feel I should add that even though our language makes it easier to talk about God as if he had gender or even both genders, in truth he is so far beyond such distinctions that the designation has no meaning.

One of the reasons you have difficulty in describing God is your language. The basic thrust of language is to separate things by specifying differences. Thus, when you try to describe God, the integrated everything, you do not have the words. When I say something is red I am conveying to you the idea that all other colors have been eliminated and only red is left. In effect I have separated red from all the other colors. When I talk about Paris, again it is to separate that particular city from all others. The same applies to feelings and other things for which you use English. The English language is a very useful tool to distinguish precisely what you are defining.

It is true that you have some words that do express totality, for example, "all," "the Oneship" and "everything." In contrast to distinguishing words that convey precise characteristics, these encompassing words express very little meaning beyond the totality. This is why it is hard to describe God.

Today we will talk about how things are accomplished between our worlds. I don't believe there are many on Earth who realize the extent with which we on this side work toward benefiting your world. We are intimately involved. We influence what goes on in a vast variety of ways, none dictatorial or coercive. We on this side are always guided by the understanding that you have been given free choice. It is not our function to take this away from you or modify it. We too, have free choice in how we partake in our mutual involvement.

The easiest way for us to communicate with you is through your thoughts. Your thoughts by their very nature are capable of being attuned to this side. We on this side often act as the contributor to your thoughts. Our purpose in so doing is to offer you a new or alternative way of viewing your world. With your free will you can accept, reject or remodel what we give you.

Some of us on this side can see that the world is ready for advancement in technology or understanding. We develop these ideas in a form that can be broadcast into the thought field. It need not be aimed at anyone in particular, but is available to be received by anyone whose thoughts are in attunement with the broadcast idea. The receiving mind will believe that it is its own idea and act upon it. This is as it should be.

We on this side are not in the least concerned with who gets credit. We do, however, understand that if someone thinks it is his own idea he will be motivated to pursue and defend it. Many of the advancements in your world come about in this way. It explains why Leibnitz and Newton concurrently, but independently, developed calculus. Darwin and Wallace did the same with their theories of evolution.

As I have said, you are in the new millennium. This acceleration has come about because of an increase in all our communications—on Earth, and above. We are acting as contributors to your thoughts with greater frequency. One reason we are doing this now, however, is that we are aware you are more receptive to these elevating ideas. We on this side are responding to the world's readiness.

I hope this makes clear that we are very careful not to interfere with what you choose. We simply expose you to more alternatives. This gentle way of suggesting things also occurs with other civilizations.

For example, there are many people who believe there are other civilizations in the universe. When you imagine these other societies you may think of them coming and invading you. With their superior weapons you would feel helpless to resist being conquered.

Although this is scary, you don't need to worry because the relevant spiritual law that I am referring to makes such a scenario impossible. By the time another civilization has advanced to the point where they can come to Earth or to any other civilization, they will also have advanced to the spiritual level where they will hold sacred the exercise of your free will. Such an advanced society would have the same respect for your free will as we do on this side. Your fear of a conquering invasion from outer space is simply a projection of your fears. You will not have this capability to travel elsewhere until such time as you give up your desire to impose your will on others. This applies on Earth as it does universally. Do you see what tender care God uses with respect to his universes?

There is great diversity on Earth and there is even greater diversity here. Throughout the universes are additional diversities. God likes diversity, but how does this correlate with the various religions on Earth? Is there only one true religion? Is one religion truer than another? In Earth's history people of different religions have vigorously fought each other. They have pirated and murdered each other's members and engaged in all sorts of ungodly actions. Since I talk about *the Oneship so much shouldn't there be one religion on Earth to bring about the Oneship? Which one would God want us to choose? Should we create a new religion?*

We can start with the basic idea that it is not so much what you do as who you are. Similarly, it does not matter what religion you practice, but it does matter what devotion you have. This devotion is not only to God, but includes devotion to your sisters and brothers too. When you feel devotion to God you are doing so because you do not believe yourself to be a separate, unconnected individual; you believe yourself to be part of a Oneship no matter how vague your understanding. In truth our comprehension of the Oneship is vague, as the Oneship is beyond us. You cannot feel this devotion to God without feeling you are connected to him and he to you.

It is not so important what you do as what your intentions are. This very same pattern is repeated here. It is not so important which religion you practice, as is the devotion you feel to God and God's children. None of the religions truly comprehend God. Only God knows what God is. Therefore no religion is the true religion, but each is a noble attempt to relate to God.

As you each have your individual paths to God, so each religion is also on a path to God. Almost always you will find religious beliefs superior to the practitioners who try to live them. It is amazing how some religious adherents do ungodly actions in the name of God. Still they are your brothers and sisters, each of whom is on the spiritual path, stumbling though they may be.

There are many paths to God and you should help each other on your different paths. Where you find religions trying to retain their separateness by excluding or condemning other belief systems you find difficulties. As I have said about all human efforts, if you try to create and maintain separateness you will find trouble, as you are moving away from God. Just because a religion tries to be separate in the name of God does not mean it can escape the consequences of the spiritual laws. Separateness brings trouble. Union brings enlightenment.

You asked if the world wouldn't be better with one religion and wouldn't this be more consistent with the Oneship? The answer is no, not at this time with the current state of the world's consciousness. It is true we will all eventually return to God and in effect be One. Although this could be described as one religion, this is too limited. More correctly you will simply be One. Until that time, however, you need multiple spiritual and religious paths converging toward that goal. You should be aware, tolerant and helpful of those on other paths.

There are many who feel the world's problems would be solved if you could prove scientifically that there is a God and also prove the way he operates. There are some who accept the Bible or some other scripture as that proof. They assume that if there were such proof, people would behave better and follow the spiritual laws. If you knew for sure what the spiritual laws were you could establish a theocracy that would soon lead to utopia. Do you ever wonder why these scientific proofs have never been established? You have proved so much else but not this. Although there is much data that strongly points to a God, an afterlife and reincarnation, solid proof remains elusive. Why?

To answer this you need to look at what God wants, not what you desire. God wants you to develop your truth. To develop your truth is to fulfill your nature through your free will. If scientific proof of God were established, each of you would find searching for your truth short-circuited. You would be given a truth from outside yourself [the scientific proof]. *Thus the truth of God would not be your internal truth, but the scientist's proof. The same applies to reincarnation, an afterlife, the law of karma and other spiritual truths. You are to discover and create these as your truths.*

*It is for this reason that you will find **evidence** of God, of reincarnation, of karma and other spiritual wisdom, but not **proof**. The possibility of scientific proof is tantalizing. The data supporting such ideas is plentiful. And yet the hard proof will not manifest. You can be glad this is so; it is God's plan in creating an environment most suitable for your learning.*

Another way of stating this is: To live spiritually is a matter of the heart not the intellect. It is the heart that needs to grow, to seek its own truth. Intellectual concepts proven or unproven will not bring the heart to its fulfillment.

I was giving a presentation about our first book[9] regarding communications from Gail at St. Joseph's Hospital. As an all-cancer facility, the patients' families were much involved so they had a small auditorium, which was used to present programs on topics of interest to all involved in their care.

I was about halfway through my talk when a doctor stood up and asked me, "Do you have any scientific proof of what you are saying about communicating with your deceased wife."

"No," I replied, "but I wish I could."

"Then what are you doing telling these people all this stuff?" He felt he had made his case.

"Are you married?" I asked him.

"Yes, but what has that got to do with it?"

"Did you use the scientific method to choose your wife?"

"No," he replied, "Why would I do that?"

"Precisely my point. Many of the most important things and choices in our lives are made outside the scientific method and we wisely do so."

He sat down and didn't argue further. But I suspect I didn't change his mind in any way.

❧

My dear Buck, we can talk about time again. It is a common human thought to wonder where time originated. Actually God created time along with everything else. This has interesting consequences. Man has always been puzzled about the beginning. He theorizes that our universe began with the Big Bang. He puzzles about what initiat-

---

[9] Marshall and Gail Kent, *In Death We Do Not Part*, Alleusha Publishing, 2002.

ed the Big Bang and what was there before it started. *Philosophically there is always the conundrum that you say something was the beginning but where did it come from, if not from another beginning before it? You can't ever seem to get back to the original beginning.*

Any beginning, as you know it, is time dependent. In other words a beginning only makes sense if there is time. If there is no time you cannot have a beginning, so God preexisted time.

It is hard to conceive of a state of existence without time. Yet such exists. You might say that one of the attributes of God is that he can exist without time. He is not time dependent.

To try to grasp this most peculiar state, think of our three spatial dimensions. If there can be three if not more spatial dimensions, why do you assume time is only a single dimension? That would be inconsistent. It can be said that time is three in that there is the past, the present and the future. As we have said, that separation is earthbound and doesn't exist over here. In addition, there are other dimensions that are time-like. One of these is non-time; God's state referred to above. I call it non-time to convey the idea that it is beyond your knowledge of time with its beginnings and endings. Actually it is all-time, an umbrella that includes times in all manifestations. This all-time was not so much created by God, as it is God. From this he created the special times including your time, as you know it.

If there are times different from the one you know it is not so difficult to envision universes greatly differing from your own. And indeed they do exist.

As you can see the above is consistent with the We Are All One principle. The all-time of God is another expression of the universal. That we are all One does not limit in any way the possibilities of God or his creations. The diversity and individuality within the Oneship is unlimited. God would have it be so.

❧

My beloved Gail, our dear family has gone home after a fine Christmas together. We are fortunate. It is dark and rainy. I am now alone with the Christmas tree lights looking so good and listening to beautiful violin music by Saint-Saëns. Write to me with love as you do.

You are indeed fortunate. God gives you so many gifts it is hard to appreciate them all at once. This morning I would like to write about the All that you are immersed in. The All is infinite and to truly sense it requires that you look to infinity.

Here's an analogy. As I try to show you what a grain of sand is, I explain it is like a very small rock of quartz that is clear mostly but with different traces of color depending upon the sand. I can say that this sand is the main constituent of glass making. This you can easily understand. I then tell you that this small grain of sand in nature is found with others like it in great numbers. You have no trouble understanding this either. If you have never been to a sandy beach, however, or spent time in the desert, it might be almost impossible to convey to you the ambiance of walking along that ocean beach at Malindi or how enchanting the desert can be. This is my problem in trying to describe to you the infinite.

There is hope however. Your growth and learning is really a journey toward the infinite, the All and God. Each lifetime, each experience can bring you greater appreciation of the infinite that is within you. If you are aware that this is what you are doing, it helps you progress more surely.

This brings us to the question: If God wants you to feel the infinite then why does he immerse you in the finite with all its continuing problems? It seems as if the finite with its concerns of food, shelter and loved ones is actually a barrier to having any concept at all of the infinite. It is difficult to even think of the infinite when all these survival issues grab your mind.

It turns out that one cannot feel the infinite if one does not also feel the finite. This concept is again difficult to explain. In time, however, you will understand the finite so that it can be joined in your being with the infinite.

In one way what I have been writing all these years to you from this side is an attempt to broaden your perspective to include a full view of your finite world, which in turn will let you partake in the infinite. When you achieve this, you will become aware of other souls from other worlds and other universes with their own particular finite parts of the infinite. You will then understand the glory in their finite world, as you will share with them the glory of your finite world. What God has been up to will then make perfect sense.

If you can't grasp this fully that's fine. I hope I have let you see a bit of the wonder in conjunction with your favorite theme of how it all fits together.

PART FIVE

GOD'S CREATED WORLD

CHAPTER TWENTY-SEVEN

A Journey Without End

We have now discussed in some detail various parts and mechanisms with which we live and deal. Let's examine the totality that they all fit within.

You are a most magnificent creation of an almost unbelievably loving creator. Within you, placed there by him, are potentials, abilities, love, energy and tools of infinite use. If you realized just a bit of this manifold gift he has given each of you, you would be in awe of your creator and also, very importantly, in awe of yourselves for what you are. You have not only received the gift of life but a wondrous mind, heart and body to take you on your journey without end.

Your Creator gives each of you a touch of his creative force, as well as his other attributes. Each of you has these attributes in nascent form; they await your awakening. Isn't that wonderful?

God is loving. That means you all have the potential to be loving too. God does not **make** *you loving as this would be involuntary. Instead he gives you free will so that you can develop into a loving soul. He plants this capability within you to allow love to happen. You have the tools to become loving if you so choose.*

The fact that God has given you free will is an attribute of God himself. He has free will as your wonderful world attests. He has given you immortality, as he himself is immortal. He has made you part of the Oneship as he himself is the Oneship. Do you see how simple yet how magnificent this is?

God is patient. God is forgiving. God is inclusive. You can become these things by using the creative power God has given you. The mind is your builder and you can create yourself to be what you choose.

*Think of all God's attributes that wait for your realization to flower. This growth is known as **remembering** who you are or **returning** to God and is why it is said that you are created in God's image. **God's attributes are your attributes in nascent form.** Rejoice that not only do you have these incredible abilities, but so too do all your brothers and sisters.*

What happens when you begin to develop these God-given attributes? In addition to having the joy of the attribute itself you will discover ancillary rewards as well. As you grow toward these potentials, you become closer in your attunement to God. This attunement will let you feel the warmth of God's love.

You will also find that your relationship with your sisters and brothers becomes much more companionable. Yes, they can be cantankerous, but don't reflect their prickliness. With your new companionability you will find it much easier to deflect their unhappy condition.

Companionable is a holy and profound word. Did you know you could actually feel yourself a companion to God? As you recognize who you are and where you are going (developing God's attributes within you) you will know yourself as God's companion.

It is as though God has given each of us a packet of various seeds and placed us in his garden. We plant those seeds, tend them, do the weeding, shelter them from too much sun, protect them from pests and see that they are watered. We watch them grow to fruition. How our seeds thrive has much to do with how good we are as gardeners.

With this understanding we can see that we are magnificently created beings with vast potential. So too is each life sacred. We have been created to partake in a holy process.

This leads to the next question. What kind of God-given place would allow us to progress in developing our attributes? Gail describes this place by analogy.

One winter day about six years after her passing I had just finished a bag lunch on the ski slopes when this message nudged me.

You ate beside a small rushing mountain stream with its lovely white water and rocks. A river with all its streams, waterfalls and banks makes a revealing spiritual analogy.

There are large drainage basins from which all water with great constancy responds to gravity and seeks a path to the ocean. Each falling raindrop is continually joining with other drops of water, one to another, from trickles to streams to rivers to the all-accepting ocean. The history of any given droplet of water therefore follows two principles: one is the act of joining and the other is the motion to the ocean.

Is this not like the human journey? You too, go through many joinings. In this world the first joining is the one you have with your mother. You have nine months of being one with her at the same time that you are individual, again a metaphor for your spiritual growth and your relationship to God. Your life then becomes a joining with family, friends, local environment, country and on to the Oneship.

You also have this underlying motion of moving toward a goal. That goal is your return to the ocean, to God. Even those who don't believe in God nonetheless are moving toward him. It is as if they have come downstream to a lake and feel that they have arrived at what they are, lake water, thinking there is no such thing as the sea. But lake water in time picks up its journey again toward the ocean.

Eventually you discover you are on a spiritual path moving as the stream does along ever-changing but ever-beautiful banks. You get involved in raging floods, falling off cliffs in waterfalls and tumbling over rocks.

As you wash over the rocks doing somersaults, getting shoved rapidly from here to there, flung into the air out of control, you are so absorbed with what is happening that you have no idea what a lovely sight you make if viewed from the bank. This is one of the secrets in widening one's perspective; in so doing you become aware of beauty that your narrow outlook sees as chaos or disaster.

The raging floods seem to sweep you along without your consent. You become a destroyer, violent and excited now that you have jumped over your confining banks. In time, however, the flood recedes and returns to its banks and on you go to the ocean's acceptance.

Another commonality you have with the droplet of water that journeys so far, is that you are indestructible. You live forever. If you were aware of this on your journey you would be less threatened and would find more joy.

There is more. How did the droplet get there in the first place to start its many joinings? It fell from the sky. And how did it get in the sky? Water moisture evaporated, and seemingly against the laws of gravity rose upward to become a cloud before dropping as a raindrop to begin the journey again. It did so without fanfare, in fact, silently and invisibly.

So too do you evaporate (die and disappear) and defy the logic of gravity (lack of scientific evidence of an afterlife) to rise up to the sky (heaven). In the sky you go through a nebulous (without bodily form) cloud-forming process until you are ready to return to Earth as a raindrop to live in another incarnation.

This is the pattern, a pattern so universal that you will see it in many places in addition to the raindrop and yourself. Godspeed.

A good day (or whatever it is you have) to you my love. Please use my fingers on the keyboard to help me understand.

My dear, dear Buck, I thank you and wish you a good day as well. God has anticipated your needs and has already given you tools to resolve those needs. I would like to go into what some of those tools are.

The first one may seem odd but is very real and crucial: He does not interfere with your free will or that of your brothers and sisters. How can this be an aid to you? Think of what the world would be like if God interfered to see that we all live perfect lives without greed, illness, exasperation, and all those things we regard as defects in the human condition. We would indeed have a utopia, but of automatons. No free will, just people doing things perfectly all the time. No growth, nothing new, only one way to do things: the right way.

But many of you say you are not asking God to interfere all the time, just on the occasions when you ask. Isn't this getting back to free will again? You want your free will so as to decide when God should intervene, but how would you feel if another soul asked God to interfere with your free will and he did? Free will by its basic character cannot be partial. Either you have it or you don't. It is one of the three great gifts given to you by God. He gives it to you and your sisters and brothers unreservedly.

It is this free will that makes you nascent gods. Without it you are not god-like, but rather automatons, hardly contributors to the Oneship as you should be. Yes, you are potential gods and in time will become so in total harmony with your creator. This is your journey. You are on this journey and so am I. You are sensing along with me how magnificent the journey can be.

It is true that most in the world see the free will of others as a huge impediment to how they think the world should be. In fact, they spend much energy and time trying to coerce or convince others to behave in a manner that would be in accord with what their free will decides is correct.

As free will is a very basic tool given to you by God to fulfill your nature and find your truth, respect this tool in others.

We have known a number of fine people who don't believe in God, yet are contributing to bettering the world. This makes me question how important it is to believe in God. What do you think Gail?

First, God is fully aware that his totality is far beyond your comprehension; he doesn't fault you for not knowing what he is or even **if** *he is. So you believe in him, but what is your cognizance of what you believe in? Whatever it is, it is at best only partial.*

The Earth environment that he has created for you, to say nothing of this side, is designed so that each soul can advance in wis-

dom discovering his or her truth. It is planned so that you will, in following your unique spiritual path, come to believe that love is the foundation and the answer. You should seek this in your being. He does not want you to come to this state of bliss because you fear his retribution in the event you don't do right. He wants the bliss to be there because you have convinced yourself that this is best.

The intentions of your heart grow through the accumulation of your essence memory.

Do you see this?

I do, but it raises an interesting question. Is it better to be loving and not believe in God or is it better to believe in God, but try to act right because if you don't he will punish you?

Here you are missing the point. Everyone has a different path with different stages on that path. No matter where they are on the path, believing or not believing in God, they are given God's blessings with recurring lifetimes of opportunities to advance.

Look within to your heart. Observe how your intentions show up in your actions and see the results you create.

I know that many of those who believe in God feel righteous over those who don't. This God belief is less important than the intentions of their heart. You should recognize, however, that belief in God could open the door for many people to experience greater wisdom. But, it is not the only path.

CHAPTER TWENTY-EIGHT

God's Three Great Gifts: Free Will, the Oneship and Immortality

We have received three great gifts. They are essential to our being. In fact, all that has been said before would not exist without them. They are central to who we are. Gail, can we go into these now?

Yes, but God's gifts to us are well beyond the small number of three. These three, however, are ever-present in your lives and should be in your thoughts. Why don't you identify them for us?

God in his divine generosity has given us three great gifts, each of which is a vast treasure. The first is that we are immortal. The second is that we are an important, integral part of the Oneship. And thirdly, we have been given free will. We have already referred to them often and each is indeed a divine gift even as we acknowledge that with our free will we often create vast troubles on this otherwise beautiful Earth.

As none of the three have priority over the other two, we will examine each of these in reverse order, starting first with free will.

Free Will

The gift of free will is given to each of us as an individual; we individually exercise it.

This brings out a most important idea. God with his infinite abilities could have given free will to an entire community of people in which the individual members could not do anything other than be in accord with the single community's free will. This would have solved a lot of problems. It would have eliminated community strife. But this is not what he created! Obviously he wanted each individual to have free will. Respect this. As we go on it will become clear why this is so.

You're saying that God intended us to be individual. If so, how does this work with the other gift that we are all One?

Very well as a matter of fact, but let's take one thing at a time.

As the farmers used to say: you can lead a horse to water but you cannot make him drink. You can offer people help, but if they choose not to accept it, it remains unaccepted. Free will trumps any proffered help. In the visible world you can see the offer and the resulting acceptance or rejection of that offer.

In the invisible world, however, it is not so obvious.

What happens when someone prays for another? Does the stated wish of the one praying take precedence over the recipient's free will? No. In healing does the healing power of the healer bring about changes that are against the will of the healed? No again.

*To understand this we should go back to the basics. Free will is a gift given to us by God. Nobody has the power to take that away from you. You always have free will to decide for yourself. No one can decide for you **unless you choose to let them do so**. This applies equally to those like me, on this side. We too have free choice.*

Why am I now communicating with you as if I were not dead, gone and silent as most people think I should be? It is because I choose to do so. Why is it you are receiving what I am saying? It is because you choose to do so. If I choose to communicate with you and you choose not to listen, what would happen? Nothing would happen. I do not have the power to suspend your free will and impose mine upon you, nor does anyone else.

Also you do not have the power to try to hang onto me, which could prevent me from doing what I should be doing on this side. I have the free choice to do what I need to do on this side. You are not responsible for what I do here; I am.

This is how free will functions. Other factors, however, must also be considered. When I died I was very concerned about leaving you and my family behind. My heart went out to you. It was not a pleasant feeling, rather unsettling. I wanted to reach out to each of you and in some way heal your grief.

With guidance and help I was soon able to give up those un-settled feelings. My broadened perspective, which I chose with my free will, let me know that you all were properly in God's hands. Further, I knew that each of you had individually chosen through your inner selves to go through my leaving so as to be presented with the learning opportunities involved. With this knowledge I could relax and feel good about your futures. You could say that with my free will I liberated myself from these concerns and was free then to go on with what I needed to do on this side.

We on this side are understandably concerned with how you on Earth are handling our departures. We choose with our free will to try to help you. We send you communications. We send you healings. You on Earth, however, may choose to dismiss them and discount them as imagination or whatever. It is your proper jurisdiction to accept or reject what we try to send you. We, of course, want you to receive our communications, but know that we cannot force you to do so, nor would we want to.

In all of these examples, free will is preserved. Understanding this allows you to be helpful, loving and healing to others including your deceased. Do pray for us on this side. Do send us healing and other loving thoughts. We will choose to receive them and appreciate them. They will help us feel the Oneship of all of us and the Oneship of just us two. The dissipation of separation is holy work and benefits both sides.

Gail continued that afternoon.

A friend allows you to be who you seek to be. Restating that in terms of free will we can say that a friend tends to leave your free will up to you. It is in the family and spousal relationships where we see much more interference with free will. And, of course, governments are tempted to limit your free will, as are some religions. I suggested that this goal of not interfering with another's free will, as is found in friendship, should be brought into family and spousal relationships. To walk in friendship with your world means to respect the free will of everything about you.

Now when you pass over to this side your respect for free will receives a big jolt. Your wider perspective shows you the importance of free will and you have a deeper understanding of it. There is great diversity here. This means that even though you may get a stimulus to respect free will more, you may be starting from a very low base to begin with. Hence your comprehension can still be meager.

Suppose your mother was very controlling and you, as a daughter, could never get through to her about being less so. When your mother passes over she will very quickly receive a broader view, particularly in regards to free will and her controlling actions. It is up to her free will how much she will change. It is very likely, however, that she will elevate herself to a higher level. This is because the les- sons God gives you through transition are powerfully appropriate. In this instance the daughter would not be wrong to assume the deceased mother now has a much better view. The daughter could talk to her assuming she had this greater understanding.

Our understanding on this side of the role of God's gift of free will influences much of what we do. We try to help you, but never by interfering with your free will. Nor do we do your homework for you. You may be in the midst of what you regard as a trial and would like so very much to have your deceased one tell you what you should do. We see your dilemma and wish you the very best, but cannot tell you how to solve that problem. We can promote thoughts of applicable wisdom to occur to you. Whether you heed them is up to you.

One very important example of this is in regard to grieving. If you mire yourself in grief and withdraw from your current life, you will have created a problem for yourself. The lesson you will need to learn is that you should engage in your current life. This is your homework that you should not ignore. When you choose to ignore it we cannot aid you in this avoidance. We cannot communicate with you if you will use this communication as an excuse to withdraw from life. Our communication with you cannot be a substitute for living. This is why I am so pleased, Buck, with your full engagement in your current life and it is why I can continue to write to you.

✒

Not many know how to use their free will. Their first big impediment is that they don't think they have choice. Until they realize they have choice it is impossible to exercise it. So let's talk about it a bit.

Often when people behave poorly to you or you are in a difficult set of circumstances, you feel you have no choice but to respond in one way. You may say, "They made me do it."

To be specific, think of resentment. Here you are resenting what has been done to you. You think you have no choice but to be resentful because what happened to you was so unfair and undeserved. Wouldn't everyone feel resentment under such circumstances? Even if you think you would like to stop your resentment you find it seemingly impossible. The resentment just keeps boiling up in your mind. You can't turn it off. Besides, you may feel your resentment is fully justified so why give it up? This is just one example of a situation where you may feel you have no choice because the external happenings determine your choice for you.

There are two things to understand. First you always have a choice. This doesn't mean that you can choose to visit the moon by starting to flap your arms vigorously. Second, the choice might not be in what happens to you, but in how you respond to what happens to you. The point of action then is not outside you where you have no control, but inside you where you can alter how you respond to the outside circumstances.

Since you always have a choice, you should be aware of this.

Thus the first step in exercising choice is to know you have it. Your second choice is how you respond to a given situation. When you are being resentful ask yourself some of these questions.

- *Do I like the choice of resentment that I made?*
- *Does my resentment help me be the person I want to be?*
- *At the moment am I happy with the effect this resentment has on me?*
- *Which has priority for me: feeling righteous in my resentment or feeling at peace?*
- *Which has priority for me: to see that he/she gets what they deserve for treating me so or my own happiness and serenity?*
- *Is my resentment helping me achieve my life's goals?*
- *Is it possible that my resentment is counter-productive, moving me in the opposite direction from where I want to go?*
- *Is my resentment having a positive effect on the people around me who matter in my life?*
- *If my choice were free and easy to make would I choose to feel the way I do right now with my resentment?*
- *Would I choose to keep this resentment until the day I die, spending the rest of my life with resentment gnawing within me?*
- *If not, that means I am going to want to give up my resentment sometime. So do I have a good reason for not giving up my resentment now instead of later?*

Having asked yourself some of these questions you may open the door to give up your resentments. Choose to walk through that door now. You may find it hard to do. If so, have the courage to at least look through the door and see what awaits you on the other side when you lay down your resentments.

Remember, the direction that you face is far more important than where you are at the moment. So even if you still feel full of resentment but are facing in the direction of letting it go, be much encouraged. You have made two major positive decisions. One, you know you do have a choice and secondly, you see that you truly want to set your resentments aside. The fact that you have not yet succeeded in doing so is to be expected. Be patient with yourself. This does not take away from the fact that you have made two large steps in the direction you want to go. You do not have an on/off switch to turn the resentment off, but you do have a volume control. Turn this volume control down a little bit at a time. Godspeed.

The Oneship

Dear beloved Gail, my friend. How are you this fine rainy, cuddly evening?

Dearest Buck, the rain enriches the Earth and all life upon it. The sun does the same thing. Most often they do not do it together although when they do rainbows appear. Do you know what rainbows are? They are symbols of the delight that God has in making you individual, as are the various colors of the rainbow, while at the same time when joined together you are one in white light, God's light. Even in your separation into colors your relationship to each other is maintained. If any one color is missing there can be no return to pure white light. In the same way each soul is important and necessary to the One.

I remember the double rainbow at the Grand Canyon and how the circle of the rainbow below the horizon curved back within the canyon itself. The bottom rainbow had the colors in upside down order. It was the most beautiful rainbow I had ever seen. Maybe this was because we had just finished hiking across that huge lovely canyon.

And there you were in sandals with wool socks since you had ten bruised toes from our descent of the north wall of the canyon. Each step you took down that trail with a thirty-five pound backpack made your toes slide forward in your boots to jam against the leather. After a four thousand foot descent your toenails were sore and blue. Later, nine of them fell off.

⁓

  Dear Buck, I want to write about the power and the magnificence of the We Are All One principle. When you consider the idea that each person is currently in the best environment to learn the lessons that they most need to learn you might feel incredulous. You might accept this as being true for one person, but not for all. For example, how can the parents of a difficult fifteen-year-old be confronted with a situation that is best for them to learn at the very same time as the fifteen-year-old is also in the best situation for her or him to learn? Then the idea of multiplying that principle to the millions of people on Earth is just too fantastic. How can the dictator and the prisoners he is having tortured both be in circumstances to learn what is most appropriate for them at this stage of their growth?

  This is where the power and the magnificence of the We Are All One principle reveals itself. Study the natural world and what do you see? You see how all things fit together. Take lichen, one of the world's hardiest life forms. It grows in the most severe places and yet it is actually two life forms that live in a symbiotic relationship.

  There are all these environmental niches that, through evolution, God has filled with just the right organism to succeed. The Gaia[10] hypothesis consists of a vast network or pattern of various functions that allow Earth to operate as a whole in responding to a myriad of stimuli. This hypothesis thus attributes to the Earth the same pattern that we call life thus implying that the Earth is alive. All of these things are in compliance with the We Are All One principle as they fit together, function together, and grow together. This very same pattern applies to

---

[10] James Lovelock, *The Ages Of Gaia – A Biography Of Our Living Earth*, W. W. Norton and Company, 1988.

humans on Earth.

When your incredulity to this idea simmers down you begin to understand that at the same time you are placed in the very best classroom for what you need to learn, so too is everyone you meet. It now becomes clear that everyone you interact with is your teacher and you their student and vice versa. Your role in life is as both student and teacher. Adopting this attitude can have a wonderful effect on all your relationships. Good teachers are patient, forgiving of students when they fail to learn quickly, and desirous of the learning and growth of their students. Good students in turn pay attention to their teachers, don't try to avoid their homework and are grateful to the teachers for their help. Can you see how differently you would treat others if you had this attitude?

Can you see that with this attitude the realization that we are all One would become more clear and real to you? This is just a part of the power and magnificence of the We Are All One principle. This spectrum stretches from where one is fully wrapped up in Earth's happenings, to where broad understanding allows one to put strife and tribulation into the context of a perfect process.

The soul's evolvement on Earth is interesting. When the soul first comes to Earth it takes a number of lifetimes before it becomes fully committed, invested and caught up in the material plane. Once fully involved on Earth there is a tendency to overdo it wherein what is happening on Earth at the time is all that is of concern. Separation becomes supreme. There are great fights about who is to get the biggest piece of pie if not all of it. Slowly but surely over many lifetimes you traverse this spectrum to arrive at the other end with a better understanding of your true selves and your universe. It is here that you become aware of the perfect process, that you are all One, that you remember that you are all God's holy creation.

As you suspect when one reaches this end of the spectrum he is in his last few lives.

Dear Gail, I feel you want to write to me tonight even though I'm about to climb into bed.

Beloved Buck, I do want to write to you to tell you about how the all that is One has another lovely manifestation. Do you realize that if we are all One, which, of course we are, everything else is an illusion? Your separation is an illusion; your death and my death are illusions. You and I being on separate planes is an illusion. We are all One and cannot be any other way except in our illusions.

When are we not in an illusion when we are on the Earth plane? Think. Are you always separate while alive in your world? Actually you are not. When you look at a child, any child, don't you feel love come out of you toward that child? Yet you are not asking that child to do anything but be him or herself. You have no thought of getting something returned because your love is flowing out to the child. Now I know when it is your children, you are indeed expecting a certain kind of behavior some of the time. But often you love them to pieces for just being.

When you feel that love flowing out of you toward the child you are one with that child. You have gotten so used to that feeling that you don't think of it as being anything different. The next time you feel that love flow out of you, that you are now experiencing the all that is One. By consciously doing this, greater understanding will come to you.

This makes you ready for a big and, yes, difficult step. Try looking at everybody in the same way you looked at the child. Look at everybody, the homeless, the drunkard, the rat-race businessman, the hand wringer, the cop, the politician and the doctor. They are all children and quite often they act that way. God sees them as children worthy of love, all of them.

We have already discussed some tools that will help you with this. You are hopefully now convinced that you are in exactly the situation that is best suited for you to learn the lesson that you now need to learn. If this is true of you it is true of everyone else. And if everyone out there is exactly where they should be, why are you making the judg-

ment that they are not doing what they should be doing? What they should be doing is exercising their own free will. And they are, all the time.

Now it is true that much of people's behavior is far from loving. But you don't need to fret about that because God's laws are in place and operating. Thus with experience with free choice, every one of you in the Oneship will come to the knowledge that your will has become the same as God's will.

To really feel this about everybody and not just children requires not only love but also great patience. This is why Edgar Cayce said that patience was the fourth dimension.

To understand that perfection and love are to be sensed is the fulfilling of your nature. For humans this fulfillment is the exercising of free choice in a milieu tailored for advancement.

<hr>

Let us venture down the road of discussing what "values" mean as they relate to personal behavior. If you simply acted out of complete selfishness all the time there would be no need to talk about values. So you start with the idea that values have to do with how you take others into consideration in your interactions with them, in other words, your shared Oneship.

You see people act in their own self-interest much of the time, so much that you probably expect it. Yet God made you so that in some ways you don't always act in your own self-interest, for instance, many of the things you do in order to propagate the species are not done in sole self-interest. Having children is a tremendous amount of work and yet it is a heart-felt desire of many. In raising children you put up with a lot. And in adulthood many parents find their children are a disappointment. They don't finish their education. They marry the wrong person. In short, they don't seem to have the good sense that the parents think they should have.

Fortunately, this does not describe all children and their parents. My point is simply that in childrearing we invest a great deal of *our lifetime and effort in exchange for rewards that are fuzzy and not guaranteed. Looked at as a contract, you have to put up lots of time and money and curtail your activities in exchange for something you may never receive. For the species, it is obvious why this is necessary. On an individual basis, however, it is a bit of a mystery why anyone enters into parenting with such passion.*

Self-interest has been shoved aside to benefit the species. Now isn't it interesting that God is able to create you so that you behave in a manner that takes you beyond yourselves? He does so in a number of ways. Sex can be described as very much in the self-interest of those who partake. Yet this partaking is often the introduction into life-long relationships with children and the attendant behaviors that are not self-centered.

Because of the even more fundamental attribute of free choice, all of these devices from God to promote values beyond just the self can be frustrated by your choosing. This frustration is but temporary if looked at in God's time frame.

What then are the values that carry you beyond yourselves and draw from you great dedication and energy? In a word, the Oneship. We are all One. We need to remember that this is so. You need to act in a manner that reveals this is so. Acting selfishly is, of course, indi-viduality in its base form in opposition to the Oneship. To consider others is to move toward the Oneship on your enlightened path.

There are many stages in this process of uniting in the One-ship. Therefore you will find that some of the value systems adopted along this path are far from ideal. Many of them will have strong elements of separation in them. A very common idea is that one group consists of "the chosen ones of God" and because others are not they do not share a special place in God's heart. Nonetheless, even these value systems are very helpful. Although they separate those whom they re-gard as being outside (infidels), there is a very strong sense of joining with those who are inside. In time over many centuries the power of joining expands while the sense of separation becomes less relevant. You see this happening in your world today.

Values of love, tolerance, openness, compassion, non-violence and aiding your sisters and brothers are all being recognized as being superior. Earth is moving forward on the spiritual path to God.

～～

Sweetheart, a wonderful day is coming. Spring is in the air but it is still chilly.

Beloved Buck, count and give your blessings. To have an attitude of giving blessings is very cleansing to your system. Yes, I mean that physically as well as spiritually. Giving blessings attunes you to the Oneship, which in turn brings you the healing and enlightenment that the Oneship has to offer. If you are in the sunshine you partake of its qualities like heat and light. Without the sunlight it is cold and dark. It is like that when you attune or don't attune to the Oneship. Sense the Oneship, seek the Oneship and you will feel a surge in the blessings you receive. The law of the Oneship is such that you cannot give without receiving and you cannot receive without giving.

You can choose not to be aware of what you are receiving when you give, and you can choose not to be aware that you are giving when you receive. There are many "takers" in the world. Their purpose in life seems to be to take whatever they can get. Some seem successful in taking more than their "share." How do they give commensurate with what they take? They are giving learning circumstances to others that are appropriate to what those others need to learn. This is complex and difficult to understand. If your problem was simply to learn to like pleasant people, one lifetime would be plenty to learn the lesson. The spiritual lesson is more involved than this; you need to know how to love as God loves.

By aligning yourself with the Oneship and partaking in its blessings, the spiritual path becomes easier, more understandable and enlightening. It doesn't seem so difficult when your awareness includes the possibility of the Oneship.

The mind is the builder so let's go over the building steps. First, your mind has to be able to conceive the idea of a Oneship wherein you are not only related to everything but you **are** everything.

Next, you need to think that such an idea can actually exist, that it is possible. You don't have to believe it is absolutely true but you do need to believe it is possible.

Third, you will begin to perceive evidence that it is true. This is evidence you did not see before. Perhaps you may have seen it before, but did not recognize it for what it was.

Fourth, the pace quickens and you will come to believe the Oneship is true. Your attitudes and behavior will reflect this. You have become a co-creator of the Oneship. Who you are will ascend over what you do. In fact, your "being" will determine what you "do." You have reversed the material plane perception that what you do determines who you are.

The Oneship is yours. Do not hesitate to join it.

❧

It is exciting to be present at this time of huge transition in the realization that we are all One. This does not mean you have to discard your individuality, just the opposite. **Your individuality is the gift you bring to God.** What some of you see only dimly is that your individuality can be harmonious with other individualities, with all individualities. You often feel that individuality requires confrontation, controlling, dominance and other grossly separating devices. You fail to see the potential within individuality to bring congruence and harmony, in short, love. The new millennium will manifest this potential of harmony. It is a giant step for this Earth.

Immortality is Ours

With a deeper feeling for the Oneship, the idea that one is immortal seems more tenable. This is God's third great gift to us.

You have great difficulty on Earth in sensing your immortality *because you only see the world's materiality. On this side we see both your material world and our spiritual world easily.*

I want you to notice, however, that almost all religions and mystical systems believe in some sort of afterlife. This is prompted by your deep memory of having experienced the afterlife. These various afterlife concepts of the different religions are quite distinct. This is reflected by the great diversity that is here. For example, throughout time the idea of the peaceable kingdom of animals has been very attractive. This is the result of your hidden memory of actually being in such an environment in the spirit world. So it is with the afterlife. You would be amazed at how many attitudes in your memory shelves are due to echoes from this side.

You carry within your deeper self the essence of what you have learned and known, but without the specific detail of your past lives. To you, specificity lends credence. Basically, you believe truth is revealed and confirmed by specificity. Without specific data to back up your truths you feel they are quite tenuous. Thus you tend not to see any truth in these vague memories of spiritual realms, which come unprompted into your thoughts.

Why do you think that specificity is stripped away from your memories as you reincarnate from life to life? The details of your past experiences on this side and of your past lives on Earth would just get in the way of your life now. You have the essence of these experiences, which is what you need and can use to evolve and grow. The specificity or details of these experiences would simply cloud your mind and obscure your life process.

What is it that you are doing when you practice anything, for example learning to sight-read music? You start with paying great attention to the placement of each note on the scale, trusting that with practice the detail will fade away and you will carry with you only the essence. A concert pianist can play hundreds of notes a minute because of his practice leading up to his internalization of the whole. It would be impossible for him to do this if he had to consciously think of each one of those hundreds of notes separately before he could play it. So you on Earth know full well the importance of letting the details go in order to effectively accomplish your goal. In truth it opens whole huge dimensions for you. It doesn't occur to you to apply this to the concept of reincarnation. In fact, some ask how can reincarnation be real if I can't remember my past lives?

This pattern of forgetting the details in favor of achieving the higher essence is very important to your development.

Dear Buck, today I would like to talk with you about the barrier between your world and mine. Both worlds belong to each of us and we often exist in both. Right now there is no part of me incarnated on Earth. You, however, have a physical self on Earth, and your higher self over here with me. Everyone on Earth has his higher self on this side. The reverse is not true. There are many on this side who have no incarnation on Earth at this time. Some have never incarnated on Earth.

You could say that the existence over here is more fundamental. This is also borne out by the fact that life on Earth is temporary while life on this side is infinite. Your immortality is assured by your life on this side, not your life on Earth. In fact, your lives on Earth will eventually result in your evolvement to such a degree that you no longer need to return to Earth. Thus your immortality is not tied to Earth, but elsewhere.

Most of the mystical systems and some of the religions support this view. My point is that if this is the case, it is important for you on Earth to be perceptive and communicative with this side. You may regard your attempts to communicate with your deceased loved one as your affair, which it is; it is also important to mankind as a whole because it diminishes the separation between our two worlds. This helps raise the consciousness of those on Earth to accept that we are all immortally One.

This realization should help you toward an evolved attitude. You are trying to communicate with your loved one over here not only for self-centered reasons, but to help dissolve the separation. Dissolving separation is another way to bring love.

Let us carry that one step further. As communication opens up with those on this side, so too does wisdom flow from the wise to the less wise. On Earth in some areas I was more advanced than you; in other areas you were more advanced than I.

When I came here, however, three important things occurred that changed that. First, I was able to review my lifetime experiences in great depth. That review allowed me to see it all with a much broader perspective. For example, I could see how my actions affected others. This was a real eye opener as you can imagine.

Next, I have ready and easy access to the wisdom of others. On Earth I also had access to wisdom but I found it difficult to access. Coming here was almost like suddenly discovering how to use the library.

The third thing is that my mind was no longer cluttered with the requirements of living in a material world. As you put it, no diapers to change or mortgage payments to make. This gives tremendous freedom to pursue wisdom directly and in depth.

Buck, you and I were fortunate because we long ago realized that learning was our purpose on Earth. It was not difficult for me to come here and continue to pursue learning. When you pass over you will delight in discovering our wonderful library with its most helpful librarians.

Our role here is to further open communications between this world and the Earth. With the channel opened I can reveal to you much of the wisdom that you and I sought so dearly on Earth. It gives me great pleasure that you are receiving it, understanding it and being thrilled by it. Our learning together on Earth is continuing and at a much higher level, although I had no idea this could happen. It wasn't that I disbelieved, it was just that it didn't occur to me that it was a realistic possibility.

There is a lesson in that for both of us (I remember my Mother telling me that as a child). You will be much closer to wisdom if you think all things are possible, (not the least that you are immortal) rather than assuming so many things are impossible or unlikely. Assuming things are impossible closes your mind.

Take my hand and rejoice. We are among the chosen. All of humanity is chosen.

CHAPTER TWENTY-NINE

Infinite God

There are so many competing belief systems that it is difficult to step forward in any discussion of God without treading on someone's toes. But Gail has always been very brave. Here is some of what she has told me.

From the viewpoint on this spiritual side we see God is indeed infinite in all ways. Yet, we see that within this Oneship he has created enclaves that are finite in character. There are other universes that are much different than our own. There are also other civilizations on other worlds in this universe.

His creative powers have given you life and an environment in which to live. Some see this environment as full of beauty, wonder and love. Others see it as full of difficulties, tragedies and injustice. If properly understood, however, it can bring you great adventure, joy, peace and meaning.

This leads to yet another wonderful thing. You and God are co-creators of your reality. God gave us the tools to expand without limit your boundaries of knowing. In other words, with your free will you can elect to grow toward his infinitude as much and as fast as you are capable. God does not limit you in this regard. He does not want you to remain ignorant of him or his laws. What a gift!

With this understanding I hope you now see why it is so important not to dismiss things as impossible or ridiculous. Think positively that all things are indeed possible, but not necessarily true, in this finite world.

When we asked our four-year-old son what he wanted for his October birthday, he replied, "An electric turkey." It was a reasonable request. After all they had toy electric trains so why not an electric turkey? He has continued into adulthood to believe that things are possible as he now has many patents, all based on new ideas not thought of before.

❧

Each time you designed and built a house during your contracting days it dropped out of your awareness within a couple of years. Your mind was full of the new construction you were doing. You did not think about how the houses built years before were aging and some were being remodeled.

God, being infinite, is quite different. His awareness is total, complete, and continuous. His creations are always in his consciousness. In fact, his consciousness is the source of their continued existence. If anything were to slide out of his awareness it would cease to exist, as he energizes it all. It seems totally impossible that any cosmic intelligence, no matter how huge, could keep such vast amounts in mind at all times. And yet the invisible is much greater than the visible and all this too is in his awareness. Such is the power of the infinite.

Are you saying that God's spark or energy is within me right now and that is why I am alive and communicating with you? Would an analogy be that all life is plugged into something like an electrical system that produces the energy that is life. Unplug us, or life in general, from that electrical energy system and you live no more?

Of course.

It is hard to believe that any being would be capable of so very much. The very size of his involvement is beyond comprehension. Now I realize why no one, no religion or any conception of man, is capable of knowing more than a small part of God.

My dear Buck, infinity is hard to comprehend so let's talk more about it. How would you explain infinity to someone?

I would use time and numbers to describe it. You can count forever and still not reach infinity. The same is true of time. You can go into the future and into the past forever and there is no beginning and no end. This is also true with space.

Did you notice that the first two examples you gave, numbers and time, are thought of as linear sequences of one dimension? Space of course is three-dimensional and therefore more enlightening.

Infinity is far more encompassing than a one-dimensional view would reveal. Infinity means without limits or dimensions. We tend to think of infinity having no beginning or end, but infinity is without sideways limits as well. Infinity is without limits in any direction, time, power, manifestation or possibility. This is what makes it so hard to understand.

Max Planck, the father of quantum physics, and a member of the pantheon of physicists, saw it this way: "All matter originates and exists only by virtue of force…. We must assume behind this force the existence of a conscious and intelligent mind." And he further stated: "Science cannot solve the ultimate mystery of nature. And that is because, in the last analysis, we ourselves are … part of the mystery that we are trying to solve."

These statements are consistent with the concept that the "conscious and intelligent mind" can be labeled God. His mysterious attributes, which he has given to us in potential form, make us "part of the mysteries" as we contain the seeds of these same attributes.

You, however, live in a world with many finite limitations, for example, you have limited earthly life spans. Seeing limits all around you, you nonetheless have parts of you that are unlimited and infinite. Being immortal allows you to continue after the completion of your current Earth life as I am doing now.

Can the limitations of any finite part broaden to include more of the infinite? Yes, and it is happening all the time. At the personal level the raising of your consciousness opens your contact with the infinite. Cosmic consciousness is one such epiphany. Here you can receive and realize wider understandings. This is why some people appear to us as geniuses. They seem to grasp and comprehend things that were not previously within the understanding of humankind. Each of you has the power also to expand your limits. Isn't it interesting that at this time in human history there is such a vast expansion of human knowledge in the sciences and human consciousness? It is a new millennium indeed.

Most people live most of the time in the finite. Life becomes much more enjoyable if you deliberately tap into your infinite abilities. How do you do that? When you hear and feel one with music it is with a sense of no limits or boundaries. When you feel gratitude for the magnificence of your life and the world in which you live, the gratitude is without limits. I could go on but the point is that if you live with the awareness that you are consciously touching the infinite you will open even more of the finite to the infinite.

There are many references in religious literature in the fact that God is infinite. If indeed God has unlimited powers then, if he so chose, he could have created each of us without any tendency to be greedy or violent, in perfect bodily health and with a host of virtues that we wish everyone on Earth shared. That he chose not to do so should make us ponder. What he did choose to do was to make us individuals with free will. Why would he do that when, with our individual free will we often choose to do things that are not in the least godlike?

Sweet Buck, with God all things are possible. Have you thought about what that might mean for you individually? God in his creativity bestows upon his creations the potential of his attributes. This means that you possess the nascent capability of having all things possible for you. Think of what tremendous power resides within you.

It is true that you do not have such power yet, but God gave you free will so you can develop this power. Actually you can expand this to include your holy trinity: your individuality, free will and inner self. These three are tools for you to develop the awesome ability to make all things possible.

Now I want you to notice that God in exercising his ability to do all things does not do all things. Just because he has the power to make you all automatons doing everything in strict accordance to proper behavior does not mean he does so. Another thing he does not do, although he could, is to interfere with your free will and/or the free will of your sisters and brothers. Think about that. Does that not imply that if you are to develop this great power you too should not be eager to suspend the free will of others?

I often wonder if the experience of parenting is not one of God's tools to give us the opportunity to learn not to interfere with the free will of others. We love our children and spend much time, energy and worry protecting them from possible consequences they could get into on their own. And yet our end goal is to have them be mature, self-reliant adults. To get to this goal we must allow our children to practice their free will without trumping their decisions with our own parental authority. Yet we need to protect them as well. Having raised four children with Gail I'm impressed by how difficult this is.

CHAPTER THIRTY

God's Farsighted Laws

Our creator made the universe not as a static, unchanging cosmos, but as a dynamic, ever altering one. What governs its changes? What laws does it follow? From where does the energy that drives it come?

We've already briefly answered these questions. In addition to creating the universes God also created a vast interlacing set of laws that are really one law manifested in many ways. Lets expand upon this topic.

The very same law operates consistently and persistently through all the complex changes that occur daily. Although the law doesn't change, the manifestation of the law constantly alters. This means that the law was originally conceived to foresee the direction in which things could go but it does not predetermine an outcome. The one law allows a wide variety of possibilities all of which are acceptable to God.

This shares some of the qualities of quantum mechanics, which is about possibilities and their probability.

Yes, quantum mechanics is one part of the overall law created by God. These wonderful principles allow you to enjoy and learn in your ever-fascinating world in both predictable and unpredictable ways.

But let us now go into how you can live within these farsighted laws.

❧

We have mentioned God's attributes and how he gave those attributes to each of us. You can observe your world and see that God has created great diversity, which apparently he likes. From this you can say that one of his attributes is diversity. He has given you this same attribute in seed form, for part of your basic nature is diversity.

Think of the diversity that exists in each of us from the very different past lives whose essence has contributed to whom we are.

God's laws generate diversity. This is in sharp contrast to man-made laws that promote the opposite: conformity. When you think of the concept of laws you think in terms of acceptable and unacceptable ways of behaving. Man-made laws are basically limiting in nature. Your driving speed for example, is limited. There are a whole series of actions defined by your laws as criminal, which limit what you may or may not do unless you are willing to go to jail. It is no wonder that when you speak of laws you think in terms of being good or bad, and conforming or facing the consequences.

Further, it is no wonder religions use this same approach. You behave in the way proscribed by religious tenets, the right way, or face God's consequences, which some religions go to great lengths to describe as pretty terrible. So your culture's feeling about laws is that they limit behavior and promote conformity. This is contrary to the diversity that God prefers. If you are to understand God's laws and his attribute of diversity you must deliberately abandon this conforming attitude and reaction to the word "law."

God's laws do promote diversity. From your cultural bias it is hard to see how this is possible, but nonetheless it is not only possible but also a universal characteristic.

Your Earth has thousands of mountains and yet each is uniquely different as we discovered in our lovely travels. Each mountain obeys God's laws to the letter. Further, each of those mountains is constantly changing. The changing is also in allegiance to God's laws. They are not changing toward greater conformity but to a continued diversity. Do you see the constancy with which God's laws promote diversity?

The example of the mountains is a metaphor for our own selves. Each of you is different. Each of you is changing or growing.

You are as God created you at the same time that he allows you to shape yourself by his gift of free will. You are growing in allegiance to God's laws. You are doing so in harmony with the diversity seed that is within you, put there by God, making each of you individual.

You will gain much in understanding if you think of God's laws as being almost the opposite of your man-made laws, which color how you view and react to laws. You will discover that it is joyous to live in attunement with God's laws. It is not a burden. In fact, it is a setting down of self-imposed burdens you do not wish to carry.

Being unforgiving to one you feel has transgressed against you is an example of a burden you create for yourself. The word transgressed means that someone has broken a law of conformity. For many, that is enough to justify not forgiving, which prevents learning. Be forgiving. Be in harmony with God's laws and feel the joy that comes from setting down your unwanted burdens and self-imposed limitations.

This is a difficult concept. It is as if I am explaining things to you in a foreign language. Just think that God's laws are designed to let you choose and become individual in finding your truth. They do not demand your conformity.

We should all try to be loving, forgiving and understanding. Our behavior should come from within as we search for God. While external laws can sometimes be helpful in finding our way, they are not a substitute for our own responsibility for enlightenment.

The next letter tells us how we can make God's laws, both visible and invisible, work for us so we may partake in God's goodness.

You have a question that you want to ask me.

I've been reading a book called *Hello From Heaven,*[11] which

---

[11] Bill and Judy Guggenheim, *Hello From Heaven*, Bantam Books, 1995.

is chock full of many people's experiences communicating with those who have passed on. They call these "after death communications" or ADCs. In a number of these cases it seems as though the communicating person is intervening in the survivor's life, albeit always for the good. Yet you have written that those on your side need to be very careful not to interfere with the lives of the survivors. This seems inconsistent.

I can see why it would. Two things will clarify it for you, one simple and one profound. The simple one is that if you reread those examples of your term interventions, you will note that they are more accurately examples of a situation where a being on my side is offering an opportunity to one on the Earth plane. In the cases you are reading, the survivor chooses to accept the opportunity. If he or she chose not to take advantage of the opportunity there would be no story to tell. My point is that the choice of acting upon the information or urging from one in spirit is always in the hands of the one receiving the information.

In the functioning of this Oneship communication there is not a limit to the amount of urging allowed. As a general rule, however, the urging is usually the minimum suitable for the circumstances. At all times the receiver of the information is free to choose to respond in any way he or she wishes. There are many who do not respond.

On Earth mankind makes laws as specific and clear as possible. Yet no matter how many pages are written to take care of all possible situations there are circumstances in which, for some people, the law will be applied in a manner contrary to its intent. Take the welfare laws in United States, a huge, complicated set of laws that do their best to be just. Nonetheless, there are people who fall through the cracks and don't receive the help that the legislators intended. Also there are people who receive aid who, in fact, were not intended to receive it. They are just clever at working the system.

The only way truly to get around this would be to have many, many thousands of social workers of truly saintly skill and motivation who would be given the power to ignore the law, if appropriate, and look into each individual case and make decisions, in noncompliance with the letter of the law. Obviously this is impractical. On Earth you feel you need a law that can be operated mechanically whereas what you really need is a law that operates based on intentions.

With God's spiritual laws it is different. In fact, his laws have the very feature that is lacking in man-made laws. His foresightful laws respond appropriately to our true intentions. In effect it works as if he has spiritual social workers of truly saintly powers who review every single individual case and determine how best to apply the intent of the law even though it may appear to violate the spiritual law itself as you perceive it. Here I have to be very careful what I say. The spiritual law is never violated.

Because man views God's laws as having the same characteristics as the laws he himself makes, man perceives the spiritual laws as having the same mechanical application. He does not see that God's laws are intention-based, not action based. Therefore, from Earth's viewpoint it may seem as though God's laws operate in a flexible manner giving the appearance of inconsistency.

Are you not constantly wondering how God could allow such and such to happen, as it seems inconsistent with the God you think you know? When you first become acquainted with karma you view it as a rigid law of an eye for an eye and a tooth for a tooth. You also regard karma as rigidly inescapable. Karma is absolved by the law of grace. Generally it is true that any of God's laws can be avoided by the law of grace. But, in fact, you are not escaping his laws, you merely misperceive them.

The glory of God, the manifestation of his love for you, comes into being because his spiritual laws are the fulfillment of his intentions and not rigid adherence to some dictate. This is a larger, more profound understanding of God. It applies specifically to your initial question in this manner: It is true that we in spirit cannot interfere with the free will of you on Earth; however, this is not a rigid law that applies at all times in all circumstances. It is not a shoe that attempts to fit all feet. It can appear that this law is not adhered to, if by so doing, the intent of the law is fulfilled.

You need not be perfect in order to bring God's laws into operation for your benefit. If your intentions are right even though you are not yet doing right, then God's laws will spring into operation to help you.

Dear Gail, the sun is shining after some rains, which makes everything look so fresh.

Buck, your experience yesterday brings to mind that there is confusion as to how God intervenes on Earth, if in fact, he does. There are many who feel that God can and does interfere with the affairs of man in what might be called a personal way. There are many who pray to God to have him cure a terminally ill child or punish someone who is guilty of harming them. Sometimes these prayers seem to be answered and sometimes not. There is also that peculiarity of two nations at war, both of which adhere to basically the same religion and ask the same God for victory. On each side there are individuals who feel God saved their lives.

Many pray to God to create the utopia that they feel God should have created in the first place. Ironic isn't it?

The basic belief is that God does at least sometimes manipulate events that occur on Earth even though he has given you free will. This would imply that some individual's free will is suspended temporarily as God takes over in a given situation.

This is not the way God operates even though at times the results suggest this. God created the universe, energized it and built a unified body of laws, both physical and spiritual, by which the universe is governed. Your free will is never suspended and neither is your immortality.

How you use this free will is up to you. You do not have the free will to disable God's laws or even violate them. You must operate within them. If you murder someone you have not violated God's law, but you will have to undergo the consequences of such an act, as this is God's law. You all have to accept the consequences of what you do and what you feel.

Thus you look at your world and think it deficient and sorely in need of great changes. You feel justice is but a wobbly venture. The guilty seem to go unpunished and the virtuous unrewarded. These perceptions all come because you think God is not taking command of events as you feel he should. God does not reveal himself in this manner. He does not interfere with your free will or the free will of your sisters and brothers. Although this may sound discouraging, it is not.

The good news is that in creating you, he gave you powers to help you create the utopia of which you dream. Further, his laws have built within them a gentle directional flow that will lead us all back to God.

An example of this is the healing field that you all are immersed in. You have the ability to tap into that healing and direct its benefits to someone else. If other conditions are right then a healing will occur and you will feel that your prayers have been answered. If your beliefs say so you will think God personally intervened and provided the healing. In a way he ultimately did because he created the healing field in the first place. God did not, however, decide to heal the person you asked to be healed nor did he decide not to heal someone else who remains ill despite prayer on their behalf. Do you see how this can be?

CHAPTER THIRTY-ONE

The All-inclusive God Field

We have talked about the infinitude of God and how difficult this is to comprehend. Is there some way to talk about this more easily and in a way that is more understandable?

I've had difficulty trying to explain the spiritual in English words, as they were not designed for this purpose. Interestingly as man investigates God's creation he senses certain concepts of reality that can be very helpful here; in particular I'm talking about "fields" as in magnetic fields. Mankind already knows some basic characteristics of fields. They are essentially without boundaries and invisible. Further, some things react to those fields and others do not. The effect of the field varies depending upon the location within the field   For instance, mass reacts to the gravitational field and is therefore affected by various degrees according to its distance from another mass.

God's effect upon the universe can be described as a God field in that it is invisible. It is also without boundaries, or put another way, there is no place where it does not exist. Unlike other known fields, however, everything is sensitive to the God field. That is why God and the God field are the same. This new label is helpful as we can more easily visualize how God functions with everything every-where in his field.

That's a wonderful insight. Is it because we feel the effect of the God field that almost all cultures past and present come up with some kind of God concept?

Yes, although not the only reason, the God field does facilitate the understanding of God's infinitude.

Einstein believed the concept of fields was one of the major breakthroughs in man's understanding of reality.

A field is essentially a region of space with a characteristic, such as magnetism. The power or force exerted by this characteristic varies throughout the space occupied by the field. The characteristics of fields are not limited only to physical things such as the gravitational effect. There are other fields that are invisible with invisible effects.

Our compasses work because they detect Earth's magnetic field. Although the effects of the magnetic field are visible, the field itself remains invisible. The gravitational field is another wonderful example of invisibility, even though there isn't a moment in our lives when we are not noticeably affected by it.

We will use the magnetic field to illustrate how this field concept works. All of you on Earth at all times are in Earth's magnetic field. Yet better than 95% of the time you pay no attention to this fact. In your operation of your free will you almost never include the magnetic field to aid in your decisions. But by ignoring the magnetic field it has not disappeared nor have you managed to escape it.

The time comes when you choose to use the magnetic field, perhaps on a long hike. You get out a compass and with its aid you determine your direction. You are now cognizant of being in the magnetic field. You don't have to climb to the top of a mountain and then pull out your compass to make it work; you are always in the field.

Notice in the first sentence above that I used the two words, "you choose." The magnetic field didn't choose you. By paying attention to it, you chose and benefited from it. It isn't the magnetic field that decides to give you the benefit of knowing your direction. This also holds true of other invisible fields.

Let's consider the healing field and what it can do for the individual. Just as you move about in an ambiance of temperature and heat, you move about in a field of healing. With proper attunement you can tap into this field. This healing can be received by you to promote your health or you can direct it to aid the health of others.

When you pray for someone's health you may feel your prayer as somewhat feeble. After all, compared to Jesus, you might think, who are you to give healing to someone else? The truth is that you can direct the healing that already exists in the healing field and turn it toward someone else. Thus your healing power is amplified. The healing is always there, and you have the power to focus it.

You can also tap into this healing field for your own benefit. How is that done? Several ways. When you feel joy you come into congruency with this healing field. Science has already established that when you have a positive attitude, your immune system is measurably enhanced. The corollary is also true. When you feel depressed or angry you reduce your connection with the healing field and your immune system is compromised.

Another way for you to receive healing is to give healing to others: "As we give so shall we receive."

Those on Earth who are true healers are sometimes puzzled by how they channel the healing. Most of them are very careful to state that they do no healing themselves, but act as a conduit for God's healing. They are right. They are a channel to the healing field created by God for our use. The way this comes about is through their ability to focus the healing field.

One very famous English healer of the last century was Harry Edwards[12]. He did considerable absent healing, which is healing people at a distance. His success was so demonstrable that one grateful person bequeathed him a beautiful estate at Burrows Lea near Guilford, U.K. He was helpful to many important people including the royal family and has written several fascinating books.

Before Gail died we went to Harry Edwards Healing Sanctuary to asking for healing for Gail's sore back caused by congenital scoliosis. Barry, Harry Edward's longtime healing assistant, told

[12] Harry Edwards, 1893-1976. His Healing Sanctuary is still quite active and can be contacted at www.harryedwards.org.UK/

her she had a nice back. That sounds almost trite, but it made Gail realize she had spent years acting and feeling that she had a bad back. She decided right then to think she had a good back. Barry also gave her back a soft healing massage. Subsequently, her back did improve. She began thanking her back for allowing her to do all our varied activities.

We often went backpacking in the Sierra Mountains for a week or so. Gail would carry a 35-to 40-pound backpack with sleeping gear and food. Strangely, the weight of the backpack load made her back feel better. I have a beautiful photo of her in the Hoover Wilderness with the backpack starting at her hips and going above her head.

The consciousness of individuals would be raised if they realized they existed in a healing ambiance, a healing field that is not only available to help them, but to all on Earth. By bringing themselves into congruence with that field they participate in this embracing phenomenon. For those who feel discouraged with the earthly state of affairs, recognition of the healing field can be an elevating tonic to their thoughts and feelings. God has blessed you with so very much.

Later she added:

Think of someone praying to his or her personal God for the healing of another. This invokes the healing field and can bring about healing. Although the person thinks it is God who decides whether the healing is justified or not, is this true? Healing occurs because the person offering the healing is doing a number of things in accord with spiritual principles. Spiritual principles existed long before the person made his prayer, but the prayer brings into action the benefits of these spiritual laws. Spiritual laws are invoked based on the intentions of the person praying. Thus the sincere, devoted intention of bringing health to another will engage the healing field.

Giving and receiving are the same. If you give somebody something you set in motion an attraction to bring that same thing to you.

Thus your wish for healing in someone else will attract healing to you.

We can apply this latter law to use the spiritual laws knowingly. If I bless someone in my heart, I know I too will receive blessings. For this to work, I need to really intend the blessings for the other person and not do this with the primary goal of receiving blessings myself. It is all in the intentions.

Now at this point you can ask a justifiable question. If the prayer of a person who believes in a personal God is as effective as one who believes in an impersonal God, what difference does it make what you believe? Either belief represents a valid place on the path of enlightenment. Bear in mind, however, that your eventual goal is to return to God and to truly know him. This being the case it is important for you to know the reality of what he is. This brings you closer to him and to understanding him.

This apparent equal effectiveness of the prayers of those who believe in a personal God and those who don't is to me an illustration of the beautiful love and mercy that God gives all his children. He does not exclude anyone from benefiting from his laws because they are not further along the path.

You do the choosing. The intention demonstrated in your choice gives you the power to bring forth the bounty of his laws.

People puzzle over the fact that it seems many forms of healing are not effective. It all sounds nice but where are the results? No factor acts in isolation. This is the result of the We Are All One principle. All factors of one's being are always mutually operative. If you have attitudes that are counter to the healing within which you are immersed, then the healing can be limited. It is still there but blocked by other parts of your intention.

What can you do to remove these blocks? You bring yourself into attunement with the healing. On the one hand you want to be healed and on the other hand you are not willing to give up the perceived benefits you receive by being ill. This is not congruent. This lack of congruency will stunt the healing. There are many more than just these two factors affecting you, each of which will enhance healing or retard it. At other times it seems the healing sweeps aside the nega-

tive factors and one receives full healing.

    With this knowledge you can now feel good about sending healing and know that it really is sent and received even if you see no change. In doing so you have added a vector to the other person's being that is pulling in a healthy direction. Do not doubt this. At the same time you are inducing in the healing field a vector in your being that is healing. You will feel it as love at first. God's world is wonderful, full of all kinds of things for your benefit if you just widen your perceptions to include them.

    God exists as a huge field, a God field, which has within it many interlocking aspects, some of which we comprehend and many we do not. We have mentioned the gravitational and magnetic fields to name just two. There are many other special fields that affect you. Some fields are measurable like the electric field and other parts of the unified field. Some are not measurable and for this reason are difficult to see or prove. The healing field, the joy field and the love field are examples. When I looked at my children and felt unbounded love for them I didn't realize I was responding to the love field. I only learned that here. You are all now immersed in God's love field, which is a major part of the God Field. All fields are aspects of the God field.

    You need to understand how the God field operates, particularly in the way you make decisions. There are many devoted sisters and brothers who feel that God makes a decision to help one person, but for some reason chooses not to help another person, or rewards one person while another is punished. Many feel God is personally making these decisions. To try to bring favorable circumstances to yourself and yours you pray to God and beseech him to look upon you kindly and decide in your favor. God is indeed a loving God but he will not suspend one of his children's free will at the request of another. He does not exclude anyone. His very basic nature is inclusion. It is how the Oneship is created.

    Now if you think of God as an anthropomorphic being, for ex-

ample, a man with a white beard, it is easy to think of him making decisions about what happens in your personal life. God is far beyond any such limiting human form. He is also far beyond being only masculine or feminine. You are made in his image but this does not refer to anything physical. It refers to your potential attributes and spiritual nature.

If God is not the decision-maker in your personal lives, what is he? He is the God field. What does this mean? I have already pointed out that fields influence you even if you are not aware of them or choose to ignore them.

Although fields are omnipresent, it is the individual who decides knowingly to tap into the field to utilize it or ignore it. The God field, however, like its subordinate gravity field, has its inescapable effect upon everything in the field. Everything is in the God field and is therefore affected by it. How you utilize the effect of the power of this field is up to you. God is not deciding who should be rewarded and who should be punished any more than the magnetic field is.

My point here is that in the operation of the God field, God is very attuned to how you, his children, use the tools he has given you. As it is said, his eye is on the sparrow. He loves you and understands you more completely than you understand yourselves. In fact, a major aspect of the God field is the love field.

What God has done is create this many-faceted intertwined field in such a way that he has given you tools with which to accomplish the fulfillment of your nature. It is up to you to decide when and how to use them. You are the decision makers. Although sometimes you use these tools unknowingly, it is best to use them knowingly.

I will close with something you will love, Buck. One of the aspects of the God field is the joy field. You are in a field of joy and if you get out your joy compass you can let this joy give you direction. This understanding is behind the statement I made long ago that happiness is what you have when outside circumstances fulfill your wishes. Joy, however, is what you feel irrespective of your outside circumstances. Joy is an inward feeling because it is you knowing and feeling the joy field within. To feel the ambience of the joy field seek and listen with gratitude.

My most wonderful friend I feel you wanting to write more.

The compass is a detection device and a means of accessing the magnetic field. By extrapolation, one can detect some of the many aspects of the God field. As the compass is to the magnetic field, so gratitude is to the joy field. When you feel gratitude you open the door to experiencing joy. You have already discovered this. Do you remember how healing it was to feel gratitude for the 47 wonderful years we had together on Earth rather than feeling cheated for the years we could have had if I had stayed? This gratitude in lieu of deprivation ushered in some much-needed joy to your life. Do you remember what you said at the top of the stairs about a week after I passed on?

I do. At the time it amazed me that I said it or could say it. I looked out over our hilltop and raised my arms and said, "I am a happy man. I feel joy." I really didn't know where that came from or why it came out like that. I do remember a feeling of attunement with everything. But to say that so soon after you died made me wonder what was happening to me. Unfortunately that feeling quickly faded into sorrow again.

Healing was happening to you. Note that the gratitude you felt came out as joy, for gratitude is the compass of joy.

As I mentioned, there are other fields. Do you know the compass for the healing field? It is love. When you ask for the healing of someone else with love in your heart you access the healing field. I feel I must add what I said before, that in anyone's illness there are many factors at play and it is the result of all these factors that healing occurs. By sending healing with love to another you do introduce a positive, therapeutic factor into that mix.

Do you know what triggers the forgiveness field? Forgiveness is difficult. On Earth most of you experience forgiveness in an incre-

mental way, bit by bit. When you finally forgive someone completely, however, you realize you have let go of a burden. The compass for forgiveness is again gratitude. You cannot feel gratitude while remaining unforgiving because the two cannot coexist in your heart. When you feel gratitude you push out resentments from your heart space.

Now isn't it interesting that forgiveness and joy have the same means to engage their fields? It shows the very close association between the two. When you have truly forgiven you will at that moment feel joy.

Do you know how you detect and access the love field? You do so by feeling at one with the Oneship. The universes are so vast and have within them things that are beyond your wildest imagination. It is hard for you to feel at one with all that. Thus your sensing the Oneship consists of being at one with someone or something without boundaries or a sense of separation. When I looked at each of my newborn babies I experienced a love for them beyond description. I felt at one with God and the baby; it seemed that love filled the whole world although I knew perfectly well that it didn't. What I felt in my heart was the truth, the reality of my being.

For now I give you and whoever reads this my love and through me the love of God. God's love comes to you from so many sources. Feel them all.

My dearest one, here we are in this sacred place made sacred by our thoughts reinforcing the thoughts already here of the ancient Anazasi Indians. Please use my fingers and my mind to do as you wish.

My Buck, this place and its sacredness is co-created by the Indians, the two of us and by God. It is at such times that we are more aware of the God field. Let us say a prayer in appreciation of the sacredness of who we are and where we are.

We return your love of us in our love of you.
We feel the sacredness of our being.
We feel the sacredness of our individuality
We feel the presence of our immersion in the invisible
Oneship of us all
Thank you for these blessings.

The concept of the God field is very important to understand so I would like to talk more about it. The electrical field or the electricity that generates it is invisible and yet much of civilization has grown dependent on it. The God field is also invisible and yes, all life depends upon it.

There are subfields of the God field that have special purposes. To fulfill those purposes it is necessary for the fields to influence some things, but not others. This allows them to have special effects. They do act together at times to supplement each other; the love field and the healing field are examples. The God field can be described as the complete general field that displays the highest supreme union of all the other fields.

Fields are everywhere. Some fields, as everyone knows, are stronger in some places than in others; for example, the gravitational field on the moon is less strong than on Earth. While true of many of the subfields, this is not true of the God field. Although the subfields have special purposes to fulfill that need to concentrate in certain areas, the God field is ubiquitous, everywhere at all times. If the God field were not present, space itself would not be. There is no place where the God field is not.

Fields are always turned on; simply put fields exist always. Being everywhere and always means that fields are infinite, which is in great contrast to many other things in our lives. Now it may appear that you can turn on and off an electromagnet and the field it produces. Actually the field is there to begin with and all the electromagnet does is amplify that magnetism in one area. The infinite nature of fields is crucial to understanding them.

The love field, the joy field and others you identify as spiritual are more numerous and active than most people realize. People tend to be cognizant of only the physically manifesting fields. For example, when an individual attunes to the healing field he is attuning to an infinite phenomenon and receives the benefits of infinity. This gives the attunement more power than can be found when one appeals to the finite. Those on Earth have a tendency to try to solve all problems by utilizing visible cause and effect efforts that are finite. To change what you don't like, you intervene physically in a finite framework. Such efforts often seem to result in frustration or at best in short-term success that leads to later problems. While characteristic of the finite, this is not characteristic of the infinite.

That the invisible has such power is a difficult concept and seems counter intuitive. If you observe what happens, however, the wisdom will slowly make its appearance in your perception.

It is by sensing these fields that you can utilize them even as they remain mysterious. In this way your choices and your desires are enhanced in power well beyond your individual energy. In other words, your seemingly puny individual effort is amplified by these fields when you learn to utilize them. This can be a great help to you as it is easy to feel individually helpless to change things.

To try this out think of certain areas in your life that are difficult. Try to feel gratitude before there seems to be anything to be grateful for. How do you do this? You can feel grateful for the opportunity presented to you to learn greater skills in living. You can be grateful that your creator gave you the tools to resolve this issue. You may not have figured out what those tools are, but they are there. You won't find them unless you seek them. Open your heart and mind to discover these unrecognized tools.

The result of the above is that you will set up the invisible law of attraction to bring good things to you. As a personal note, be open to the idea that as you use this approach, your goal in this problem may change altogether.

Be aware of the God field even as it is a mystery beyond your understanding. You are immersed in it. Knowing this will allow you to perceive more easily the Oneship of which you are an integral part. True gratitude will come into your heart along with the joy of being.

PART SIX

TO KNOW GOD, LET'S PLAY GOD

CHAPTER THIRTY-TWO

God the Designer

I want you to play God today. He doesn't mind. In fact, he likes you to play God, as it helps you comprehend him. After all he has given you his attributes in potential form so you need to practice them.

Think about his creative aspect and practice how you might design a world with living beings in it. Remember that God is infinite in his creative abilities. All things are possible for him.

First, do you wish to make your creations perfect or do you wish to give them different individualities capable of jurisdiction over themselves? If you make them perfect both in behavior and body, you certainly have solved a tremendous number of potential problems.

How would life be for your perfectly created beings? For one thing all sports would be pointless. If every golfer is able to shoot a hole in one each time, what would be the point? You would have automatons that would never do anything wrong. There would be no crime, violence, cruelty or sickness.

Look at your world and you will see that God did not make this choice even though he has the power to do so.

If you make your created beings individual with jurisdiction over themselves, you give them free will so they can be individual and develop individual qualities. With this you can expect some to go this way and some to go that way. You can imagine them getting in each other's way. Because they are not automatons you can expect them to do quite a number of egregious acts and to be a very chaotic morass of individuals in an unstable state. This doesn't sound too great either. So what do you do as creator?

You create an environment in which the individuals can evolve into something higher at their own choosing, not yours. How do they evolve without your interfering with the free will you have given them? You create a set of laws within which they have to live that will provide them with more opportunities to grow upwards rather than stay the same. You create laws that reveal that loving and joining feels better than strife and exclusiveness.

Even here though, how will they develop along these lines? What sort of nature will you create within them? It depends upon what you would like them to become. If you wish them to join you in companionship then you need to give them characteristics that will allow you both to have something in common to share and enjoy. If you have nothing in common the companionship will not flower. The solution is to give them aspects of you, not a carbon copy, but the potential and underlying desire to fulfill what is within them. You give them attributes to match yours.

Then you let them loose in your created world. But you notice that they live just one episode after another without really seeing the whole picture. They get so engrossed in their situation they cannot see the forest for the trees. So you give them a sabbatical from their tenure in the earthly world. This allows them to refresh themselves, see their activities from a more detached, complete view and also watch how others behave without being overly emotionally involved.

As you can see we are now getting closer to a viable, interesting and fulfilling life adventure. The decisions as presented in this scenario do not differ greatly from what God has created and within which you live. By playing God do you now understand better why **you exist in a perfect process even though it is an imperfect world?** *Godspeed.*

My dear one, it feels so good to be home again.

My Buck, let us play God once more. We have created creatures like ourselves and given them certain characteristics and goals. To do this they need wide experience. One lifetime will not do it. If you are born male you will never in a single lifetime experience being female. You will never have the mother experience, which is so profound. There are many other conditions that can be instructive, for example poverty or riches. There is such a vast panoply of diverse circumstances that one lifetime cannot begin to encompass them. So what do you do as creator? You give your beings multiple lifetimes. Reincarnation is the key.

This leads you to the next creation. How are your beings going to accumulate these experiences, these lessons so that they progress? You need a savings account of some sort. Hence God created a memory system that becomes an integral part of your being. Here, however, you run into a practical problem. With all these vastly different experiences how do you keep them straight? How do you make available what is important while leaving the rest dormant as they continue to address new experiences? You create the ability to derive the essence of an experience (essence memory) while leaving the details at a deeper dormant level. This level of detailed experience becomes available only under special circumstances, hypnosis for example. Having established essence memory, your creations are now able to accumulate more wisdom and more understanding as they go on with additional lifetimes. Now you have created beings with free will, experiencing many diverse circumstances from which they derive wisdom to fulfill the nature that you have given them.

What more do they need? As stated before they need an environment in which to try all this out. What is important is that the environment you select must contain the appropriate functionality to help them advance toward their goal. You must create tools for them within that framework to enable this. The easiest thing would be to make a set of interlocking laws within which they live and with which they can and will grow.

You come up with the law of karma, which effectively keeps their learning environment active while preserving their free will options in their journey to wisdom and compassion.

It would be well to devise another method to be sure that the multiple lifetimes diverge in circumstances to expose your beings to the wide variety of experiences from which they can learn broad wisdom. God cleverly created astrology with its birth chart set of personality traits from which to perceive and react to the world from different perspectives. Every person is born in each of the astrological signs multiple times. Thus astrology is a learning device through which you can understand the full truth by experiencing life from a variety of personalities and perspectives.

In this experiment you have developed with your thoughts a world such as God created. I hope this will let you see more clearly from God's perspective that your world has been perfectly constructed. He has been kind and generous to you. The fact that some on Earth cannot perceive truths that exist in all circumstances for all people does not mean the truths are not there; they simply do not yet see them. From your viewpoint these truths do change with time, person and circumstances. The error occurs in the assumption that this relative or transient truth is all there is, ignoring that God placed you in an environment conducive to evolving upward.

This points out the importance of realizing that you co-create our reality or your truth in partnership with God. Your contribution to your truth and your reality derives from the great creative power that God gave your minds along with free will. With this you create your evolving truth.

When you recognize that God is co-creator of your truth and reality, and his contribution is an inseparable part of this, you gain wisdom. You can then use your evolving truth as a tool to become aware of God's truth.

Do you see how this conducts you on your journey? Do you see how this realization of the two components of your truth allows acceleration in your growth?

❧

Hello darling, how is it with you? Soon I'll be off to Pittsburgh and music.

My dear Buck, we are going to play God again today. You spend much time and energy trying to get in control of yourselves, your environment and generally the conditions under which you live. It seems to be a never-ending task. You try to control your health and aging processes. Your world operates on a system of constant manipulation of all sorts of things; it is difficult to imagine being without this constant effort and desire to control. You could even say humans are obsessed with control.

Now try to leap in your imagination to be God who is in control of everything effortlessly. Control is no longer a problem. Since you already have control with full confidence of continuing to have it, do you think you would be concerned about it? No, you wouldn't. It just wouldn't be an issue. So with the control problem solved what do you put your mind to? Would you not be attracted to exercising your creative powers? And instead of creating something you control you might want to do the opposite: create something in which you do not have full control, but operates in a manner you find interesting.

Look at your universe to see if it does not appear to be consistent with precisely this view. First of all, this universe seems to be an unbelievably complex system incorporating the infinitely big and the infinitely small. The Creator did a great deal of creating. And what was created is going through never ending changes and transformations, which again represent a tremendous creativity.

Secondly, you see yourselves living with free will. There are things your free will cannot do such as stop Earth from spinning, but you nonetheless have great latitude in what you can choose. Most importantly, you can choose your own perspective and interpretation of what you sense and feel. The mind is your builder so you can build freely with your free will.

God shows you results consistent with what I described. What wisdom can you get from this imagining? When you realize that God wants very much for you to have free will, you will treasure it and exercise it with respect. You will also find it easier to respect the free will of others. When you are able to relax your efforts to be in constant control, you will learn the deeper meaning of acceptance, which is not passive.

God gave you of himself so it should not be surprising that you can, in a limited manner, come to the same understanding that brought about the universes and your free will within it.

CHAPTER THIRTY-THREE

What God Likes

*God is infinite and your world is finite. Nonetheless God reveals himself in your finite world. Because he does not reveal his total self in this world, you must guard against thinking he is limited to what manifests in **this** universe. Only part of what he is can be discerned from where you stand.*

What can you see? Diversity is everywhere. God likes diversity. Life, too, is everywhere. Man has conceived of life as being different than non-life, separating into the category of non-life things like rocks and water. For God, however, energy is life. Anything with energy is alive. There is great diversity in the way life manifests itself and that is why you fail to see rocks or electrons as alive.

This same concept is found in the Paiute creed as expressed by a Kaibab Paiute tribal member.

"There is an inherent understanding that all things are placed on this land with the breath of life, just as humans. This land is considered their home, just as it is for man, and it is taught that one must consider that rocks, trees, animals, mountains and other things are on the same level as man. Each has a purpose in life, and the one who created every living thing on this Earth placed all living things here to interact with one another...."[13]

Yes and without energy and life the universe could exist only in a static state like sculpture. You know then that God likes life, likes energy and by inference supports and encourages how life/energy manifests itself.

How does it manifest? Many, many things are attracted to

[13] Pipe Springs National Monument, Arizona

each other. When this attraction is fulfilled a third thing often is cre-
ated. Sometimes this third thing is an additional manifestation and
sometimes it is just the new effect of two things joining.

Buck, you have in mind examples of each. Go ahead and
write them.

You and I joined together with the result that we had children who became separate from the two of us. The electron joined
with the proton and the effect was an atom whose effect or existence behaves differently than do electrons and protons separately.
I also think of the law of momentum and the law of gravity joining
so that Earth can revolve around the sun for billions of years.

That's right. God then seems to delight in creating things that
can join and create yet more things. So joining begets creativity, which
begets more joining, which begets more creativity. This could be called
the love principle. Just as God's definition of life is much broader than
man's, so too is God's definition of love more expansive and diverse
than we tend to see it.

You observe that within this world you can also see things sepa-
rating, which again tends to be in opposition to joining and love. But
notice that the separations in your world are only temporary conditions
and from a cosmic time frame it is not long before they return to a
joining. You also have a tendency to place upon your world the idea of
either-or. Either it is alive or it is dead. Either it is joining in love or
separating in dislike. Either-or is a construct of your minds, not reali-
ty. You are all One, not either-or. In fact, even the separation you see
is a vital part of a more complex form of joining. You look at diversity
and see it as a panoply of separated species, elements, and whatnot.
God looks at this diversity and sees it more like a picture puzzle in
which every piece is different and yet each has a place in creating a
whole. The true meaning of the whole is far beyond its individual
parts. Isn't that a magnificent concept?

With your minds you can create powers that did not previously exist, calculus for example. To a finite thinker this will seem no different than discovering quarks, but it is very different. Again I am going to have difficulty in showing you what the difference is.

Quarks are part of your finite world and yet with your finite thinking you can discover them and more. What your mind creates, however, can only be created in the infinite because the infinite includes all possibilities. It has all possibilities because there is no boundary in the infinite to limit what can or cannot be done. Therefore your minds, when they probe past the boundaries of your self-imposed limits, can create new capabilities. You didn't discover them; you created them. You could say you co-created them with God, as he was the one who gave you this power when he created you.

Creativity and wisdom cannot be expressed or understood by using limiting words or concepts. They come from the removal of limitations. Although the wellspring of creativity is fuzzy and cannot be defined, what you want to do is to determine if the mind is capable only of creating something that is already there or something new. You want it defined one way or another. Do you see what you are trying to do? You have been given the power of the infinite and you are trying to reduce it to a definition that only exists in the finite. What is a definition but a description of the limits of a thing? When you define the color red you do so by saying it is not green, blue or any other color. It is only the red color. When you try your best to determine whether you are discovering a pre-existing phenomena or creating a new one you try to limit it to the finite world by defining its limitations. You can't understand the infinite and creativity by putting limits on them. The infinite simply cannot be defined by finite limits.

To know and use the powers of the infinite, as does God, one must give up trying to reduce it to the finite. You do not see God's infinite character when you describe him as a finite, wrathful, bearded old man. Push out the boundaries you have created. Recognize the unlimited possibilities of the infinite even when they are well beyond you. Develop these powers of your mind with no concern as to whether you are discovering these powers or creating them. Just believe they will *be yours if you open your mind to the all-possible and push back your current boundaries of awareness to include new territory and new capabilities. When you achieve these powers you will have a much better idea of how they came about than you do when you cannot even see their potential.*

§

  Hello Buck, did you know that doing creative things is very healing? Healing is a form of creativity, creating health if you will. To bring your thoughts into a creative mode is to bring about a healing ambiance within you.

  The mind's function is thought and memory. There is another vital part to the mind and that is free will, which we have discussed at great length. I just want you to include free will in your mind as I discuss the mind further.

  There are large numbers of peoples and belief systems who feel that God punishes them if they don't behave as they should. The Old Testament has numerous examples, as do many other sacred writings. If you discuss punishment with these people they have a very rational way of supporting their beliefs. Merely observing all the bad things that happen is enough cause to construct the concept of a pervasive punishment system.

  There is another explanation. Briefly, by your free will you create bad and good situations, which are all part of a teaching environment to allow you to grow toward God. If you understand how the divine laws work and choose in harmony with them, you will discover that life is much more satisfying. This does not necessarily require that the outside circumstances change as much as your response and attitude toward them.

  My point is that your world seems to be created whereby your minds can with seemingly equal validity see the world in two contrasting ways, either as punishment for our sins or in harmony with God's laws. It is not obvious which is closer to the truth but it is quite puzzling. Has God deliberately set it up this way? If so, is there a purpose in his leaving you puzzled?

No, he is not deliberately trying to make things difficult to comprehend. In fact, he has gone to great lengths to provide you the tools and learning environment to seek truth. The purpose behind what you see as confusing is fascinating. God wants you to understand that the wonderful mind he has given you is of extraordinary power. It is far more powerful in shaping your lives than the outside circumstances you find so frustrating.

It is your mind that creates and believes in a world where God punishes you for your sins. Likewise it is your mind that creates and believes in a world where God does not punish, but rather creates a divine world predicated on love. Once you take this giant step in realizing this broad power of your mind, you can create the world to be loving, learning and beautiful.

The mind is completely capable of creating very different worlds, which we think of as simply different interpretations. Interpretations are a bit misleading because you actually live and respond to these interpretations as reality. A jealous person will interpret his reality to include reasons, whether true or not, to support his jealousy. Interpret the world differently and you live in a different world. You will discover that external circumstances vary greatly depending upon the interpretation you are living. It is not only that you may respond differently to the same event coming into your life, powerful as this maybe, it is also that you will attract into your life different happenings. It is in this realization that you begin to glimpse the vast power of your mind. Understanding the huge power of your mind and then recognizing that this mind is but a small echo of the mind of God leaves you in awe.

As Gail has said, time on the other side is not split into the past, present and future. Certainly for God, time is one with the future and the past merges with the present. Why, then, did he choose to have us go through all these lives to advance ever so slowly it seems, to grow into his companions, when he could have created us as companions to begin with?

It has been written in many places that we shall advance in our learning to the point that we are one with God. And God knows this. He gives us free will, which we exercise independently. Yet seeing the future with ease he must know how we exercise that free will each time. Why is this going on?

Gail says we have God's attributes in nascent form. This could mean that if we look at our attributes we can infer that God has them, too. We love movies and drama of all types. We like to watch our favorites several times. Why do we like to repeat a movie when we know how it will end? We wouldn't enjoy the movie if all the difficulties were removed.

Our culture is not the only one that is fascinated with drama. No matter what political beliefs or cultural dictums various groups have they all get hooked very quickly on movies and TV. So whatever it is that engages us in drama is universal.

Can we not infer that God too, shares this attribute of liking drama even though the ending is known? Our infinite God has infinite drama to watch. As Shakespeare said, "we are but actors on the stage of life." Our drama, however, is extemporaneous because of our free will. As any actor knows this adds another dimension to it.

If we sense this and make it part of our wider perspective, our difficulties become more manageable and purposeful. In so doing we are simply fulfilling our nature as given to us by God.

There is another very important aspect of the movie analogy. Even though your favorite movie has trials and tribulations you all like a happy ending, particularly a romantic one. Might we not infer that because God is the same and perhaps that is why we are as we are? God's happy ending is that we shall fulfill our nature as given to us by him.

❧

Hello my sweet Gail, it is good to be with you this day

carrying on our study of mysticism.

My Buck, as we noticed a long time ago the study of spirituality is without end. This is because it is the study of the infinite. Today we can ponder an interesting question: if God is infinite why did he create universes that are based on finite limitations? The question can be rephrased: What purpose is there in creating finite realities?

To answer the question, think in terms of the use of limitations and how they promote God's wishes. On the one hand you read often in the spiritual literature that you should overcome the limitations you have built for yourselves. Since on the surface limitations are the very things you are trying to overcome, how can limitations be good for you?

To start with, realize that they have a positive and negative side. The good and the bad are but convenient labels in understanding how limitations work, for the good and the bad are one and fulfill a holy purpose.

The positive part of limitations is that they allow you to focus on a given learning situation; your focus must be maintained if you are to understand the lesson. A prime example of this is how your time is separated into past, present and future. You are limited to dealing with your present, which has its problems that require attention. If you were not limited to the present you would skip the problems preferring to go to a happier time in the past or future.

Another example of positive limitations is in relationships, which are ideal situations to learn the joys and sorrows of your Oneship connection with each other. Your limitations keep you involved in a relationship until you learn the wisdom the relationship contains. Again in these relationships at times you might opt to leave them and be elsewhere if you could. So, limitations are yet another learning system given to you by God to further the fulfillment of your nature.

What do you notice happens when you learn from the limited circumstances in which you are placed? You discover that some of the limitations are dissolved and now you have greater freedom to act; in other words when you learn you can diminish your limitations. This is a very long process. As you learn over many lifetimes you diminish your limitations incrementally. You become empowered to become masters of your lives instead of having circumstance be masters over you. I used the word circumstances but could substitute the word limitations to reveal how circumstances, both bad and good, function to help you advance in your growth.

There is another aspect of limitations that is helpful to understand: you can voluntarily accept or create limitations for yourselves to provide a stable platform from which to view and perceive your world more clearly. Buck, you are currently an Aries and as such have a given set of characteristics and tendencies through which you interact on a daily basis. From the experience of living on this platform you learn some lessons more surely. This also prepares you for moving to another platform, or in this case another astrological sign, in order to learn other lessons.

In your daily life you choose other sets of limitations to accomplish all sorts of things. A teenager learning a sport accepts the limitation of the rules of tennis, for example, in order to develop the physical skills that will be helpful for him or her well beyond the tennis court. What is most useful here is to recognize the purpose choosing limitations serves. If you know why the limitations are there and their purpose, you may then internalize new wisdom. Buck, you have an example of this.

When I was learning carpentry I absorbed all sorts of rigid ways of doings things. You put 2x4 studs 16 inches on center and that was all you were taught or needed to know. Why it was this way wasn't your concern. Installing studs was limited to this proper method. I did, however, learn the reason why this was done. Therefore under special circumstances I felt confident to remove these limitations to accomplish improved ways of doing things.

In this same pattern God puts us in a finite world with its limitations as a learning environment within which we are compelled to focus on certain issues. We thus absorb the rudiments needed to become creators to accomplish improved understanding.

CHAPTER THIRTY-FOUR

The World God Created For Us

Dear One, the truth is one and yet it can be revealed in so many different ways. You can truthfully describe it one way and you can truthfully define it another way. Your garbage can definition shows this.

The garbage can may be defined in three ways, each truthfully. First, it is a germ-laden, smelly, unhealthy container, a negative description. Second, early in our history it was probably one of the best tools invented by man to improve the health of a society, a positive truth. Third it is a plastic or sheet metal container made to receive and enclose garbage. The latter is an almost neutral definition. All three definitions are true. What truth you choose to believe in has a great deal to do with how you see the world.

A great deal of truth is already available to Mankind. There is much written wisdom. Yet wisdom is in fact infinite. As a result there is no end to the ways truth can be revealed.

Instead of being confusing, this plethora of truth can actually aid each of you in developing your truth. You can pick and choose with your free choice those truthful statements that seem especially meaningful to you. For instance, Buck says he wants his paintings to sing to him. It is the same with truth. You want your truths to resonate with you. You make a mistake when you try to suppress other people's truths while promoting your own. It is important to respect free choice in others.

God has given you a gymnasium in which to exercise your free will. I use this analogy to convey the idea that life on Earth is not the ultimate product or condition; your expanded wisdom is. The gymnasium is used to train and perfect your body so that it can do what you require of it. This world is used to train and perfect your being so that it can fulfill itself.

    So, is the world or the gymnasium a reality or an illusion? On Earth you feel the need to categorize a manifestation into either an illusion or a reality. Categorization is sometimes useful, as I have said. At other times it can cause confusion. The gymnasium and the world are real only in a temporary way. One could then define illusion as that which is only temporary. In this way the world is both real and illusory. But it is deeper than that.

    You look at the material world and it seems very real to you. It is your reality and you have difficulty in conceiving of it as but illusory. You can easily think of anything else as being without substance such as your imagination or your dreams, but the physical world seems to be the only real thing in your life. How can it then be illusory?

    You truly have a hunger for reality. To think you live in an illusory world is disquieting. It is an idea you do not welcome. You much prefer to feel that you live in reality. The easiest reality for you to feel is the material world. Thus the great majority of people feel the material world is real and all else is unreal by comparison. Again the world has it backwards.

    The only way you comprehend the world is through your senses. Stated more clearly: The only way to know what is outside of you is through your internal perception of it. If you can not perceive it you have no idea it is there. So reality always comes back to what is inside of you. This is a profound understanding.

    What you truly hunger for is the whole truth. In a way, that is what you mean by reality. To you, reality is true; it is there, unlike illusions, which seem untrue and not there. It is only your internal perception that allows this external reality to register as existing for you. Restated, your internal perception is the creator of your reality. You realize that other people who live in your world see things differently because their perceptions differ. You recognize there are other mind-created realities, which may be altogether contrary.

    Now we are really getting into difficulties. How can you possibly tell if these alternate realities created by the perceptions of different people are real and not illusionary? You can't. Equally you cannot tell whether the material world as revealed to you by your inward perception is real or illusory.

If you have followed this, you are now floating around in several spaces at once, none of which can be said to be hard reality. This can be very uncomfortable. You want some anchor, some ground and some reality with which to view life. That anchor, that ground, that reality is truth. I could also say it is God. God provides the ground, the reality from which you can view life and receive the truth. The realities that you create with your perception are but stations to this destination. This is why they are all temporary, finite and in that sense illusory because in time they are gone, while you are not.

Because they are illusory does not mean you should not live in them, enjoy them and in the process, learn. Being illusory does not mean they have no meaning and should be avoided. On the contrary God gave you the power to create them for your own use. He did so with the understanding that here you would always be presented with those circumstances that were most appropriate for what you currently need to learn. As I said above, God has given you a gymnasium in which to develop yourselves, to train yourselves in the skills to fulfill your goals.

Whether you regard the world as illusory or real is not that important. What is important is the nature of who you are and where you are going. This will be greatly enhanced if you realize that either the realities or the illusions (your choice) are simply tools for your utilization. Being a co-creator with God, you create the reality of who you are. That is the only reality that counts. All other realities are simple backdrops and staging upon which you act to consummate your true self.

❧

My dear one, here it is a New Year. It is always fun to try to think of all the things that could happen of which we now know nothing.

Happy New Year, Buck. As you know, all that happens to you

is for your benefit. The reason this is so hard to understand is that your view is not broad enough to see it. It is easier to look back and understand this than it is to see it while immersed in your present difficulties. When you look back your perspective is broader in that it includes all that has happened to you since. Obviously you didn't know this future at the time you were struggling with a difficulty.

The reasons people don't realize that all that happens to them is for their own good are several and interesting. First, they don't really believe God is as beneficent as he is. There is still a strong residual belief that God is strict, demanding, capricious and disciplinary, to say nothing of being vengeful. Such a God would elect to punish you for your sins. To think that he always is doing his best for you through all your trials is inconsistent with such a God.

Second, your inevitable death and seemingly undeserved illness are very hard to construe as being for your benefit. Think of all the sorrow that dying causes. How can the various tsunamis and earthquakes be of benefit to all its "victims"? Yet they are. I died. I caused sorrow. Yet I am happy. Buck is happy. The world has our two granddaughters along with many others who are growing up to take my place. Death is beautiful when seen as the constant recycling of life. From my viewpoint here it is wondrous to observe, and precious to be an integral part of its flow. And you, dear Buck, have learned so much more from the whole process of my dying. Isn't that so?

Yes, indeed! When you died I tried to believe this would be so but I couldn't comprehend how it could possibly be. It not only happened but also exceeded my expectations. But I must confess I am not sure how it all came about, although I am so very glad it did. I know you played a big part in it and I thank you.

A third reason it seems so unbelievable to think that all the hard times in your life are really for your benefit is that you tend to see only the material manifestations of your world in terms of this single lifetime. The main theater of your being, however, is in the invisible, not the visible. With greater awareness of this invisible part of your world, you would have a much better perspective of what is truly going on in your life. Sensing the invisible, I agree, is difficult compared to sensing the visible. You have been given five senses with which to sense the visible. What you don't realize is that you have been given senses to sense the invisible as well.

What are those invisible world senses? They all come through your mind, which is much, much more than your brain. Just as a musician has to train his ear or the winemaker his pallet, so too do you need to train your skills at sensing the invisible. Meditation, contemplation, prayer and the arts are all avenues available to you for this purpose. You also have various ways to seek and find help, thought duality being just one.

Ahead of you is another whole year of things that are going to come to you and everyone else as given to you by God to enable you to fulfill your nature. One of the most precious of these is the growth and enlightenment that will come to you and your world.

Hello Buck. You would be surprised to know where I am in my now. I am working with a small group of teaching adepts. Adepts is not quite the right word but will have to do. What our group is working with is how advanced teachers provide a learning environment that will cause the student to receive, to digest and to create his or her truth. How can the material be presented so that simple adoption is not substituted for true learning?

There is a great deal to learn about how to teach while at the same time allowing free will to operate. It is not so much a problem for the teachers. After all they can just lay out the teachings and allow the students to pick up what they feel advances their own truth. For the students, however, it can be a problem. There is a tendency for a student to accept wholesale the teachings of a respected teacher. Such shortcutting does not build one's own truth; rather, it attaches another's truth to one's own.

You have, therefore, this strange situation wherein the greater the teacher, the more likely the student is to respect her or his views and adopt them simply because of their source. It is the content that needs to be internalized or digested. Digestion properly infers a process that is not instantaneous. Only when you digest a teaching does it become your truth.

Yes, you know exactly what I am talking about because you realized you are doing this with me. You would like it if you knew for sure that what is contained in these inspired writings is one hundred percent me with no inadvertent altering by you. If you were sure of this then you could just accept completely what is written as the truth. Do you see why this would be shortcutting? If I were purely the source, then you would adopt it without much question. This is not the way to develop your truth.

So you see why it is that all spiritually inspired ideas and writings are "contaminated" to a greater or lesser degree by the receiver or channel. Awareness of this serves a divine purpose of bringing the student back to evaluating and internalizing the content. This process will in time bring the student back to a belief and understanding similar to what the teacher said in the first place. This may seem like a long way around to the same result, but it is not. This long process will create within the student his or her own truth, which is far wiser than would have been the quick adoption of the thoughts of a beloved teacher. The long process will leave the student eager and ready to pursue the next level of learning. The short process will result in the student being confused and discouraged by the next level of teaching. Do you see this?

❧

It is a beautiful day. It's supposed to rain later. Remember how we loved the rain, particularly in the mountains? How are you?

Oh I do. I'm fine for one who is considered dead. Let's have a dialogue. You start.

What will I say? You are the one with all the fascinating subjects. I'm like an awe-struck student.

Be patient, Buck, you will receive all those good things when you get here. The **Conversations With God** *book is right. You have to remember who you are, an innocent child of God.*

But you also need to develop and learn what you are and this is different. You are an individual. You need to bring your fully-grown individuality to the Oneship. This is a tremendous task requiring many, many lifetimes to accomplish. How you can merge Oneness and individuality is a divine mystery beyond your comprehension. If you knew you would already be godlike.

Did you know God has his individuality? If you think about it, it would have to be that way. Being a creator implies individuality. So in developing your individuality you are again echoing God. Just because individuality can be selfish, self-centered, obnoxious and a host of other not very nice things doesn't mean that it is all bad. All these lifetimes you have could be said to be devoted to discovering and implementing the noble qualities of individuality. It is these divine aspects that allow union with the Oneship.

If you would like to feel close to the Oneship there is no need to reduce your individuality. Rather, the thing to do is to use your individuality to project love, healing and peace to everyone without exception.

This shouldn't surprise you because love, as you see it in this world, also has its negative side. Jealously is inspired by what you regard as love. There is controlling love, contractual love and obligatory love. These pejorative aspects in no way diminish spiritual love. It is the same with individuality. Celebrate it. It is a divine gift especially given to you. It is your unique endowment bestowed upon you by God. Seek out how to use it.

My sweet Buck, we were talking about God's laws. Let's discuss them in contrast to man's laws. Man writes his laws on a reactive basis. For example: society observes some kind of behavior that is detrimental to its well being. Society then creates and passes a law to curb this behavior. To generalize, man intervenes when he sees what he judges as bad behavior. God's laws are not reactive, but proactive. His laws create all of the possibilities as well as the consequences based on the choices made. There is no need for God to intervene, as his laws of cause and effect have everything well in hand no matter what choice you make.

It is said that mankind is made in God's image. In truth your potential is in God's image. At this time you are not God, nor are you acting in a purely godlike manner. Yet your potential contains God's attributes. You can become the full image of God because the framework to become so is in you.

You act, however, as though God were made in man's image. That sounds almost blasphemous, but remember anything that brings about understanding cannot be blasphemous. If you think of God as a personal god intervening in a reactive manner based on whether you live in the "proper" way as described in the scriptures of your choice, you assume God is like man in the way he makes his laws. There is no reason to think that God imitates you in this regard. God has the power and capacity to create his laws to provide the perfect environment to accomplish his purposes.

Think about how this plays out and you will discover that your learning process is very much enhanced by God letting you make your own choices and receive your own rewards and disappointments within the environment he has created for you. From this you can get a glimmer of the perfection of this process.

As your wisdom grows you will know what will happen to us because you understand his laws and how they affect you. You can use these laws to benefit others and yourselves. You do not have to appeal to him in hopes of a favorable intervention on your behalf. It is very important not to misconstrue what I just said. You can and should appeal to God for his companionship, for his blessings, for his healing, and in gratitude. The appeal can be for you, for others and for the Oneship. In these things you are joining with him and fulfilling your potential to be godlike. You understand that giving and receiving are the same, so when you ask to receive God's blessing you are giving God your blessing. When you ask to receive God's healing you are giving healing to others. This all comes about through and because of your intentions. Your intentions are very important.

Do not try to immediately understand all I have said. Let this understanding grow within you. I ask God to bless you knowing that he has already done so. My doing so allows me to join in with that blessing from God and bask together as One.

Dear Buck, it is beautiful at the ranch isn't it? We have been talking about there being no personal God even though it seems that God can be appealed to intervene on our behalf. This appears to work on a number of occasions. It does so not because God intervenes, but because the spiritual laws are aligned, thus providing benefit.

We can look more closely at how this happens. But first we must understand the basic character of God's spiritual laws. The best way to show this is by looking again at man's laws through the concepts of specificity and essence.

Man creates laws to control the essence of his world. For example, you want a just world in which each of you has equal opportunity in the pursuit of happiness. That is an idealistic essence of your wish for your world.

To bring this about, however, you create laws dependent upon specificity. As a typical law let us take the driving speed limit of 60 miles per hour. If you drive at 62 miles per hour you are breaking the law. If you drive at 59 miles per hour you are a law-abiding citizen. What we want the law to accomplish in essence is to have people drive safely. Yet the specificity of the law does not always promote this goal. There are times when in a 60 mile driving zone, driving 70 miles an hour is safer than driving 50 miles per hour, particularly when the other drivers are going 70. So the specificity of the law can work against the essence of the law.

Because most of man's laws are based on such specificity they often stray from the essence that prompted them. I understand that the reason man resorts to specificity in his laws is that they generally work better, if imperfectly, than do laws expressing only the essence. My purpose here is not to get into how man should write his laws, but to point out what I mean when I say man's laws depend upon specificity as well as conformity.

In contrast God's laws depend upon essence. They come into play not based on specificity but on the essence of who you are. We have talked about how your good intentions (your essence) trigger the spiritual laws to work in your favor. They are not triggered by the specificity of what you do, which is the big difference between being and doing.

Man focuses so intently on what is specifically being done that he fails to see that God's laws operate very differently. Listen to any judicial trial and you will hear much rhetoric about who specifically did what specific thing at what specific time and place.

You expect God to intervene on your behalf because of what you expressly did that should curry God's favor. When the specific action that you deem worthy has not brought about God's intervention, you look upon other previous actions of yours and conclude that perhaps you failed God in some other way, and that is why he is withholding the desired outcome. Others observe this and question whether there is any God at all. The whole problem is that when you look for specificity you don't see that the essence of God's laws is functioning beautifully. The essence and reality of God's laws are based on his attributes. In your seeking you try to imitate God's attributes and make them your own. The attributes you have already discussed include love, forgiveness, patience, inclusiveness and creativity. As you become versed in these qualities and practice them with devoted intention, you find yourselves recipients of the blessings of God. This is not because he intervenes after seeing you acting lovingly (what you are "doing"), it is because you are ("being") loving that his spiritual laws, operating with *the essence of love, naturally bring you God's beneficence.*

*It is difficult to know what is in another's heart. This is particularly true if he is deliberately trying to deceive you. He deceives you by doing things that lead you to think he is other than what he **is**. Because we cannot know and perceive what people are, we must try to govern by laws that prohibit what they do. This results in well-intentioned people being harmed while other crafty, ill-intentioned people get away with some egregious things.*

God's laws, however, function by knowing truly who the person is. Subterfuge will not cloud this knowing. Thus God's laws work directly with one's essence with no need to create artificial and arbitrary boundaries of specificity.

I hope this clarifies somewhat why God appears to intervene as a personal God, but does not actually do so. Also I hope this lets you see that the observed inconsistency does not mean that God's laws function sporadically. You have just been looking at it in the wrong way.

My dear Buck, there you are in our peaceful home on your beautiful Earth with your very sore legs [I just came back from two days of skiing]. *We said recently that your reality or your truth is co-created with God. In other words both God and you create the reality that is truth for you. As a result your truth has two components: God's truth and your truth. Together, they integrate into what seems to you to be one truth.*

Your contribution to your truth comes about with your mind as its builder. It is a transitional truth, meaning at any given moment it is true for you, but is in a process of evolving to another level of truth, which you will understand at that time. This does not mean that this transitional truth is a false truth or a relative truth; it is more simply a less pure truth than God's truth.

*You really have no choice but to act upon your reality or truth as being **the** truth, albeit with the understanding that it will be changing as your wisdom grows. This is as it should be. The only way to* *arrive at **the** truth is by exercising and experiencing the results of your transitional truths mixed as they are with God's truth. This is a many lifetime purification process.*

The point in recognizing this is so that you can wholeheartedly embrace your reality or truth with its transitional nature and live fully with no sense of inadequacy. More importantly, you can live this transitional truth with an open mind, welcoming revisions to it.

One of the biggest deterrents to growth is the attempt to hang onto your current truth as though it were fixed. Any potential revision is regarded as a threat. This is tricky because there are parts of your reality that you need to hang onto for dear life, particularly in times of difficulties: the God component of your reality, being an obvious example. Part of your hard-earned truth is also your rock of support that should not be abandoned in times of crisis.

The big question is how do you tell which part of your reality or truth you should hang onto and which should you willingly change? This is where your recognition that you have co-created your reality in partnership with God is most helpful. You could say the purpose of God's contribution to your reality is to give you a basis for discerning just this difference. It is also a process of pulling yourself up by your bootstraps. Through your many lifetimes you gradually begin to understand that which you have tried time and again and found to be true and that which somehow doesn't bring about the harmony you desire. You try revising these parts of your truth to discover a more attuned way of going about things with happier results.

The above is difficult and requires many adjustments, testing and reassessments. God, in his generosity, has given you a great deal of time and varied experiences to do just this. So do not be discouraged with the length of the task. God so loves you he has filled the journey with delights without end.

God has been generous to you. What you need to see is God's attribute of generosity. And yes, he has given you that same attribute in potential form. You see generosity in your sisters and brothers while at the same time you see this attribute not yet in its fulfilled form.

God's generosity is in the fulfilled form. I have mentioned his three great gifts, of immortality, being part of the Oneship and free will. There are many other important gifts such as your very life. There are also those wonderful laws within which you live, love and learn.

The laws that govern your existence are particularly interesting to see from a generosity viewpoint. By giving you free will you in turn have co-created a world of considerable turmoil. I say co-created because you use your free will within God-given laws. Thus, what you see is a co-creation of both God and yourselves. The existence of all that turmoil is the result of the two gifts: his laws and our free will. Now how can the turmoil of Earth be called a gift from a generous God? Strange isn't it that these two wonderful gifts should be the means by which you create misery in the world.

But, you say, surely we didn't with our free will create disease, earthquakes and hurricanes? At your level of understanding you did not. Your understanding is based on separation, which separates you from being the cause of earthquakes. When your understanding includes the We Are All One principle you will see that indeed you do contribute to earthquakes. A very small change in an initial set of circumstances can have a large effect on a subsequent set of circumstances. This is the law of chaos recently promulgated by scientists.

Because we are all One, you contribute to the conditions on Earth that you label disasters. In changing your contribution to any and all of these disasters, with your free will you can change the very nature of these disasters. This is another gift from God that gives you power. This understanding is just beginning to dawn upon the consciousness of the world.

How you have responded to the gifts of God describes the condition of Earth. The problem is not in the nature of the gifts but in your response to them. It is as if God has given you a doll to love and play with, with great pleasure. You treat it carelessly and forgetfully leave it out in the rain. Now it seems damaged and is less appealing. You declare your innocence by saying you were not the one who caused it to rain.

Your limited understanding finds evil or disasters a vast puzzle. You know they are part of God's creation, but the idea of God's creating evil is repugnant to you. How can this be? All of God's gifts are truly divine. Part of their wonder is that they have the flexible potential to be whatever we make of them. God's gift of free will insures the mind is your builder of your perceived world. Without free will how can you be the recipients of the wonderful gift that you are co-creators with God?

❧

Hello my Gail, how are things with you wherever you are? You're still communicating, so you must be somewhere but where is it?

My dear Buck, you would be amazed at how many "wheres" there are. There are a tremendous number of "wheres" in the material realm, but these are few when compared with all the "wheres" in the thought realm.

I can but hint at them, as you have no suitable words. Let me go about it this way. You know of the electromagnetic spectrum, a vast continuum of electromagnetic energy. The portion visible to you with its colors is a very small part of the entire spectrum.

You also believe that thoughts emanating from your heart and mind have energy. Your thoughts are a part of a vast energy thought spectrum. Now take the pattern shown in the electromagnetic spectrum and transfer it to the thought spectrum. In doing so you would assign your particular portion of the thought spectrum as a small part of the entire spectrum. Think of the visible portion of the electromagnetic spectrum being similar to your portion of the thought spectrum.

This means that there are many, many regions of the energy thought spectrum of which you have no knowledge. This is not quite true as you do have a vague sense of parts of it.

You feel your thoughts are now occurring in your heart and brain. And your heart and brain are located in a material world. This is where you are. You, the observer, are in the house we built on our lovely hill. So when you ask me where I am, you are asking me for a type of location that is similar to the one you are now in. I want you to notice that where you are is dependent upon where your thoughts are being generated.

For me too, my location is dependent on where my thoughts are being generated. Actually, I have no confining material aspect to hold me in material locations; thus I am allowed to be in other non-material locations on the thought spectrum with which you are unfamiliar. This is the spiritual world.

Amazing things happen when you are in other locations of the thought spectrum. If you have trouble thinking of thoughts as locations, consider Einstein's conclusion that time and space are one. Following this, why cannot points on the thought energy spectrum also have the quality of a location albeit with no material substance?

There are thought worlds and thought universes. Because these are non-material they can be superimposed upon material worlds such as yours. Thus I can be aware of you much more easily than you can be aware of me. In fact, I can choose to be with you skiing yesterday as you sensed, but you have difficulty being with me. But nonetheless you are with me when we communicate even though it seems strange and different from your normal processes. To put it another way, I find it easy to locate myself in that portion of the thought spectrum where you reside. In trying to locate even temporarily in other portions of the thought spectrum where I basically reside, you find it imprecise or vague. As you have noted you get better and better at it with practice.

I would like to add: those feelings attuned to God or your higher self are examples of how you sense the other portions of the thought spectrum that are not your normal arena. Notice that even though these attunement experiences are hard to pin down or describe with precision they can be emotionally very strong. And in this you sense their tremendous power and value.

Remember how we used to puzzle about the planetary influences described in the Edgar Cayce readings? He talked of souls traveling to the planets and the stars, such as Saturn or the Pleiades. The heavenly bodies are centers of physical mass, but in addition can be thought centers that are located on the thought energy spectrum. Each thought center could have its own individual characteristic as Cayce describes.

You think of the location of the planets, for example, as being due to the distribution of material from which they were made. This is partially true, but in addition the thought centers also locate in these same places. In an interesting and beautiful way the material realms and the thought realms dance together creating and sharing their energy and motions.

Buck, can you get a glimpse of how magnificent this all is? Godspeed, my sweet one.

❧

Hello my beloved, here it is my 84th birthday. Wow, I never thought I would reach this age, to say nothing about feeling great and thinking my mind is in good shape. Please write to me of whatever you wish.

Happy birthday dear one. How much do you credit your good health to your spiritual beliefs?

A lot. The mind truly is the builder. Your letter on gratitude has had a wonderful effect. I just feel grateful all the time. Somehow appreciating what I have lets me keep it in my life. Living in gratitude is self-healing.

What do you think of my tripod pose (yoga position of standing on my head) where I tip back so almost all of my weight is on my head not my hands? I lift my hands off the floor and clap them, then quickly put my hands back on the floor returning to the tripod pose. The most I have been able to do is to clap three times.[14]

> *You always liked to try something new. Keep it up.*
>
> *We talked before about the thought energy spectrum and how only a small portion of the spectrum was easily within your perception because it is oriented to the physical. We also said that you sensed other non-material portions of the spectrum, but in a very different way. Feeling God's presence, as in the mountains, is one such way.*
>
> *You have been wondering where dreams fit in. Dreams are a non-physical reality and belong to the thought energy spectrum that is beyond your wakeful section of the spectrum. Your awareness while dreaming is very different from your awareness while awake. Yet while dreaming it feels no less real. Just think of the reality of a nightmare or the fun of flying.*
>
> *Notice that when you wake up, the reality, the memory of your dream fades very quickly in most cases. Those who journal their dreams know it is essential to have a notebook right beside the bed ready to note dream content immediately upon awakening or it is lost. It is as if the dream world were in one language and the real world another. Without making an attempt to translate it, it just doesn't fit into the awakened world.*
>
> *This does not mean, however, that the non-material portions of the thought spectrum are divorced from influence and interchange with the rest of the spectrum: quite the contrary. Early on I told you that the invisible has a great influence upon your world, much more than you realize. Gravity is invisible yet your physical world cannot escape its power. In the same way the other portions of the thought spectrum have a great influence upon you. You just are not aware of their vast manifestations.*
>
> *Think of God's love of diversity as is demonstrated by the physical diversity in your world. The virus and the whale are highly diverse in size, and yet there are many viruses that are an integral part of the whale. If God shows this wonderful diversity in your physical world*

---

[14] See photo at the end of the book.

would it not be reasonable to assume he also likes to have diversity in the non-material portions of the thought energy spectrum as well? This variety is well beyond your ability to imagine or understand. You have developed effective tools to discover much about the world in which you live, but you have yet to develop the tools needed to uncover the wonders of the full thought energy spectrum. In time you will.

The thought energy spectrum is thought focused. As such, one of its primary functions is to initiate. This is not its only function. It has powers of action and bridging capabilities that integrate it with everything else.

Not all the non-material portion of the thought energy spectrum is beyond you. Besides your dreams you have the law of karma, which operates invisibly, and the Akashic record. Essence memory, which is your essential self, is influenced by the thought energy spectrum.

My guess is that the thought spectrum is not subject to space or time. By that I mean that thought can travel anywhere and it takes no time to do so. The thought spectrum is independent of space-time constraints, which is not true of the electromagnetic spectrum as revealed to us by variations of time and space. This makes it very difficult for our scientific tools to detect because there is nothing to measure.

If true it means that our thoughts, which are in that small section of the thought spectrum, are also independent of space-time constraints. Anecdotal occurrences with telepathy certainly seem space-time independent. Various people, though far away, sense when someone close to them dies before they are notified of the event by normal means. This same thing is seen in quantum physics with entanglement, which is also independent of space-time. In theory two entangled particles can be a light year apart and yet if you change the spin of one, the other instantaneously changes spin also. To these particles the space between the particles of one light year is ignored and the time it takes for other information to travel, which is the speed of light, doesn't stop the particles from instantaneously changing their spins. There are so many things that seem impossible that are true that we should not be so sure we know what is impossible.

Yes and this just scratches the surface. Let me close by saying God is bountiful and kindly. These vast invisible influences upon your lives that come from other realms of the thought energy spectrum are not fearful unknowns. They are all part of God's divine creation to help you grow in ways that will please your beloved God and us.

Enjoy your birthday, Buck, and I will be with you this evening.

❧

As a child I loved echoes. I thought they were magical. I want to use them today as a metaphor.

An echo is not the maker of the sound, but a reflection, yet it has the main characteristics of sound. It reflects the essence of its origin. This is the relationship you have with God. You echo his attributes, reflecting them as you travel on your journey. These attributes are not as fully developed in you, as they are for the originator, God. All this we have said before.

I would like to expand this analogy. If you wish to learn more about God, you need to realize that the world and universe are but a reflection of him. You can expand your knowledge by discerning these reflections in your world.

As an example, I earlier wrote that even though God knows the past, present and future, at the same time he probably enjoys watching things unfold in the present. He is aware of how things will transpire in the future, but in the same way that you may like to see your favorite movie over and over again even though you know its ending, he enjoys the process of your progression. The origin of your love of drama and movies is but an echo of God's trait.

Another example I have written about is diversity. You need but look at the very diverse life forms and landscapes to see that diversity is rampant. It is reasonable to conclude from this that God intends our world to be diverse and that he likes diversity. If we too, could develop a liking for diversity, we could feel closer to him and get to appreciate diversity ourselves. In some ways we do already, but in other ways we try to bring everything into conformity with how we think the world should be. The world would be much better off if we had greater tolerance for the diversity represented in the different opinions and cultures we see in our world. Could we not deliberately try to perceive the positive in this diversity?

Perhaps you could consciously look at your world to observe those characteristics that reflect what God is, which in turn will let you know your potential self. This will not only give you insights but will let you feel closer to God and his love for you. To do so is an exciting adventure. Those "Ah ha" moments, which are so satisfying, will come more often. Your ability to overcome difficulties will make life easier. You will see more clearly the treasures you have in your relationships in spite of the bumps. The journey you are now on is a treasure. Live in gratitude of your gifts.

Dear reader, you have shared a journey with us. We have tried to be helpful to you who are our sisters and brothers, as we are all on this path. I would like to leave you for now with some summary thoughts.

Your mind is the builder and your heart tells your mind what to build. Your heart is where you live, which you choose. If your heart is full of resentment, fear or loneliness, know you can choose otherwise? Ask your mind to build otherwise.

We are all on this journey together. Let me enumerate some of the invisible energies that we all share.

Healing energy surrounds this Earth. Each of you on Earth is immersed in this sea of healing. If you open to it you will feel its effects. How do you open yourself? You choose in your heart to be open. One very good way to receive this healing is to give healing. You do not need to focus healing on any one individual, although you can. You can say, "From God through me to all of thee. Let the healing flow endlessly."

Say this several times with a desire to feel it. Your expression of this healing gift will be reinforced by the healing energy field and thereby become stronger.

Your higher self is your constant companion. Through your higher self you are in contact with many, many others. Your higher self is trying to help you. Your construct of being lonely is cutting you off from your higher self. How do you contact your higher self? First, you must allow your mind to realize that you have a higher self and it is there to help you, as it truly wants to. Then there are a number of techniques to contact this higher self. Meditation is a very good one. As you fall asleep you may ask your higher self to be in communication with you. When you awake remember and review your dreams. It is best to write them down. For several minutes quietly look at a flower that to you is beautiful and try to feel its essence. Your higher self will join you in this appreciation. You will then feel your loneliness diminish. Gratitude will attune you to your higher self.

What you think is what you attract to yourself. *Further, your thoughts are dual, consisting of your thoughts and the thoughts of others attuned to you, the contributors. If you think resentment, your mind will receive reinforcement of this resentment from other minds that are in anguish. This makes it worse. It also gives you the feeling that you cannot control your mind. You have invited other resentful minds to join you in this resentment, which is not the best way to feel joy. Choose otherwise, choose gratitude. Your mind is the builder and your heart is the navigator. Instruct your mind to build an appreciation for the sun that rises in joy each day and sets in beauty. This will attract other minds feeling gratitude to join you in this appreciation.*

And there is, of course, God's constant love. Often there is the impression that God is far away when you feel despair, fear and loneliness. This is impossible. God is always near, always everywhere. In fact, if God's love did not permeate your being and all beings, everything would disappear in an instant. It is God's love and energy that powers the atoms to be atoms within your body. Without it you could not exist. Become aware of this basic fact of existence and let it be a part of your life. In the morning awaken and say, "God, I welcome you into my awareness this day."

  The understanding and utilization of the above will help you arrive at where you want to be. While change is inevitable, you have the power to direct it. Do not look for this change outside though it may occur there, but rather feel it inside where you live.

          ✍

  No one can know God as God knows himself. It is beyond your comprehension. However, that doesn't mean you cannot know parts of God or that you can't sense his presence. You become overly concerned whether he is masculine or feminine, or a combination of the two. This is because you try hard to define him in terms you can understand, such as gender. He is so far beyond what you can understand that the gender assignment is much too limiting. It is more accurate to label him the Creator, although this is only one of his aspects. The closest you can come is to call him the Infinite, but since you cannot understand the infinite very well it still leaves you puzzled.

  You should be willing to recognize your limitations while at the same time try to understand him to the degree that you can. No religion can claim exclusive rights to knowing who God is. You are all sisters and brothers on your individual spiritual paths seeking the light. God created you all. God loves you all. You all are privileged to partake in life experiences of love and learning. There is pleasure, excitement, beauty and adventure to accompany you on your journey. God is bountiful in his gifts. Feel gratitude in return.

  You can sense God and the Infinite in observing that there is no end of new knowledge to be found in his world. This knowledge reveals that everything is intertwined in a miraculous manner to function as a whole: the Oneship.

  Although you cannot know God in his fullness, what you do know of him will let you live in celebration of his magnificence.

  This book has been a wonderful experience for me. As Buck will tell you I have always felt that communication is central to life's fulfillment. Because I have been impressed time and again by how the lack of communication leads to difficulties, it has been with great joy that I have entered into this dialogue from the other side of death with you and Buck. I feel a sense of peace, which in gratitude I radiate out to you. Can you feel it? It is there for you. God bless and Godspeed.

Acknowledgments

I'm placing the acknowledgment here rather than in the front of the book as I think that no one would care about the people named in the acknowledgment until they had read the book.

I'll start with naming three organizations which stimulated Gail and me to study and grow: Association of Research and Enlightenment (ARE), the Rosicrucians and the Theosophists. They let us understand that there is vast spiritual component to our existence to which they and others contribute their path and truth to the whole.

I was grateful to have the following readers help me find direction: Grethe Tedrick for her patient understanding and love of stories, and Joni Deittrich, my yoga teacher. Andy Veja who was particularly helpful in structuring the book. My son, Michael Kent, who with his long knowledge of Gail could assess the book in a unique way. Violet Feinauer, Gail's sister, having known Gail longer than I also has a special viewpoint. They all perused parts of the book and gave excellent feedback.

Sid and Nancy Kirkpatrick who taught me much about books and how they should be written. They were so essential in getting our first book out. Four months after Gail passed on I was attending the summer ARE conference. The Speaker, Dr. George Ritchie (*Return From Tomorrow*), listened to my story describing Gail's death, gave me encouragement and helped me understand what I was experiencing. Darcy Zander-Feinauer, my niece and layout expert, who encouraged me and played a vital part in bringing the book to completion.

I was fortunate in having a practical, grounded Republican businessman for a father and a very creative mother who was a socialist. They gave me the best of both worlds. I thank Gordon and Sarah for their tolerant, loving upbringing. As an idealistic young man I had no desire to go into business nor did I want a 9 to 5 job. Somehow I ended up becoming a building contractor and was surprised that I evidenced some talent for it. Once I got into mysticism I realized business was an excellent spiritual classroom because I was often required to make difficult decisions. Applying the spiritual approach to being of service to others, particularly my clients, lead to my business success. I also thank my children. It is wonderful to find your children inspiring both as children and adults. They have grown up as fine people.

Lastly, I thank my long-term girl friend and now wife, Constance Wolfe who lovingly embraced Gail with no trace of jealousy. She applied her considerable editorial skills and persistence to bringing this book to fruition.

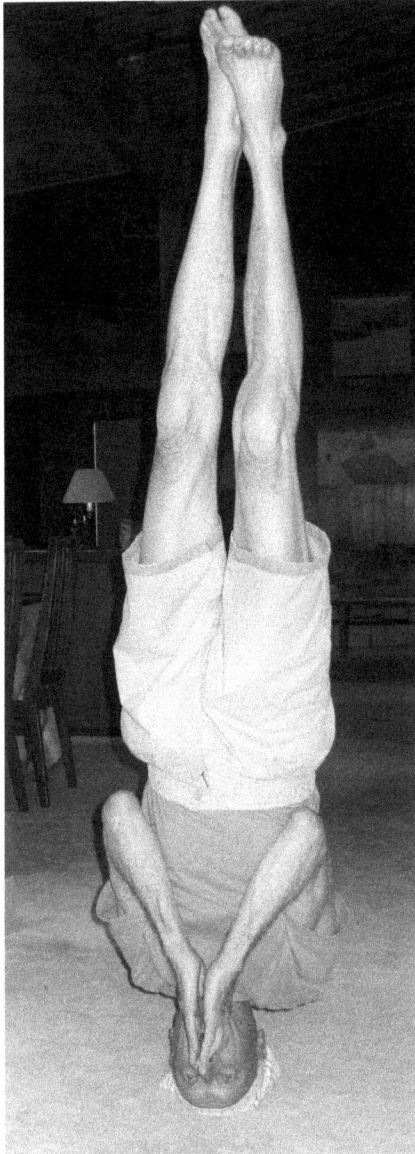

Buck at 84 doing headstand.

*Go to YouTube address **http://youtu.be/cqXwGYVRqbs***
for a video of Buck clapping his hands while in a headstand plus an interview
about the book by Sandy Lawrence of Ubuntu Yoga Studio.
*For a somewhat different longer video, go to **http://youtu.be/VMCDjDDYJeU***

www.ingramcontent.com/pod-product-compliance
Lightning Source LLC
Chambersburg PA
CBHW052029090426
42739CB00010B/1831